PEBBLES

Complete Common Worship
Talks and Activities

SUSAN SAYERS

kevin mayhew

The material in this book was originally published in the Living Stones Programme for Common Worship.

kevin
mayhew

First published in Great Britain in 2015 by Kevin Mayhew Ltd
Buxhall, Stowmarket, Suffolk IP14 3BW
Tel: +44 (0) 1449 737978 Fax: +44 (0) 1449 737834
E-mail: info@kevinmayhew.com

www.kevinmayhew.com

9 8 7 6 5 4 3 2 1 0

ISBN 978 1 84867 771 5
Catalogue No. 1501470

Cover design by Rob Mortonson
© Images used under licence from Shutterstock Inc.
Edited by John Cox
Typeset by Chris Coe

Printed and bound in Great Britain

Contents

About the author   9
Foreword   10

Year A

First Sunday of Advent   14
Second Sunday of Advent   16
Third Sunday of Advent   18
Fourth Sunday of Advent   20
Christmas Day   22
First Sunday of Christmas   24
Second Sunday of Christmas   26
The Epiphany   28
The Baptism of Christ: First Sunday of Epiphany   30
Second Sunday of Epiphany   32
Third Sunday of Epiphany   34
Fourth Sunday of Epiphany   36
Sunday between 3 and 9 February   38
Sunday between 10 and 16 February   40
Sunday between 17 and 23 February   42
Second Sunday before Lent   44
Sunday next before Lent   46
First Sunday of Lent   48
Second Sunday of Lent   50
Third Sunday of Lent   52
Fourth Sunday of Lent: Mothering Sunday   54
Fifth Sunday of Lent   56
Palm Sunday   58
Easter Day   60
Second Sunday of Easter   62
Third Sunday of Easter   64
Fourth Sunday of Easter   66
Fifth Sunday of Easter   68
Sixth Sunday of Easter   70
Ascension Day   72
Seventh Sunday of Easter   74
Day of Pentecost: Whit Sunday   76
Trinity Sunday   78
Sunday between 29 May and 4 June (if after Trinity Sunday)   80
Sunday between 5 and 11 June (if after Trinity Sunday)   82

Sunday between 12 and 18 June (if after Trinity Sunday)	84
Sunday between 19 and 25 June (if after Trinity Sunday)	86
Sunday between 26 June and 2 July	88
Sunday between 3 and 9 July	90
Sunday between 10 and 16 July	92
Sunday between 17 and 23 July	94
Sunday between 24 and 30 July	96
Sunday between 31 July and 6 August	98
Sunday between 7 and 13 August	100
Sunday between 14 and 20 August	102
Sunday between 21 and 27 August	104
Sunday between 28 August and 3 September	106
Sunday between 4 and 10 September	108
Sunday between 11 and 17 September	110
Sunday between 18 and 24 September	112
Sunday between 25 September and 1 October	114
Sunday between 2 and 8 October	116
Sunday between 9 and 15 October	118
Sunday between 16 and 22 October	120
Sunday between 23 and 29 October	122
All Saints' Day	124
Fourth Sunday before Advent	126
Third Sunday before Advent	128
Second Sunday before Advent	130
Christ the King	132

Year B

First Sunday of Advent	136
Second Sunday of Advent	138
Third Sunday of Advent	140
Fourth Sunday of Advent	142
Christmas Day	144
First Sunday of Christmas	146
Second Sunday of Christmas	148
The Epiphany	150
The Baptism of Christ: First Sunday of Epiphany	152
Second Sunday of Epiphany	154
Third Sunday of Epiphany	156
Fourth Sunday of Epiphany	158
Sunday between 3 and 9 February	160
Sunday between 10 and 16 February	162
Sunday between 17 and 23 February	164
Second Sunday before Lent	166

Sunday next before Lent   168

First Sunday of Lent   170

Second Sunday of Lent   172

Third Sunday of Lent   174

Fourth Sunday of Lent: Mothering Sunday   176

Fifth Sunday of Lent   178

Palm Sunday   180

Easter Day   182

Second Sunday of Easter   184

Third Sunday of Easter   186

Fourth Sunday of Easter   188

Fifth Sunday of Easter   190

Sixth Sunday of Easter   192

Ascension Day   194

Seventh Sunday of Easter   196

Day of Pentecost: Whit Sunday   198

Trinity Sunday   200

Sunday between 29 May and 4 June (if after Trinity Sunday)   202

Sunday between 5 and 11 June (if after Trinity Sunday)   204

Sunday between 12 and 18 June (if after Trinity Sunday)   206

Sunday between 19 and 25 June (if after Trinity Sunday)   208

Sunday between 26 June and 2 July   210

Sunday between 3 and 9 July   212

Sunday between 10 and 16 July   214

Sunday between 17 and 23 July   216

Sunday between 24 and 30 July   218

Sunday between 31 July and 6 August   220

Sunday between 7 and 13 August   222

Sunday between 14 and 20 August   224

Sunday between 21 and 27 August   226

Sunday between 28 August and 3 September   228

Sunday between 4 and 10 September   230

Sunday between 11 and 17 September   232

Sunday between 18 and 24 September   234

Sunday between 25 September and 1 October   236

Sunday between 2 and 8 October   238

Sunday between 9 and 15 October   240

Sunday between 16 and 22 October   242

Sunday between 23 and 29 October   244

All Saints' Day   246

Fourth Sunday before Advent   248

Third Sunday before Advent   250

Second Sunday before Advent   252

Christ the King   254

Year C

First Sunday of Advent	258
Second Sunday of Advent	260
Third Sunday of Advent	262
Fourth Sunday of Advent	264
Christmas Day	266
First Sunday of Christmas	268
Second Sunday of Christmas	270
The Epiphany	272
The Baptism of Christ: First Sunday of Epiphany	274
Second Sunday of Epiphany	276
Third Sunday of Epiphany	278
Fourth Sunday of Epiphany	280
Sunday between 3 and 9 February	282
Sunday between 10 and 16 February	284
Sunday between 17 and 23 February	286
Second Sunday before Lent	288
Sunday next before Lent	290
First Sunday of Lent	292
Second Sunday of Lent	294
Third Sunday of Lent	296
Fourth Sunday of Lent: Mothering Sunday	298
Fifth Sunday of Lent	300
Palm Sunday	302
Easter Day	304
Second Sunday of Easter	306
Third Sunday of Easter	308
Fourth Sunday of Easter	310
Fifth Sunday of Easter	312
Sixth Sunday of Easter	314
Ascension Day	316
Seventh Sunday of Easter	318
Day of Pentecost: Whit Sunday	320
Trinity Sunday	322
Sunday between 29 May and 4 June (if after Trinity Sunday)	324
Sunday between 5 and 11 June (if after Trinity Sunday)	326
Sunday between 12 and 18 June (if after Trinity Sunday)	328
Sunday between 19 and 25 June (if after Trinity Sunday)	330
Sunday between 26 June and 2 July	332
Sunday between 3 and 9 July	334
Sunday between 10 and 16 July	336
Sunday between 17 and 23 July	338
Sunday between 24 and 30 July	340

Sunday between 31 July and 6 August   342
Sunday between 7 and 13 August   344
Sunday between 14 and 20 August   346
Sunday between 21 and 27 August   348
Sunday between 28 August and 3 September   350
Sunday between 4 and 10 September   352
Sunday between 11 and 17 September   354
Sunday between 18 and 24 September   356
Sunday between 25 September and 1 October   358
Sunday between 2 and 8 October   360
Sunday between 9 and 15 October   362
Sunday between 16 and 22 October   364
Sunday between 23 and 29 October   366
All Saints' Day   368
Fourth Sunday before Advent   370
Third Sunday before Advent   372
Second Sunday before Advent   374
Christ the King   376

Appendix   378

*This book is dedicated to my family and friends,
whose encouraging support has been
wonderful, and to all those whose good ideas
are included here for others to share.*

About the author

A teacher by profession, Susan Sayers was ordained a priest in the Anglican Church and, before retirement her work was divided between the parish of Southend-on-Sea, the local women's prison, writing, training days and retreats.

Susan is the author of many popular resource books for the church including our ever-popular Living Stones and Confirmation Experience ranges. Her most recent publication for Kevin Mayhew is *The Holy Ground Around You, Reflective services for taking the church outside*.

Through the conferences and workshops she is invited to lead, she has been privileged to share in the worship of many different traditions and cultures.

Foreword

For this age group the world is opening out from the immediate family circle, and full of possibilities. The children are becoming aware of familiar faces Sunday by Sunday, and now they are brought in to join the big children for Sunday school. It can be a daunting prospect, and the way young children are met and welcomed, talked and listened to, when they first encounter the children's ministry in your church, will have a profound effect on their spiritual growth. It is through the good humour, care and friendliness of those they meet that they will begin to realise how God loves them.

In all your planning, keep aware of how it will seem from the children's point of view. Is the area attractive and inviting? Does the furniture fit? Is the atmosphere orderly and therefore unthreatening? Are people talking at a speed they can cope with, and giving them time to reply without pressure? Do people genuinely seem to like them and want them to be happy? Is considerate love and fairness expressed in actions as well as in the teaching? Is it a place where they can relax and feel at home? Is it fun?

These things are so important because the children will be learning far more from the way things are done and from the people they work with, than from the actual teaching content, valuable as this obviously is. It is a good idea to review your aims and objectives annually, setting out for yourselves, the PCC, the parents, and any helpers, what you are doing and why, what works well and what needs to be tried differently. If this regular review is built into the system there is no danger of outdated methods carrying on past their sell-by date just because things have always been done like that. A termly or annual training day is also helpful in refreshing leaders and preventing cases of burn-out.

This book provides you with ideas and materials for activities for young children, all based on the weekly readings of the Common Worship Lectionary. The activity sheets often include something to think and talk about together, and you can select and adapt the ideas to suit your particular group. Vary the media the children work with – crayons, finger paints, sponge painting, printing, paper and fabric collage, chalks and pastels are all fun to use. Pray for the children and their families, and read the Bible passages before you plan, so as to incorporate your own valuable insights, and use the suggested games either as they stand or as starting points to help you think of other ideas of your own.

A few general ideas about storytelling:

- Tell the story from the viewpoint of a character in the situation. To create the time-machine effect, avoid eye contact as you slowly put on the appropriate cloth or cloak, and then make eye contact as you greet the children in character.

- Have an object with you which leads into the story – a water jug, or a lunch box, for instance.

- Walk the whole group through the story, so that they are physically moving from one place to another; and use all kinds of places, such as broom cupboards, under the stairs, outside under the trees, and so on.

- Collect some carpet tiles – blue and green – so that at story time the children can sit round the edge of this and help you place on the cut-outs for the story.

If parents are going to be staying with their children, involve them in the activities, or think over the possibility of having an adult discussion group in the same room. Parents are encouraged to pray with their children during the week, using the worksheet prayers.

SUSAN SAYERS

Recommended Bibles

It is often a good idea to look at a passage in several different versions before deciding which to use for a particular occasion.

As far as children are concerned, separate Bible stories, such as those published by Palm Tree Press and Lion, are a good introduction for the very young. Once children are reading, a very helpful version is the *International Children's Bible* (New Century version) published by Word Publishing. Here children have a translation based on experienced scholarship, using language structure suitable for young readers, with short sentences and appropriate vocabulary. There is a helpful dictionary, and clear maps and pictures are provided.

Leaders may also wish to refer to the recently published Study Bible, freshly translated by Nicholas King (Kevin Mayhew, 2013).

Editor's note

Pebbles was first published in three volumes – one for each year of the liturgical cycle. Since then it has proved to be of enduring value as a resource for those who lead children's groups and it is now republished here as a single volume, alongside its companion volume for older children *Rocks*. Apart from very minor revisions the content has remained the same. This revised edition includes a CD-Rom of the worksheets for every Sunday.

YEAR A

First Sunday of Advent

Thought for the day

We are to wake up and make sure we stay ready for the second coming.

Readings

Isaiah 2:1-5
Psalm 122
Romans 13:11-14
Matthew 24:36-44

Aim

To learn the importance of being alert to God all the time.

Starter

Play this version of 'musical bumps'. Tell the children that when you show the red sign they stand still. Whenever the music stops they sit down. This will mean that they have to keep watching, as well as listening, while they jump up and down.

Teaching

Praise everyone for watching and listening so well in the game. It was because they were watching and listening so well that they knew when to stop and when to sit down. Explain that Jesus told his friends to watch and listen carefully – he will be pleased to see how well the children at (your town) can do it already!

Explain that you are going to tell them a story. Every time they hear the word 'Jesus', they put their hand up.

Now tell them this story.

The world God had made was very beautiful. It had blue sea and green grass, and flowers of red and yellow and pink and purple. There were furry animals, and shining fish, birds which sang songs, and frogs which croaked. There were people. There were clouds. There was sunshine and rain and snow. God loved the world he had made. But he saw that people were spoiling the world; they were choosing to hate one another instead of loving one another. Sometimes they chose well and were happy. Sometimes they chose to be selfish and made themselves and each other very unhappy.

'The people I have made need saving and rescuing,' thought God. 'I will come to save and rescue them.'

He got his people ready. 'Watch and listen carefully!' he told them. 'Then when I come to save you, you will recognise who I am.'

Some of the people kept listening and watching. As they grew old they passed the message on to their children. And they passed it on to their children – 'Keep watching and listening. One day God will come to us to save and rescue us.'

At last, God kept his promise and came among his people in person to save and rescue them. The people had been expecting a rich and powerful king, but God came among his people as a tiny baby, who was born in a stable and put to bed in the animals' hay. This baby, whose name was Jesus, was God's Son, who had come into the world to save and rescue us.

Not everyone recognised him, because he wasn't what they were expecting. But the ones who were used to listening out for the loving words of God, and the ones who were used to watching out for the loving kindness of God – they knew exactly who Jesus was, and they were very pleased to meet him!

Praying

Dear God,
the world is full of your love. *(trace big circle)*
Help us to listen out for it. *(cup ears)*
Help us to watch out for it. *(shade eyes and look around)*
Thank you for all the goodness and love
that we can hear and see.
Amen.

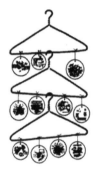

Activities

On the worksheet they can draw small and big things they enjoy seeing and hearing. These can all be cut out and stuck on to a group picture, or hole-punched and hung on to a coat hanger mobile *(see right)*.

Print worksheet *First Sunday of Advent (A)* from CD-ROM.

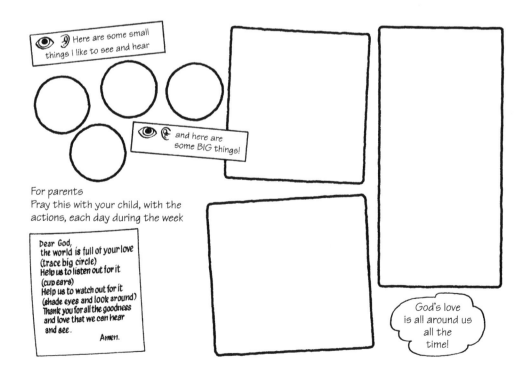

Second Sunday of Advent

Thought for the day
Get the road ready for the Lord!

Readings
Isaiah 11:1-10
Psalm 72:1-7, 18-19
Romans 15:4-13
Matthew 3:1-12

Aim
To think about getting ready for Jesus at Christmas.

Starter
Ready, steady, go! Give the children different tasks to do (such as running to the back wall, jumping round a chair, hopping to a leader). Having explained the task, they have to wait until you say, 'Ready, steady, go!' before they start.

Teaching
Talk about getting ready for Christmas, and all the things going on at home and in the shops. Everyone has long lists of jobs to do and cards and presents to make or buy. Show some of your own scribbled lists. How can we get ourselves ready for Christmas? Show the children an Advent calendar, with a week of windows already opened, and then open today's window. The Church calls this time before Christmas 'Advent', which is another way of saying 'coming'. We can use this time to work on something we find hard to do, like sharing our toys, going to bed when we're told to, or remembering to help at home. (Talk over the ideas with the children.) We can do this as a present to give Jesus at Christmas.

Praying
Dear Jesus,
when I open today's window
in my Advent calendar
I remember the present
I am getting ready to give you.
Please help me to do it well.
Amen.

Activities

Give each child some modelling clay to make the shape of them doing what they are working at during Advent. Here are some suggestions to help the children think of their own:

Praying every day
Helping at home in some way
Telling the truth
Sharing without getting cross
Going to bed at the right time
Feeding/cleaning out a pet

Next week the children will be making a box to put their model in, and the week after it will be wrapped up so that all the gifts can be part of the offering at Christmas.

Print worksheet *Second Sunday of Advent (A)* from CD-ROM.

Third Sunday of Advent

Thought for the day
Great expectations. Jesus fulfils the great statements of prophecy.

Readings
Isaiah 35:1-10
Psalm 146:5-10 or Canticle: Magnificat James 5:7-10
Matthew 11:2-11

Aim
To know that God is more wonderful than we can ever imagine, and to continue getting ready for Christmas.

Starter
Pass the parcel. Inside is a giant balloon, ready to be blown up, with the word 'God' written on it (OHP pens work well). During the game play or sing *Our God is so great* or *Think big*.

Teaching
Tell the children what it says on the balloon, and talk about how small the balloon and the word are at the moment. Is God really small and unimportant like this? No! God is the one who made the world and everything in it. (Start to blow up the balloon.)

Is that all? No! God is the one who knows and loves each of us by name. (Blow up the balloon some more.)

Is that all? What else do we know about the one true God? Collect their suggestions, making the balloon bigger with each one. Add other characteristics yourself:

- He's always ready to listen to us.
- Jesus came to show us how kind and loving he is.
- He helps us when we are sad or ill or frightened.
- He has always been alive and always will be.
- He helps us to be kind and loving and fair.

At each quality, inflate the balloon so that it is huge, and draw attention to how big God's name is now.

Our God is more powerful and wonderful and loving and kind than we can ever imagine, and yet he wants to be friends with us! And he's the best friend you could ever hope to have, because he loves you, and is always there for you and will never let you down.

Praying

Our God is so big,
so strong and so mighty,
there's nothing our God cannot do!
Amen.

Activities

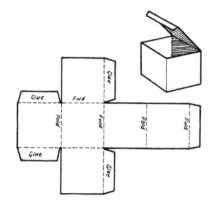

Using the net (*right*) as a guide, cut out the shapes for the boxes from coloured paper. Help the children to assemble the boxes as shown, and place their models from last week inside, talking about what they represent and how their 'present' for Jesus is going. Encourage them in what they are doing.

Print worksheet *Third Sunday of Advent (A)* from CD-ROM.

Fourth Sunday of Advent

Thought for the day

Through the willing participation of Mary and Joseph, God is poised to come among his people as their Saviour.

Readings

Isaiah 7:10-16
Psalm 80:1-7,17-19
Romans 1:1-7
Matthew 1:18-25

Aim

To see that we can help God.

Starter

Have a selection of jigsaws and other puzzles that the children can work on together, with the leader encouraging everyone to help each other.

Teaching

Draw attention to the way we all helped each other, and how good that was. Talk about what people say when they are asked to help with something. Sometimes they say things like:

'No, I don't want to.'
'No, I'm too busy.'
'No, it's too hard.'

(You could use different toys or puppets to say these things.)

Sometimes when people are asked to help they say things like:

'Yes, I'd love to.'
'Yes, I'll do that for you.'
'Yes, it sounds hard but I'll do my best.'

God needed some help for his plan to save his people. He asked Mary to help him by being Jesus' mum. He asked Joseph to help him by looking after Mary and the baby Jesus. Mary and Joseph could have said, 'No, I don't want to' (and the other refusals). The children can join in, doing the thumbs-down sign each time. But they didn't say that! They said 'Yes!' (thumbs up). So God got the help he needed, and Jesus came into the world at the first Christmas to save us and set us free.

Praying

Dear God,
when you want someone to help,
ask me.
I don't want to say 'No!' *(thumbs down)*
I want to say 'Yes!' *(thumbs up)*
Amen.

Activities

This week we are making the wrapping paper to wrap our present to God. Remind the children of their models, and print some paper with stencils or shapes dipped in paint. Wrap the box which can then be offered to God on Christmas Day. Encourage the children to keep up their resolution and offer God what they have tried their best to do. On the worksheet there is a picture to colour of Mary and Joseph going in to Bethlehem.

Print worksheet *Fourth Sunday of Advent (A)* from CD-ROM.

With love from
- - - - - - - - -

For parents to pray with your child

Dear God,
when you want
someone to help,
ask me.
I don't want to say 'NO!'
I want to say 'YES!'
Amen.

Colour this picture

Christmas Day

Thought for the day

The Word of God is made flesh. In the birth of Jesus we see God expressed in human terms.

Readings

Isaiah 52:7-10
Psalm 98
Hebrews 1:1-4 (5-12)
John 1:1-14

Activities

Christmas Day is very much a time for all God's children to worship together.

Involve all the children in the singing and playing of carols, decorating the church, and in the other ministries of welcoming, serving, collection of gifts and so on. Have nativity toys for the very young to play with, such as knitted Mary, Joseph and Jesus, sheep and shepherds.

I have included a drawing and colouring activity for today so that children in church can work at this during the sermon.

Print worksheet *Christmas Day (A)* from CD-ROM.

Christmas is Jesus' birthday

PEBBLES

First Sunday of Christmas

Thought for the day

Jesus, the expression of God's love, lives as a vulnerable boy in the real and dangerous world we all inhabit.

Readings

Isaiah 63:7-9
Psalm 148
Hebrews 2:10-18
Matthew 2:13-23

Aim

To know that Joseph worked with God to keep his family safe.

Starter

Sharks! Scatter some random shapes of newspaper around on the floor to be islands. When the music is playing everyone swims around in the sea enjoying themselves. When the music stops, and the leader calls out, 'Watch out – sharks about!' everyone swims to the safety of an island and stands there until the all-clear, when the music starts again.

Teaching

Talk about how we had to go where it was safe, when we were in danger from the sharks. People who love us look after us to make sure we are safe. We look after those we love (both people and animals) to make sure they are safe. God loves to see us all looking after one another like this, because he loves all of us.

Let the children give some examples of ways people look after them to make sure they are safe, such as marking a yellow line on the station platform to stand behind, belting us up in the car, and helping us to cross the road. When people check that we have warm clothes to go out in, and that we are getting enough sleep, or when they tell us off for doing something dangerous, they are showing their love by looking after us!

God made sure Jesus was as safe as possible in the dangerous world by having Joseph and Mary to look after him. How would they do that? As well as all the usual ways, they had some big dangers to cope with. One night, God told Joseph that King Herod was out looking for Jesus so that he could kill him. So Joseph got up in the middle of the night. He packed up some food and clothes and strapped them on the sleepy donkey. Then he woke Mary up.

'Mary! Wake up! Jesus is in danger. We'll have to leave Bethlehem and go where he will be safe. Come on!'

Mary and Joseph crept around as quietly as they could so that no one would hear them going. They wrapped Jesus up and hoped he wouldn't wake up and cry. They walked through the dark streets, very frightened, and when they left the town they walked on and on through the hills. Jesus woke up and still they walked on, for several days, until at last they got to Egypt, where they knew they were safe. King Herod couldn't come after Jesus there. They only went back home when they heard that King Herod had died.

Praying

God bless my family.
Look after us all.
Help us look after each other.
In life and death
keep us safe for ever.
Amen.

Activities

Using upturned bowls and a large cloth, sheet or towel, make a model of the landscape. Using a cut-out picture of Mary, Jesus and Joseph, based on the one on the worksheet, all the children can have a go at taking the family to safety.

Print worksheet *First Sunday of Christmas (A)* from CD-ROM.

25

Second Sunday of Christmas

Thought for the day

The grace and truth revealed in Jesus show God's freely-given love; through Jesus, God pours out his blessings on us and gives us real freedom.

Readings

Ecclesiasticus* 24:1-12 (* also called Sirach)
Canticle: Wisdom of Solomon 10:15-21
Ephesians 1:3-14
John 1:(1-9) 10-18

Aim

To know that Jesus is God saying, 'I love you!'

Starter

Show me you're happy! Sit everyone in a circle. Just using their faces, ask them to show you they're happy/sad/in pain/excited/tired, etc.

Teaching

They were so good at showing those feelings that you could tell what they were thinking inside! Our bodies are very useful for helping us tell people how we feel. How can you show your mum, dad, grandma or baby cousin that you love them? How do they show that they love you?

Jesus is God saying, 'I love you!' No one has ever seen God while they are alive on earth. He can't be seen. But in Jesus, being born as a baby, growing up and walking around as an adult, we can see God's love.

Praying

Thank you, Jesus,
for being born
into our world.
Thank you for showing us
God's love.
Amen.

Activities

On the worksheet there is a dot-to-dot picture to complete, so that they can see something clearly which they couldn't see before. Have lots of pieces of Christmas wrapping paper, pieces of ribbon and milk-bottle tops to stick on coloured paper to make the suggested collage.

Print worksheet *Second Sunday of Christmas (A)* from CD-ROM.

The Epiphany

Thought for the day

Jesus, the hope of the nations, is shown to the world.

Readings

Isaiah 60:1-6
Psalm 72:(1-9) 10-15
Ephesians 3:1-12
Matthew 2:1-12

Aim

To become familiar with the story of the wise men finding Jesus.

Starter

Play pass the parcel. At the different layers have old bus and train tickets. The prize at the end is a star-shaped biscuit.

Teaching

Tell the children that today we are going to hear about a journey. It isn't a bus journey or a car journey or a train journey. This is a camel journey. (All pack your bags and get on your camels.) We are very wise people, but we don't know where we are going. We are looking for a baby king. And we are packing presents for him. (Pack gold, frankincense and myrrh.) Produce a star on a stick as you explain how a special star has started shining in the sky and we are sure it will lead us to the baby king. Lead off behind the star, riding your camels, and pretending to go over high mountains, through water, stopping for the night, and going to sleep and so on. At last you reach the town of Bethlehem (stick up a sign) where you find the baby king with his mum and dad. (Have a large picture, or one of the cribs made before Christmas.) We all get off our camels and give the baby our presents. The baby's name is Jesus and we have found him at last!

Praying

This is a prayer the wise men might have said. We have all been invited to find Jesus as well, so we can say it with them.

Thank you, Jesus,
for inviting me
to come and look for you.
I am glad I have found you!
Amen.

Activities

To emphasise that the journey of the wise men was probably a hard one, there is a maze to help the wise men find their way to Bethlehem. The star-making activity will need star templates, and ready-cut card for the younger children.

Print worksheet *The Epiphany (A)* from CD-ROM.

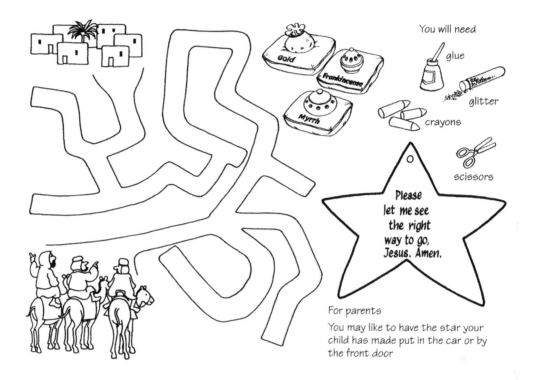

You will need

glue

glitter

crayons

scissors

Please let me see the right way to go, Jesus. Amen.

Gold

Frankincense

Myrrh

For parents

You may like to have the star your child has made put in the car or by the front door

The Baptism of Christ
First Sunday of Epiphany

Thought for the day

As Jesus is baptised, the Spirit of God rests visibly on him, marking him out as the One who will save his people.

Readings

Isaiah 42:1-9
Psalm 29
Acts 10:34-43
Matthew 3:13-17

Aim

To know that Jesus was baptised in the river Jordan.

Starter

Water play. Protect the floor and have some bowls of water and plastic bowls, funnels and tubes for the children to play with.

Teaching

Talk about all the things we could do with the water. Water is so useful to us because it makes us clean when we're dirty, we can drink it and cook with it, and we can paddle and swim in it too. Show the children some pictures of seas and oceans, rivers and ponds.

We have to be very careful with water because we can't breathe in it. We can drown in it.

That makes water a very good way of explaining what happens at Baptism: we drown to everything evil, and come up with our sins all washed clean away by God.

Talk about any Baptisms in their families that they remember – or even their own.

When Jesus walked into the water in the River Jordan, he asked to be baptised as well. So John poured the water over him, and when he came up out of the water, God's Spirit, like a dove, flew out of heaven and rested on him. God said, 'This is my Son. I love him very much.' When we are baptised, God is saying, 'This is my daughter, Eleanor; this is my son Richard. And I love them very much!'

Praying

Dear God,
I'm glad you love me.
I like being one of your children!
Amen.

Activities

Use water added to paint and make some bright pictures to thank God for water. Let the children watch the paint-making, or use blocks of watercolour so they need to keep dipping their brushes in the water to clean them and to make the picture beautiful.

Print worksheet *First Sunday of Epiphany (A)* from CD-ROM.

water + paint powder = paint!

water + paint + brush

= picture!

For parents
Draw your child's attention to all the times we use and need water this week

Dear God,
I'm glad you love me
I like being one of your children!
Amen.

Thank you, God, for water!

Second Sunday of Epiphany

Thought for the day
Jesus is recognised and pointed out by John to be God's chosen one.

Readings
Isaiah 49:1-7
Psalm 40:1-11
1 Corinthians 1:1-9
John 1:29-42

Aim
To know that we can tell others about Jesus.

Starter
Sit in a circle and play 'pass the smile'. You smile to the person next to you, and they smile to the next person until the smile has gone all round the circle. With very young children you can pass a big smiley face around the circle; with older ones you could also try a short message, such as 'God loves you! Pass it on', which they can whisper to each other.

Teaching
First tell a story about the way some good news is passed on from one person to the next. Use simple puppets (wooden spoons and spatulas with faces drawn on and paper clothes stuck on with sticky tack).

Justin was excited. That morning the postman had delivered an airmail letter from his Uncle Kent and Auntie Betty. They lived in California, in the USA, and Justin had never seen them. Every birthday they sent him a birthday card and an American present, and every Christmas they sent a Christmas card, an American Advent calendar, an American Christmas present, and a photograph of them and their family sitting smiling in front of their Christmas tree. They had a large black dog called Corby.

Although he had never seen them, Justin felt he knew and loved Uncle Kent and Auntie Betty already. He knew that Uncle Kent liked gardening and making bird tables out of wood. He knew that Auntie Betty made big chocolate cakes which you ate with ice cream. And he knew that they both loved getting the drawings and paintings he often sent them, and that they kept a photo of Justin on the fridge in their kitchen.

In this airmail letter Uncle Kent and Auntie Betty said that they were able to come to England, and stay with Justin and his family. So that's why Justin and his mum and dad were so excited!

They would all be driving to the airport to meet them. 'How will I know who they are?' asked Justin. Dad got out the latest Christmas photo. 'We'll take this with us and that will help you recognise them,' he said.

When they got to the airport they stood at the barrier while lots of people walked towards them, pushing trolleys piled high with bags and cases. Justin kept looking at the photo and then at all the people. Suddenly he spotted them. Auntie Betty looked just like the sort of person who would bake chocolate cakes and serve them with ice cream. Uncle Kent looked just like the sort of person who would enjoy making wooden bird tables. And from their smiles as they saw Justin, he knew they were just the sort of people to like his drawings and keep his photo on their fridge, because their smiles told Justin that Uncle Kent and Auntie Betty really knew and loved him. 'Hi, you guys!' shouted Auntie Betty, and Uncle Kent wheeled their trolley towards them as fast as he could, with a big grin all over his face.

It was a lovely visit. Justin liked the way Auntie Betty and Uncle Kent spoke, and were interested in everything. He couldn't wait to have his best friend round to meet them. As soon as he could, he told Imogen about them.

'Auntie Betty and Uncle Kent are here from America,' said Justin.

'What are they like?' asked Imogen.

'Come round and see!' said Justin.

So Imogen came round to see, and by the end of the afternoon she, Justin and Auntie Betty had made a big chocolate cake, which they all ate – with ice cream.

'How about you help me make a wooden bird table tomorrow?' said Uncle Kent. Justin and Imogen looked at one another. 'You bet!' they said.

Praying

Jesus, we haven't seen you
but we know you love us.
We want to get to know you
and enjoy your company.
Amen.

Activities

On the sheet they can think about how Jesus shows that he loves them, and how they can tell their friends about Jesus.

Print worksheet *Second Sunday of Epiphany (A)* from CD-ROM.

Third Sunday of Epiphany

Thought for the day
The prophecies of Isaiah are fulfilled in a new and lasting way in Jesus of Nazareth.

Readings
Isaiah 9:1-4
Psalm 27:1, 4-9
1 Corinthians 1:10-18
Matthew 4:12-23

Aim
To know that God wants us all to be safe, free and happy.

Starter
Have a selection of toys which encourage co-operative play, such as a farm, train set and building blocks. Leaders and children play together, setting up a non-threatening environment for successful interaction and contentment.

Teaching
Use a few toys as 'puppets' to act out a situation in which one is not letting the others play happily. This toy's behaviour is stopping the others from being free. First time through ask the children to spot what is happening and offer solutions to the problem. Listen carefully to all the ideas, even the extremely impractical and decidedly unchristian ones! Help them to see it as a problem to solve, rather than as a downer on a particular person. Now have an action replay, and this time have one of the other toys explain to the one behaving badly that they can't play their game if the buildings keep getting knocked over or taken away. The toy listens and says s/he would like to play as well. They let him/her have some bricks to knock down, so everyone is set free to play as they like to.

All of us sometimes make life difficult for other people. Perhaps we feel grumpy so we start being nasty to someone else. Perhaps we want something someone else has so we take it away from them. We are all learning how to live in the loving way that Jesus shows us. God sets us free so we can set one another free.

Praying
Lord Jesus,
thank you for setting us free.
Help us to let others be free as well.
Amen.

Activities

Using the sheet the children can make a moving picture to reinforce today's teaching. They will each need some card and string. Vary the amount of preparation already done by leaders according to the age and skills of each child in the group.

Print worksheet *Third Sunday of Epiphany (A)* from CD-ROM.

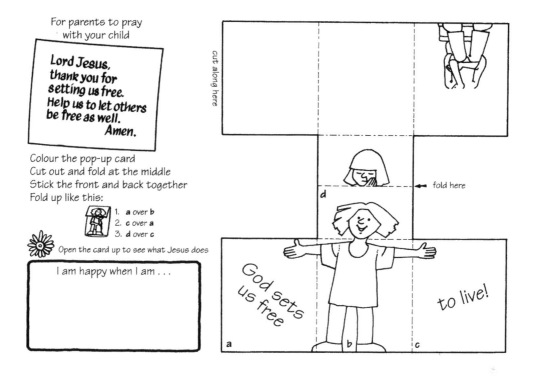

Fourth Sunday of Epiphany

Thought for the day

Jesus shows us in action the loving provision of the God who made us.

Readings

1 Kings 17:8-16
Psalm 36:5-10
1 Corinthians 1:18-31
John 2:1-11

Aim

To know that when we do kind and loving things we are being Jesus' friends.

Starter

Stand in front of the children. They have to copy whatever you do – for example, walking on the spot, jumping, clapping, nodding, wiggling one finger. Older children can take it in turns to be the leader.

Teaching

In our 'copycat' game we were doing what our leader did. As Christians, the leader we follow is Jesus. We look at him and try to be like him in the way we live. Today we are going to look at the kind of things Jesus does which we can copy in our lives.

Use the illustrations below to make large pictures, and show each in turn.

1. *Jesus helped his friends*. One day he went to a wedding and they ran out of wine. Jesus came to the rescue. He told the servants to fill the water pots with water and pour it out. When they poured it out the water had turned into wine, so there was enough for everyone.

2. *Jesus was a good listener*. When people wanted to talk to him about something, he always made time to listen to them and help them.

3. *Jesus loved everyone and treated them all the same.* It didn't matter to him if they were rich or poor, smelly or clean, old or young, ill or well.

Now look at each picture again with its heading and talk together about how we can help our friends, be good listeners and treat everyone with love.

Praying

Jesus, we can't see God,
but you show us what God is like.
Help us to be kind and loving
as you are kind and loving.
Amen.

Activities

On the sheet there are examples for the children to complete and colour in of people living God's way, and a three-sided pop-up picture of Jesus, based on the pictures used in the teaching. The children will each need a strip of card to mount the pictures on.

Print worksheet *Fourth Sunday of Epiphany (A)* from CD-ROM.

Jesus helped his friends

Jesus was a good listener

Jesus loved everyone

Stick the pictures on a strip of card made into a triangle

For parents to pray with your child

Jesus, we can't see God, but you show us what God is like. Help us to be kind and loving as you are kind and loving. Amen.

Draw a kind person feeding the dog

Draw a good friend listening to this person

Sunday between 3 and 9 February

(if earlier than the Second Sunday before Lent)

Thought for the day

We are commissioned to live so that we shine like lights which direct others on to God, the source of Light.

Readings

Isaiah 58:1-9a (9b-12)
Psalm 112:1-9 (10)
1 Corinthians 2:1-12 (13-16)
Matthew 5:13-20

Aim

To know what salt does and think about being like it.

Starter

A little makes a difference. Have a very quiet bell and give this to one of the children. Explain that whenever Suzie rings the bell, everyone freezes. Then get everyone moving and dancing around. Let each of the children have a turn at ringing the bell. It's only a little sound but look at what a difference it makes when it is used!

Teaching

Sit everyone in a circle and have a plate of plain crisps and a salt-cellar in the middle of the circle.

Explain that sometimes even little things can make a big difference – like our little bell in the game. Salt is like that. Spill a few grains (no more!) into everyone's hand to look at. The bits of salt aren't very big and we can't smell them, but we can certainly taste them. (If they want to, they can taste the salt in their hand.) What does the taste remind them of? We only need a little salt to flavour and bring out the taste of our food. For instance, a little salt on plain crisps helps us taste the nice potato flavour. They can all eat a crisp to notice this. Enjoy the eating of these together.

What would happen if we covered our food with salt? It would be bad for us, and we wouldn't taste anything except salt! So the job of salt is to bring out the good taste of other things.

Guess what Jesus said once – he said God wants us as his friends to be like salt! This is what he meant. Even if there aren't many of us, and even if we aren't very big, we can still make a big difference to the world, and help it to be a kinder, fairer and more loving place. The little bits of salt on the crisps help us to taste the real potato, and God wants us to be so loving and friendly to people that they feel happy and free. Instead of going around making people frightened, or making life hard work for them, God wants us to help people, and let them know we care about them.

Praying

Dear Jesus,
I would like to be like salt
and help people
to enjoy being themselves.
Amen.

Activities

On the activity sheet there are some little things to search for, and some pictures of Jesus' friends being salt. There is also a label to colour which they can stick on to their salt mill at home.

Print worksheet *Sunday between 3 and 9 February (A)* from CD-ROM.

For parents to pray with your child

Dear Jesus,
I would like to be like salt and help people to enjoy being themselves.
Amen.

Can you find
5
3
1

be like salt
Matthew 5.13–20

Colour in this label and stick it on your salt mill at home

Sunday between 10 and 16 February

(if earlier than the Second Sunday before Lent)

Thought for the day

To live God's way is to choose the way of life.

Readings

Deuteronomy 30:15-20 or Ecclesiasticus 15:15-20
Psalm 119:1-8
1 Corinthians 3:1-9
Matthew 5:21-37

Aim

To know that God's way is the way of love.

Starter

Using some cut-out paper arrow signs, two of the children go with a leader to lay a trail. The others then go off in pairs to follow the trail, so that eventually everyone should end up at the same place. Make sure the children are supervised very carefully, and that the trail is within sight of a leader all the time.

Teaching

We followed the way Zac and Phoebe led us because we followed the arrows they left. Today we are going to find out what God's way is, so that we can follow that in our lives.

Ask them to follow these instructions:

- Walk quickly
- Creep quietly
- Clap loudly
- Sit silently
- Smile happily
- Frown crossly

Praise everyone for following the instructions so well. Jesus tells us that to follow him we are to live lovingly. All get up and hold hands in a circle as you talk about ways to live lovingly when we are at home / at playgroup / visiting grandparents and so on. Talk about how to live lovingly with different people (such as people who are sad / have got a headache / want to play with your toys.) Then walk round, still holding hands, singing these words to the tune of *Frère Jacques*.

Follow Jesus, follow Jesus
walk his way, walk his way,
loving one another, loving one another every day, every day.

Praying

Lead on, Jesus, I will follow!
I want to live your way,
loving you and loving other people.
Amen.

Activities

On the activity sheet there are other trails to follow, and a signpost to make which helps them remember that Jesus' way is the way of love. They will each need a short stick (about 6 centimetres long) and some glue.

Print worksheet *Sunday between 10 and 16 February (A)* from CD-ROM.

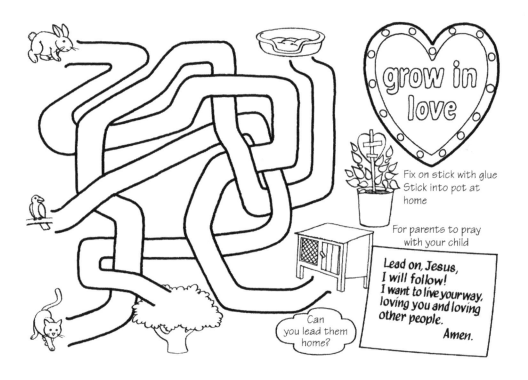

grow in love

Fix on stick with glue
Stick into pot at home

For parents to pray with your child

Lead on, Jesus, I will follow!
I want to live your way, loving you and loving other people.
Amen.

Can you lead them home?

Sunday between 17 and 23 February

(if earlier than the Second Sunday before Lent)

Thought for the day

We are called to be holy; to be perfect in our generous loving, because that is what God our Father is like.

Readings

Leviticus 19:1-2, 9-18
Psalm 119:33-40
1 Corinthians 3:10-11, 16-23
Matthew 5:38-48

Aim

To know that God wants us to love one another as he loves us.

Starter

Bring along lots of cartons and boxes and place them all over the room. Tell the children we are going to build a high tower, and let them help by collecting boxes and bringing them over to add to the tower.

Teaching

Show the children the comedy trick of having your own hands behind your back while your partner's arms pretend to be yours. Try talking and gesticulating, and try to eat or drink something! Enjoy the silliness of it, and then get everyone to look at the way we train our own arms to look after all our needs. Suppose your nose itches – what happens? One of your arms stretches out to exactly the right itchy place and scratches it better for you. Suppose you want to eat a biscuit? One of your arms gets hold of the biscuit and holds it for you, bringing it up to your mouth every time you want to take a bite.

It isn't just our arms we use. If we want to get across the room to see out of the window, we get our legs to take us over there. We don't have to wait for them while they finish what they are doing, or just sit and watch a bit more television. They do what we want straight away. That's because we love ourselves, and do our best to make sure we are comfortable.

God's idea for us is that we should love one another like that. That means noticing what other people are needing and going to help them. Let's try it.

Suppose Mum is trying to carry lots of bags out of the supermarket. (Act this out with real bags from the local store.) Get the children to suggest ways they could do some practical loving. Suppose it's time for the cat to be fed and her bowl is empty. (Have a bowl and some dry cat food.) The children can suggest how to do the loving. Suppose

Dad is feeling very fed up because his team has lost an important match. (Mime this.) How can they do the loving?

Teach the children this 'love your neighbour as yourself' code to help them remember:

- Look *(make hands into binoculars and look around)*
- Think *(put finger to head thoughtfully)*
- Do *(stretch out hands)*

Praying

The more love we give,
the more love there is!
Help us to spread your love around
so there's lots and lots and lots!
Amen.

Activities

On the sheet there is a picture to which the children can add lots of apples, lots of flowers and lots of sunshine and raindrops. There is also a picture to spot the loving going on, and the needs which are not being noticed by the people in the drawing.

Print worksheet *Sunday between 17 and 23 February (A)* from CD-ROM.

Second Sunday before Lent

Thought for the day
God is creative and good; seeking his rule, as our priority, will mean that everything else falls into place.

Readings
Genesis 1:1-2:3
Psalm 136 or 136:1-9, 23-26
Romans 8:18-25
Matthew 6:25-34

Aim
To know that God made the world and looks after us.

Starter
Using either a real baby and parent or a baby doll, have someone talking about looking after a new baby, bathing and feeding, and showing some of the normal baby equipment like rattles and shampoo, nappies and bibs.

Teaching
Talk over the loving care parents give their babies, bringing in the way they may help look after any baby brothers and sisters. Explain that God loves and looks after us like that, noticing what we need, comforting us when we are sad, and sorting us out when we get into a mess. Just as we can help our parents in the care of our brothers and sisters, so we can work with God in helping to look after one another, because we are all brothers and sisters in God's family.

Look at some pictures of God's world to see what a beautiful place God has given us to live in. We can help look after the world as well as the people who live in it.

Praying
Thank you, God,
for making us such a lovely world to live in.
Help us to look after it
and the other people who live here.
Amen.

Activities

Using a paper plate each and some salt dough (two cups of flour, one cup of salt, and water to mix) the children can make a model animal and put it in a suitable landscape, following the instructions (*right*). There is also a dot-to-dot puzzle on the worksheet. Add to the dots provided or delete some according to the age and ability of the children in your group.

Print worksheet *Second Sunday before Lent (A)* from CD-ROM.

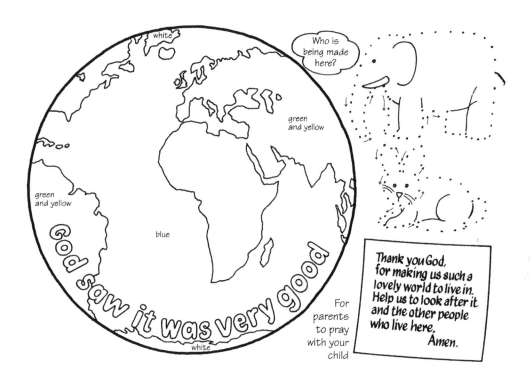

Sunday next before Lent

Thought for the day
In Jesus the full glory of God is revealed and encountered.

Readings
Exodus 24:12-18
Psalm 2 or Psalm 99
2 Peter 1:16-21
Matthew 17:1-9

Aim
To think about how wonderful God is.

Starter
Sit in a circle and pass round something natural and beautiful, such as a shell, a flower or a pineapple. Each person says one thing they notice about it. This encourages very careful observation and enjoyment of detail. The leader can draw attention to what a lot of things we managed to notice in this one bit of God's world.

Teaching
Have some quiet, gentle music playing, and ask the children to lie with their eyes closed as you take them on a lovely journey.

Imagine you find a door in a wall. There is a handle on the door and you open it. On the other side of the door the sun is shining and the sky is blue. There are birds singing. You feel warm and happy. You run in bare feet over the springy grass through the daisies and buttercups, and a bright blue butterfly flies beside you. You can hear the sound of the sea, swishing gently on the sand. Now you can see the water, and you walk over the sand to the edge of the cool water and stand in it, with the water trickling over your feet. A boat is being rowed towards you and inside is someone you know and love and trust. Perhaps it's your mum or dad. Perhaps it's Jesus. They help you into the boat and you sit there safely and happily, looking at the clear water and at the hills in the distance, enjoying the lapping sound of the water against the boat. The boat comes back to the sandy beach, and you climb out and walk back over the soft sand, over the springy green grass with the daisies and buttercups, till you get back to the door in the wall. You go through the door and close it behind you, feeling all happy and rested. The door has your own name written on it and you can go back there whenever you want.

Tell the children that when the music stops they can open their eyes and sit up, and gradually fade the music out so this is not a jolt for them. If the children want to talk about their journey allow a little time for this; it very much depends on the personality of the child.

Talk about the way God has made us a beautiful place to live in and the way he loves us. With God we can feel safe and happy, because there is absolutely nothing nasty or frightening about God. He is completely good and right and true and fair.

Praying

Go straight into the praying after the teaching, making a beautiful focus for the children using shells or flowers and candles, perhaps with a globe.

Holy, holy, holy Lord,
God of power and might,
heaven and earth
are full of your glory!

Activities

The children will need white candles or white wax crayons to draw pictures with. They then paint with water-based colours over their drawings so that they see clearly what they have already drawn, rather as we have been noticing God's glory in the starter and the teaching. There are also examples of God's glory to colour on the worksheet.

Print worksheet *Sunday next before Lent (A)* from CD-ROM.

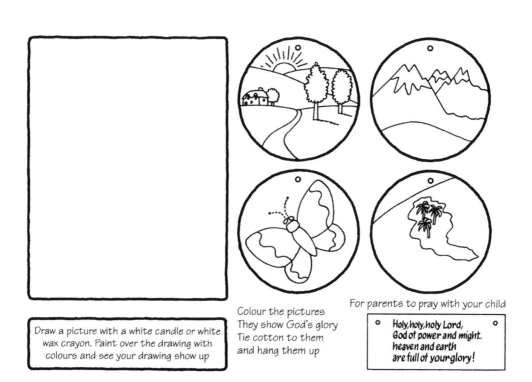

Draw a picture with a white candle or white wax crayon. Paint over the drawing with colours and see your drawing show up

Colour the pictures
They show God's glory
Tie cotton to them
and hang them up

For parents to pray with your child

Holy, holy, holy Lord,
God of power and might,
heaven and earth
are full of your glory!

First Sunday of Lent

Thought for the day

Jesus knows all about temptation; and he can deal with our sin.

Readings

Genesis 2:15-17; 3:1-7
Psalm 32
Romans 5:12-19
Matthew 4:1-11

Aim

To know the Adam and Eve temptation story.

Starter

Put out chairs all over the room, with a cross on the chair in the middle. Play musical chairs, telling everyone first that they mustn't sit on the chair in the middle, even if it's the only chair left.

Teaching

Talk about how well they managed/how hard they found it to keep the rule during the game. Today we are going to hear about Adam and Eve who had a rule to keep.

Tell the story either from a children's adapted version, in your own words based on the biblical account, or from a suitable Bible translation (see 'Recommended Bibles', page 11). Accompany the words with pictures, either from the book you are using or using the carpet tiles and cut-outs of trees, Adam, Eve and the snake. In this case the children can help by placing the trees and fruit on the background. At the point where they are told not to eat from the tree in the middle of the garden, place a cross on the centre tree.

Praying

Jesus, you want us to be loving each day
and we say, 'OK!'
Jesus, you want us to do as you say
and we say, 'OK!'

Activities

On the activity sheet they can count all the fruit Adam and Eve are allowed to eat, and there are outlines for trees and characters to make into a model. Each child will need a flat piece of card for this, and either green paper or green chopped wool to stick on it. If you prefer, you can make one big communal model.

Print worksheet *First Sunday of Lent (A)* from CD-ROM.

Second Sunday of Lent

Thought for the day
Anyone who believes in Jesus can know his power to save and set us free.

Readings
Genesis 12:1-4a
Psalm 121
Romans 4:1-5, 13-17
John 3:1-17

Aim
To know that with God no one is left out.

Starter
Have a large sheet of paper (such as a length of wallpaper) on which everyone can draw or paint themselves. Label it 'God loves us all.'

Teaching
You will need a selection of varied objects which you and the children can sort into a series of categories, such as red, soft, toys, blue, hard, and round. Each time there are some objects which are left out because they don't fit in. Now sort the children in different ways, such as those wearing stripes, those with yellow/black/red hair, brothers, and those who like chicken nuggets. All the time we find there are people left out, but with God it's different. Put a long piece of string around all the group and explain that with God no one is ever left out – God knows and loves everyone.

Praying
Dear God,
thank you for not leaving anyone
outside your love.
Thank you for loving
every single one!
Amen.

Activities
On the sheet the children draw a line of God's love around all the scattered people, and they are going to make a windmill to use in the wind, to remind them that though they cannot see God, like the wind he is real.

Print worksheet *Second Sunday of Lent (A)* from CD-ROM.

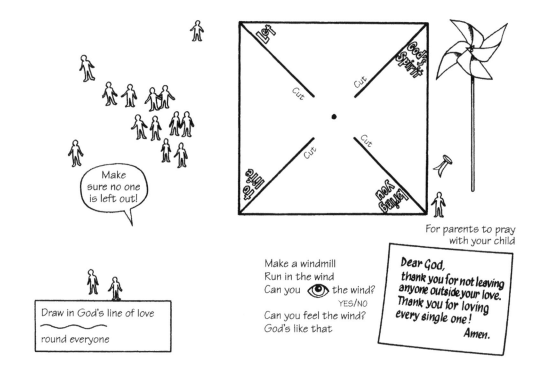

Make sure no one is left out!

Left

God's Spirit

Cut

Cut

Cut

Cut

to life

bring you

For parents to pray with your child

Draw in God's line of love

round everyone

Make a windmill
Run in the wind
Can you 👁 the wind?
YES/NO
Can you feel the wind?
God's like that

Dear God,
thank you for not leaving anyone outside your love.
Thank you for loving every single one!

Amen.

Third Sunday of Lent

Thought for the day

God both knows us completely and loves us completely; meeting us where we are, he provides us with living water, to satisfy all our needs.

Readings

Exodus 17:1-7
Psalm 95
Romans 5:1-11
John 4:5-42

Aim

To know that God can supply our needs.

Starter

Give the children little boxes to fill with little things. Either take them outside to do this (if you have a convenient church garden) or scatter suitable objects around the room so that they can go round collecting them.

Teaching

Introduce two or three puppets or character toys who are trying to use things that don't work very well and are disappointing as they keep letting them down. You can have items that are particularly relevant to your group, but here are some general ideas to start your thinking off: a pencil or crayon which keeps breaking, a leaky bucket, gloves with holes in so your hands get cold, a thin plastic knife and fork which snap, and water that tastes horrid.

Jesus is like a good bucket or like a glove / pencil that really works. (Let the puppets try these and be suitably delighted.) Jesus is like good-tasting, clear water which really quenches our thirst. We can trust Jesus to satisfy our deepest needs.

Praying

My lovely God,
thank you for supplying all our needs,
like a fresh, clear spring of water
which never runs dry.
Amen.

Activities

On the sheet there are pictures to colour which encourage discussion about the way water can supply different needs, and a 'spot the loving' picture which shows love supplying other needs.

The children can also make a water wheel. Prepare for this by cutting a yoghurt or margarine tub as shown below. The children can fix the plastic 'blades' in the slots and thread the wheel on a pencil. When held under a running tap the wheel will turn.

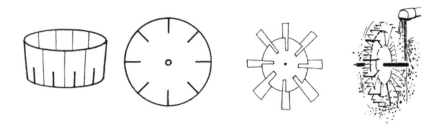

Print worksheet *Third Sunday of Lent (A)* from CD-ROM.

Fourth Sunday of Lent
Mothering Sunday

Thought for the day

Thanking God for our earthly opportunities for mothering and being mothered, we also remember the mothering parenthood of God.

Readings

Exodus 2:1-10 or 1 Samuel 1:20-28
Psalm 34:11-20 or Psalm 127:1-4
2 Corinthians 1:3-7 or Colossians 3:12-17
Luke 2:33-35 or John 19:25-27

Activities

Today is not one for learning separately but for celebrating and learning together. Use some of the all-age suggestions below, involve the children and young people in the music group or choir, as servers, welcomers, collectors for the offering, and so on.

- Stage the interview with a younger and an older mum, either just before the all-stage talk or between the readings.
- Have a family or parent and child leading the intercessions.
- Have a group of different aged people reading one of today's Bible readings, working on it beforehand to use the variety of voices effectively, sometimes alone and sometimes together.
- If posies of flowers are being distributed today, first light a special candle of thanksgiving to remember all those mothers who have died and commend them to God's safe keeping.
- Have a collection of food or toiletries for those families who are at present having to live in refuge or asylum housing, or who are homeless.
- Have a scribble wall (a length of lining paper and some crayons) for people to draw or describe qualities they are thankful for in their own mothers or in God's parenting, as they pray their thanks during a time of quietness and reflective music.

Provide shakers and bells for the younger ones to play during one or two hymns, and streamers to wave. Gather the children round the altar for the eucharistic prayer and choose hymns where the language is accessible.

Have materials for making flowers available for the younger children.

Print worksheet *Fourth Sunday of Lent (A)* from CD-ROM.

How to make
the flowers

You will need
strips of green
tissue paper
straws
glue   bright pieces of   sticky
stick   fabric, wool or paper   tape

1. Wind green paper round a
   straw and fix with tape

2. Decorate a flower shape

3. Stick it on its green stem

4. Cut out leaves from green
   paper

5. Give flowers to your mum!

Fifth Sunday of Lent

Thought for the day

Jesus is the resurrection and the life. He can transform death and despair, in any form, into life and hope.

Readings

Ezekiel 37:1-14
Psalm 130
Romans 8:6-11
John 11:1-45

Aim

To know that God gives life and hope.

Starter

Inflatable toys to blow up and then play with.

Teaching

Get all the children breathing in and out while they hold their ribs, so they can feel the air going in and out. Talk about the way we breathed air into the inflatable toys so that we were able to play with them. Just as our bodies need air, so our spirits need God's Spirit. God gives us life and God gives us hope.

Now spread carpet tiles, bath towels or a sheet on the floor, and use the pictures below to make larger cut-outs from thin card. Gather the children around the edge and move the figures as you tell the story of Lazarus being brought back to life again.

Praying

God be in my head and in my thinking.
  (hold head with both hands)
God be in my hands and in my doing.
  (hold out hands)
God be in my heart and in my loving.
Amen.
  (hands on heart, then arms and hands stretched out)

Activities

On the sheet there are some pictures of people and animals in very tricky situations. The children can draw in something that brings them hope. Also the Lazarus story can be made into a book to take home and read. The children will need coloured mounting paper already cut to size, a hole-punch and a length of wool, or a stapler.

Print worksheet *Fifth Sunday of Lent (A)* from CD-ROM.

Palm Sunday

Thought for the day

Jesus rides into Jerusalem cheered by the crowds. Days later crowds will be clamouring for his death.

Readings

Liturgy of the Palms:
Matthew 21:1-11
Psalm 118:1-2, 19-29

Liturgy of the Passion:
Isaiah 50:4-9a
Psalm 31:9-16
Philippians 2:5-11
Matthew 26:14–27:66 or Matthew 27:11-54

Aim

To welcome Jesus, the king on a donkey.

Starter

If your church has a Palm Sunday procession, then the children will be joining in with this. Provide them with branches to wave, cut from evergreen trees, and ask for one of the hymns to be one the children can cope with, such as *Hosanna, hosanna!* or *Rejoice in the Lord always*.

   If the church doesn't organise a procession, have one for the children, and take a portable tape player with you so that everyone can sing and play along with it.

Teaching

Tell the children the story of Jesus coming into Jerusalem on a donkey, either using your own words based on a careful reading of the Bible text, or one of the versions available for young children. As you tell the story, get the children to join in with all the actions, such as miming the untying of the donkey and leading it to Jesus, the waving of palm branches and laying coats on the road, and shouting 'Hooray for Jesus!'

Praying

Clip, clop, clip, clop!
Hosanna! Hosanna!
Hooray for Jesus,
   the king on a donkey!
Hosanna! Hosanna!
Clip, clop, clip, clop!

Activities

Use the pattern on the sheet to make palm branches from green paper. There is also a road drawn on the sheet and a donkey to cut out and lead along the road into Jerusalem. Children will need assistance with the cutting. For very young children have the donkey already cut out.

Print worksheet *Palm Sunday (A)* from CD-ROM.

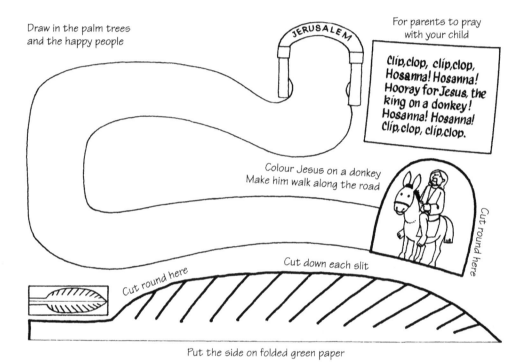

Easter Day

If possible, it is recommended that the children and young people are in church with the other age groups today. Involve the young people in some of the music and in the cleaning and decorating of the church.

Thought for the day
It is true. Jesus is alive for all time. The Lord of life cannot be held by death. God's victory over sin and death means that new life for us is a reality.

Readings
Acts 10:34-43 or Jeremiah 31:1-6
Psalm 118:1-2, 14-24
Colossians 3:1-4 or Acts 10:34-43
John 20:1-18 or Matthew 28:1-10

Aim
To enjoy celebrating that Jesus is alive.

Starter
Have an Easter egg hunt, preferably outside if this is safe and practical.

Teaching
Using a blackboard and chalks, draw the story as you tell it. Please don't be put off and think you won't be able to do it as you can't draw! Young children will be fascinated by the story being drawn, however simple the drawing, and will be quite happy to imagine the bits your drawing leaves out. So do try it!

Start with the green hill outside the city of Jerusalem with the three crosses on it, and tell the children that this is where Jesus had been killed on Good Friday. Now draw in a garden with a cave, and tell the children how Jesus' friends sadly took his body down from the cross and put it in a cave. They rolled a huge heavy stone across the front of the cave to shut it. (Draw in the stone.) The next day was the day when everyone rested. Then on Sunday (which is the same day as today), when it was very early and not even light yet, some of Jesus' friends came to the garden. They wanted to put some sweet-smelling ointment on Jesus' body. (Draw them in at the cave.)

They had been wondering who they could get to move the heavy stone for them, but they were in for a big surprise. When they got to the cave they found that the stone had been rolled away! (Rub it out and draw it in at the side of the cave.) Sitting on the stone was an angel, all full of light. (Draw in the angel.) The angel told them that Jesus wasn't dead any more but had risen from the dead and was alive! The women were very surprised. (Make O shapes for their mouths.) Then suddenly they realised that Jesus was standing there, right next to them! (Draw him in.) The women were very happy to see Jesus. (Change their mouths into smiles.) They went back to tell Jesus' other friends that he was alive, not just for now, but for ever. (Change their legs to be running.)

Praying

Jesus, you died for me
  (arms out like a cross)
Jesus, you came to life for me!
  (arms up)
Jesus, you are alive for ever and ever and ever!
  (clap, clap, clap during the 'evers')

Activities

On the sheet they can follow the footsteps of the women to find where they have gone, and draw in the flowers in the garden. They can also decorate a hard-boiled egg with felt-tip pens or paints.

Print worksheet *Easter Day (A)* from CD-ROM.

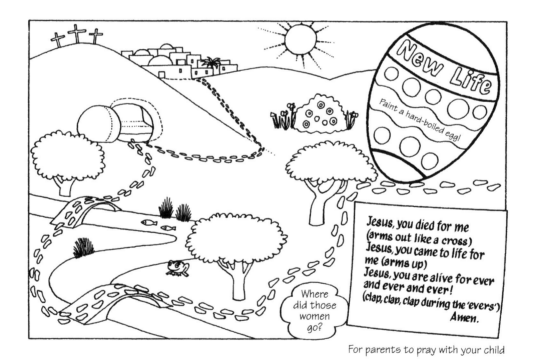

For parents to pray with your child

Second Sunday of Easter

Thought for the day

Through the risen Jesus we have a living hope which will never spoil or fade.

Readings

Acts 2:14a, 22-32
Psalm 16
1 Peter 1:3-9
John 20:19-31

Aim

To know we can sometimes trust what we can't see.

Starter

With the very young play a 'peep-bo' game. With the older children play 'hunt the trainer', telling the children first that there is a trainer somewhere in the room, even though they can't see it yet.

Teaching

Was the trainer there all the time? Yes it was, even though we couldn't see it. We can't see the air all around us but we know it's there because we are alive, breathing the air in and out of our bodies. We can't see Jesus, but we know he is here with us and he can see us.

Jesus can hear us, too, so we can talk to him. Who has some good news to tell Jesus and the rest of us? Have a time of sharing the children's news, in Jesus' company. Jesus loves us, so we can trust him with the things that make us sad as well as the happy things. Have a time of telling Jesus about some of the things that make us sad. After each one lead the children to ask for Jesus' help, either to comfort the person or animal, or simply to be there with them and bring some good thing out of a bad time.

What shall we sing to Jesus? All sing a favourite song (it doesn't have to be a hymn), singing our best, just for Jesus, who is listening, and loves to be with us.

Praying

Who cares if I can't see you?
   (shrug shoulders with hands open)
I certainly know that you're here!
   (nod)
Who cares if I can't touch you?
   (shrug shoulders with hands open)
I certainly know that you're here!
   (nod)

You love me.
  (hands on heart)
You listen to me.
  (touch ears)
You see me
  (point to eyes)
and you talk to me.
  (fingers to mouth then out from it)
So who cares if I can't see you?
  (shrug shoulders with hands open)
I certainly know you're here!
  (nod)

Activities

The children will need a piece of white candle each.

On the sheet they can draw Jesus in wax in the picture of the Pebbles in their group, and then, with a light watercolour wash, paint over the picture so that Jesus can be seen. Protect the children's clothing before they start.

Print worksheet *Second Sunday of Easter (A)* from CD-ROM.

Third Sunday of Easter

Thought for the day
Jesus explains the scriptures and is recognised in the breaking of bread.

Readings
Acts 2:14a, 36-41
Psalm 116:1-4,12-19
1 Peter 1:17-23
Luke 24:13-35

Aim
To know what happened on the road to Emmaus and the effect it had on the two disciples.

Starter
Play with various puzzle games such as jigsaws and shape puzzles. Or play Kim's game, where you set out a number of different objects on a tray and let everyone look at them for a while. Then cover the tray and see how many things they can remember. The children are having to work things out, and experience that this isn't always easy.

Teaching
Set up a length of lining paper on which you have drawn Jerusalem at one end (with the green hill, the crosses and the cave in the garden) and the little town of Emmaus at the other end. Draw a windy road going between the two places. Use this as you recap on the events leading up to the Resurrection and also for today's teaching.

Remind the children that on the first Easter Day – Easter is the day we all have Easter eggs – Jesus came to life. He had died on the cross on the Friday and his friends had put his body in the cave and fixed a great big stone like a door to shut the cave. And early on the Sunday morning, when the women came to the garden what did they find? They found the stone rolled away and Jesus' dead body wasn't in the cave because he wasn't dead any more – he was alive! Alive so that he would never die again. (They will be able to help you with the story. It will be interesting to discover which details they remember best!)

Today we are going to hear about two friends of Jesus who lived about seven miles from Jerusalem. On that same day they were walking home. (Have two toys to walk along the road, starting at Jerusalem.) They were very sad because their dear friend Jesus had died. Just then another traveller caught them up and they all said hello. The stranger said to them, 'Why are you both looking so sad?' 'Haven't you heard?' they said, 'We're sad because Jesus is dead. He was so kind and good, and he told us good stories to teach us about God, and he made people better, and we hoped he would be the leader of our country. But he was put to death on a cross, even though he hadn't done anything wrong at all. Some women said they saw him alive this morning but we don't know whether to believe their story. It's all a big puzzle, and we don't understand it at all.'

As the three of them walked along, the stranger talked. He helped them to understand the things they were puzzling over. He helped them understand that Jesus had said he would have to go through pain and death, but that he would come through that to be alive again. The two friends started to feel a bit happier and a bit more hopeful.

Just then they got near their town. The stranger began to wave goodbye. 'Oh, don't go!' said the friends. 'Come in and have something to eat with us.' So he did. At the meal, the stranger took some bread and thanked God for it. Then he broke it . . . and suddenly the two friends knew exactly who the stranger was! (Can the children guess?) Yes, it was Jesus, and he really was alive!

Praying

Walk with me, Jesus,
today and every day.
I want to walk with you, Jesus,
right through my life!
Amen.

Activities

On the sheet there is the road for the children to make the two friends walk down with Jesus. To make the friends stand up, stick them on card as shown. Then they can tell the story again, and to their parents in the week.

Print worksheet *Third Sunday of Easter (A)* from CD-ROM.

Fourth Sunday of Easter

Thought for the day
Jesus, the Good Shepherd, has come so that we may have life in rich abundance.

Readings
Acts 2:42-47
Psalm 23
1 Peter 2:19-25
John 10:1-10

Aim
To know that Jesus is like a good shepherd who loves his sheep and lambs.

Starter
Have hidden around enough toy lambs and sheep (or pictures of them) for each child to find one.

Lay down a mat which can be a sheep pen and tell the children that there are lots of sheep all over the hillside which need bringing home for the night. Send the children off to collect one sheep each and put them safely in the sheepfold.

Teaching
Praise them for being such good shepherds when they brought in all the sheep, and talk with them about why sheep need to be safely looked after at night if there are wolves, foxes and bears around. (They may have pets which need putting away at night for the same reason.)

Talk about the way shepherds are people who look after sheep. How do we look after our pets? Bring out the need to care for them every day and night, and not just when we feel like it.

Show them a picture of Jesus as the Good Shepherd and explain that Jesus looks after us like a good shepherd looks after his sheep – so we are like Jesus' lambs, and he is our shepherd, taking great care of us all the time. He gives us sleep when we are tired, food and drink when we are hungry and thirsty, and other lambs to play with.

Praying
Dear Jesus, you are my shepherd
and I am one of your lambs.
Thank you for loving me
and looking after me.
Amen.

Activities

The children can make a sheep mask to wear, based on the shape drawn on the sheet. They will also need some glue and chopped white wool. There is a picture to which the children can add other sheep and lambs, either by drawing, or by sticking on pre-cut shapes.

Print worksheet *Fourth Sunday of Easter (A)* from CD-ROM.

Fifth Sunday of Easter

Thought for the day

Jesus is the Way, the Truth and the Life, through whom we can come into the presence of God for ever.

Readings

Acts 7:55-60
Psalm 31:1-5, 15-16
1 Peter 2:2-10
John 14:1-14

Aim

To know that Jesus is like a road that leads us to heaven.

Starter

Gather a collection of vehicles to play with – model cars and lorries, and a sit-and-ride or two. Have a time of car play, either all over the floor, or on a road mat if you have one.

Teaching

Take the children to look at a road, either looking through a window, or going outside (in which case ensure that the children are holding hands with adults or some of the older children, and are well supervised). Talk about what the road looks like, and where it is going. Then come back inside.

Roads are very useful things. You can drive along a road easily without bumping into trees or falling into the sea, because the road is a clear way. A road will take you straight to the shops, or the park, or to church. It stops you getting lost in the mountains if you keep on the clear roadway.

Jesus said he was like a clear roadway that we can travel on to heaven. The Jesus road is clear and strong. If we travel the Jesus Way through life, then, like the best roads, it will take us safely home, at the end of our life here, to live with God for ever in heaven.

Mark a road with chairs, and all walk along it, repeating the prayer in time to the marching.

Praying

Left, right, left, right,
Jesus you're the Way!
Left, right, left, right,
we'll walk your Way today!

Activities

On the sheet they can try drawing roads from one place to another, and there is a 'Jesus knows the way!' badge to colour. It can then be stuck on to pre-cut thin card, and attached to their clothes with a piece of double-sided sticky tape.

Print worksheet *Fifth Sunday of Easter (A)* from CD-ROM.

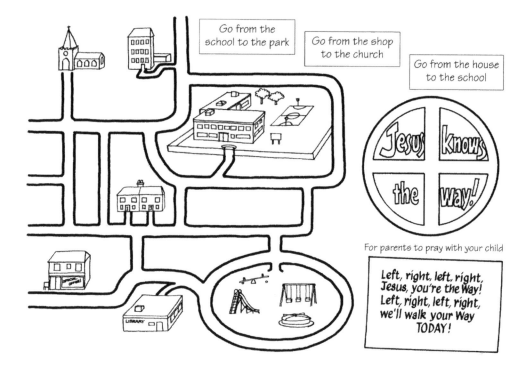

Sixth Sunday of Easter

Thought for the day
The Spirit of truth, given to us, enables us to discern the living, risen Christ.

Readings
Acts 17:22-31
Psalm 66:8-20
1 Peter 3:13-22
John 14:15-21

Aim
To know that we can go on getting to know God more and more till we are old.

Starter
Bring along some clothes belonging to people of different ages to be sorted in order. They should range from baby clothes and nappies to walking sticks and warm sensible slippers, taking in some fashionable items for teenagers and smart office clothing along the way. Have some fun deciding which age would wear them, and end with them in a line, from youngest to oldest.

Teaching
Those clothes told us a story. They told us that we don't stay the same as when we are born. We get older and bigger and grow up. As we grow up we learn all sorts of things. Like what, for instance? Share their ideas of what they think we learn. As we grow we also get better at doing things, like moving about, talking, singing, eating tidily and dressing ourselves. What would they like to be able to do which they can't quite manage yet?

Another important thing we do as we grow up is to make friends. We get to know people and we like them. We get to know them a bit more and like them even better. Friendship grows like we do, as we spend time with our friends and talk, and play together. Friendship grows as we help one another, too.

It's just the same with our friend, Jesus. First of all we don't know him very well. People tell us about him and we think he sounds nice. But we make friends with him by spending time with him and talking and playing with him. Bit by bit we get to know Jesus better, and find that we love him more and more. Even now, the leaders are still getting to know him. Think of some elderly Christians they know at church, or invite one or two along. Even these people are still finding they're getting to know Jesus and love him more.

So as you grow, and grow out of your clothes, right through until you are so old that your hair is white and you need a stick to walk with, you and Jesus can go on being friends, and he'll show you more and more of what he is like, all through your life.

Praying

When I was a baby,
(crouch down small)
I know you loved me, Jesus.
Now I am as tall as this,
(stand at normal height)
I know you as my friend.
When I am as tall as this, or this, or this, or this,
(measure with hand at levels above head)
or even when I walk like this,
(pretend to walk with stick as an old person)
we'll still be best of friends.

Activities

On the sheet there are people to put in order of age. Then they can count the friends of Jesus, so they realise that they all are his friends, whatever the age. There is also an illustration of a height chart to make. Each child will need a pre-cut length of paper which has the heights marked on it, and the words: 'Jesus' friends grow'. The children decorate the chart with paints or stickers.

Print worksheet *Sixth Sunday of Easter (A)* from CD-ROM.

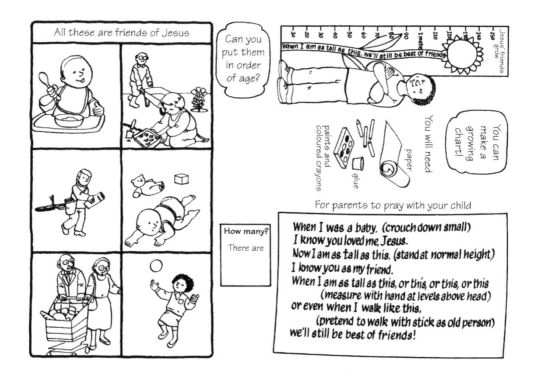

Ascension Day

Thought for the day

Having bought back our freedom with the giving of his life, Jesus enters into the full glory to which he is entitled.

Readings

Acts 1:1-11 or Daniel 7:9-14
Psalm 47 or Psalm 93
Ephesians 1:15-23 or Acts 1:1-11
Luke 24:44-53

Activities

It is likely that Ascension Day services for schools will not need a separate programme for children. However, I have included a drawing and colouring activity for today so that children in church can work at this during the sermon.

Here are some suggestions:

- Any artwork or writing that the children have done on what the Ascension is about can be displayed around the building, and time given in the service to looking at it.

- Have a beautiful helium balloon at the ready. Write on it an Ascension message that the children would like to send. After the service two representative children can let the balloon float away.

- Children can wave white and yellow streamers during some of the hymns.

Print worksheet *Ascension Day (A)* from CD-ROM.

PEBBLES

Seventh Sunday of Easter
Sunday after Ascension Day

Thought for the day

God's glory is often revealed in the context of suffering and failure in the world's eyes.

Readings

Acts 1:6-14
Psalm 68:1-10, 32-35
1 Peter 4:12-14; 5:6-11
John 17:1-11

Aim

To know that Jesus went back into heaven.

Starter

Guess who's coming through the door. Introduce a number of different toys and then bundle them all behind a 'door'. The leader says, 'Guess who's coming through the door', and the children all shout out who they think it is. Vary the length of time they shout, before making one of the toys walk through the door. Repeat until all the toys are outside. Sometimes a toy can go back behind the door again and come out for a second time.

Teaching

What a lot of coming and going there was in that game! Remind the children that since Easter (which will seem a very long time ago) when we remembered Jesus coming to life again, we've had stories of him coming and going, meeting his friends. Sometimes they could see Jesus and sometimes they couldn't.

It went on like that for about the same time as from Easter Day to now. Jesus' friends were starting to understand that Jesus could still be with them, even if they couldn't see him.

One day Jesus was with them all outside. It was time for Jesus to say goodbye to his friends and go back to heaven. 'Don't worry,' he said, 'I won't leave you on your own. I will ask my Father and he will send you the Holy Spirit to give you strength and comfort. It means that I shall be with you all the time, wherever you go.' Then, as they watched, Jesus was lifted up from the ground and a cloud hid him from them. They knew they would not see him again in the same way, but they knew he would be with them, loving them and looking after them.

Like those friends of Jesus, we can't see him with our eyes, but we know he is just as real and alive now as he was then. And when we ask him to be near us and help us he is right there, straight away.

Praying

Jesus, you were born as a baby
  (*rock baby in arms*)
you worked as a carpenter, sawing the wood.
  (*saw wood*)
You died on a cross and you rose again.
  (*arms out, then jump and clap hands*)
You are loving and kind and good.
  (*put up fingers, counting to three*)
In heaven and on earth your glory shines.
  (*point up and down, then trace big circle with fingers stretched out*)
You are loving and kind and good.
  (*count on fingers again*)

Activities

On the sheet there is a picture of the Ascension for the children to add to and colour, or they can complete the picture as a mosaic. For this, pre-cut pieces of different colours from old greetings cards, and place the different colours in separate tubs. The children stick on the bits with glue sticks.

Print worksheet *Seventh Sunday of Easter (A)* from CD-ROM.

For parents to pray with your child

Jesus, you were born as a baby (rock baby in arms).
You worked as a carpenter, sawing the wood.
(saw wood).
You died on a cross and you rose again.
(arms out, then jump and clap hands).
You are loving and kind and good.
(put up fingers, counting to three).
In heaven and on earth your glory shines.
(point up and down then trace big circle with fingers stretched out).
You are loving and kind and good.
(count on fingers again).

Day of Pentecost
Whit Sunday

Thought for the day
With great power the Spirit of God is poured out on the expectant disciples.

Readings
Acts 2:1-21 or Numbers 11:24-30
Psalm 104:24-34, 35b
1 Corinthians 12:3b-13 or Acts 2:1-21
John 20:19-23 or John 7:37-39

Aim
To celebrate the birthday of the Church.

Starter
Play with balloons, enjoying the way they float about in the air.

Teaching
Bring in a birthday cake with two candles on, each candle standing for a thousand years. Explain that today is the Church's birthday. 'Church' doesn't really mean the building, but the people inside. It means a group of Christians who are filled with God's love. That first happened at Pentecost, nearly two thousand years ago, when God's Holy Spirit was poured into the followers of Jesus, until they were filled with his love. So that's how old the Church is – nearly two thousand years old! Sing 'Happy birthday to you' to 'dear Church', and while the cake is being cut up, try the finger rhyme which reminds us that the Church is really the people inside, filled with God's love. (And all of us here are part of that Church.)

Here's the church,   open the doors

here's the steeple,   and here's all the people

Praying

We are the Church
and you are our God.
You fill us with love every day.
We are the Church
and you are our God.
We're a body of people who pray.

Activities

Today's sheet can be decorated and made into a Pentecost birthday hat, which the children can wear into church. They can also have another game, dancing and jumping about to some recorded praise songs. Every time the music stops, call out a name, and everyone prays for that person in the group. (Thank you, God, for Jessica. Fill her with your love.) Make sure every person is prayed for.

Print worksheet *Day of Pentecost (A)* from CD-ROM.

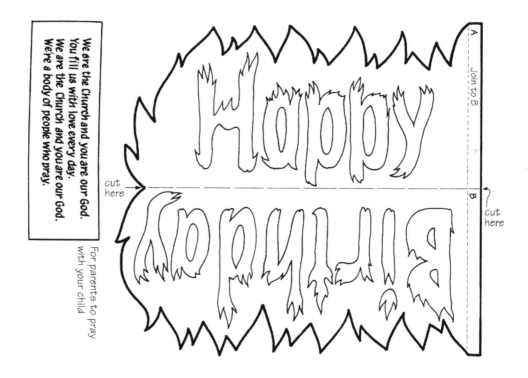

Trinity Sunday

Thought for the day

The mystery of God – Creator, Redeemer and Sanctifier all at once – is beyond our human understanding, yet closer to us than breathing.

Readings

Isaiah 40:12-17, 27-31
Psalm 8
2 Corinthians 13:11-13
Matthew 28:16-20

Aim

To know that God is the greatest.

Starter

Play with sand and buckets, spades and pots, or with water, filling and emptying, and discovering that big amounts won't fit in small containers.

Teaching

Use examples from the starter activity to show how we can't fit big amounts into small containers. Our God is much greater and more wonderful than we can imagine, so it's not surprising that all he is won't fit into our little human minds!

But even though we cannot ever understand all that God is, we can certainly be best friends with him, and snuggle up in his loving, and know that he loves us and cares for us. It's all a bit like this.

There was once a puppy called Pete. He was very soft to stroke, very wriggly and he ran about a lot, and liked eating. Best of all he liked eating rabbit-flavoured crunchy biscuits, but he wasn't allowed many of those in case he got fat. Pete belonged to Oliver, who thought he was the best puppy in the world. Pete thought Oliver was the best boy in the world. They loved each other. Sometimes they played with a ball. Oliver threw the ball and Pete went racing after it, with his ears flying out behind him. He could catch the ball while it was still in the air! Then he would hang on to the ball so Oliver couldn't get it back, wagging his tail because it was such fun. But if Oliver started to walk away, Pete came racing over and dropped the ball at his feet, waiting for Oliver to throw it again.

Every day Oliver disappeared for a while. He didn't really disappear, of course; he just went to nursery school for the morning. Pete was puzzled and sad whenever Oliver disappeared, and he was happy and waggy as soon as Oliver came back. Because he was a dog, Pete couldn't understand things like people going to nursery school, and, however long Pete lives, he will never be able to understand things like that, any more than we will ever be able to understand everything about God.

But what Pete did know very well indeed was that he loved Oliver and Oliver loved him, and they both enjoyed being together. Whenever they played and laughed together, whenever Oliver fed him (especially rabbit-flavoured crunchy biscuits!) and whenever Pete fell asleep on Oliver's feet, he knew that he was loved and owned by someone very special, just as we know we are owned and loved by a wonderful God.

Praying

Our God is so BIG, so strong and so mighty,
There's nothing that he cannot do!
The rivers are his, the mountains are his,
the stars are his handiwork too!
Our God is so BIG, so strong and so mighty,
there's nothing that he cannot do!

Activities

On the sheet there is a pattern which the children can trace round and round to get a feel of how God is unending, and they can look at and colour the pictures to see the different aspects of God.

Print worksheet *Trinity Sunday (A)* from CD-ROM.

Sunday between
29 May and 4 June

(if after Trinity Sunday)

Thought for the day

Wise listeners build their lives up on the strong rock of the word of God.

Readings

Deuteronomy 11:18-21, 26-28
Psalm 31:1-5,19-24
Romans 1:16-17; 3:22b-28 (29-31)
Matthew 7:21-29

Aim

To know that Jesus is like strong rock to build on.

Starter

Bring along plenty of construction toys, such as building bricks, blocks or simply lots of boxes and cartons, and work with the children to build.

Teaching

Jesus was once talking to his friends and he told them this: 'All the things I teach you to do are very important, and will help you live a good life. Wise people will listen to what I teach them *(cup hand to ear as you say this)* and then do it *(open hands up)*. Foolish people will hear what I tell them *(cup hand to ear)* and yet do nothing about it *(fold arms)*.'

Explain that you are going to tell them all something, and they can choose whether to listen (cup hand to ear) and then do what you say (open hands) or just listen (cup hand to ear) and do nothing about it (fold arms). Tell them that you have some sweets in a tin. Only children who put their hands up will be given one. They can now choose whether to put their hands up or not. Then give out sweets to those with their hands up.

It is wise and sensible to do what Jesus tells us, because he loves us and knows what is best for us all. But lots of people are not very wise. They hear what Jesus says, and yet do nothing about it.

Jesus said, 'If you listen to what I tell you *(cup hand to ear)* and do what I have said *(open hands up)* you will be as sensible and wise as a person building on a good strong rock. If you listen to what I tell you *(cup hand to ear)* and yet do nothing about it *(fold arms)* you will be as silly and foolish as a person building on wobbly, moving sand!'

Let's see what happens if we build on rock (which is strong, like this floor). Build up on this and see how firm the house is. Let's see what happens if we build on wobbly, moving sand. Have a floppy surface such as an old pillow, or rumpled blanket and pretend that is sand, because it is wobbly and moves about a bit, like sand. Even if you carefully manage to keep your building together while you are building, as soon as the pillow or blanket is jogged the whole building collapses. (*Do this as you speak.*)

So if we are going to build up good strong lives, let's not be foolish, listening to what Jesus says (*cup hands to ears*) and doing nothing about it (*fold arms*). Let's make sure we are wise, listening to what Jesus tells us (*cup hands to ears*) and doing what he says (*open hands*).

Praying

Jesus, I don't want to be foolish, hearing what you tell me
> (*cup hand to ear*)

but not doing anything about it.
> (*fold arms*)

Jesus, I want to be wise, hearing what you tell me
> (*cup hand to ear*)

and doing it in my life.
> (*open hands*)

Activities

Each child will need a strip of thin card so they can stick their house models on to it and stand them up. Also on the sheet, a picture with some people doing what Jesus said, and some not, helps them notice the godly way of living and the contrasting selfish way.

Print worksheet *Sunday between 29 May and 4 June (A)* from CD-ROM.

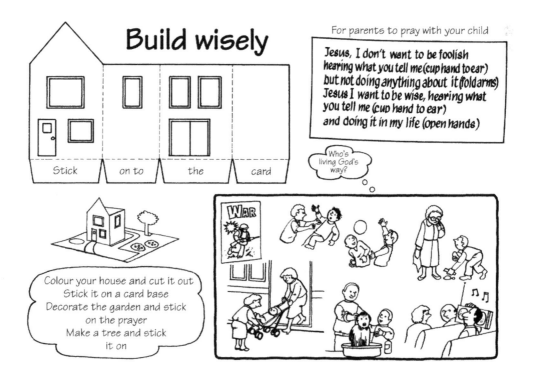

Sunday between 5 and 11 June

(if after Trinity Sunday)

Thought for the day

Jesus' life of healing and compassion acts out God's desire for mercy rather than empty sacrifice.

Readings

Hosea 5:15–6:6
Psalm 50:7-15
Romans 4:13-25
Matthew 9:9-13, 18-26

Aim

To know that Jesus made people better.

Starter

Sit in a circle and pass round a teddy with bandage on him. Each person holding the teddy can share with the others about a time they were poorly, or what it is like to be poorly.

Teaching

Hold up a picture (from a children's Bible) of Jesus healing someone which is covered up by a piece of card. Explain that before Jesus came, people couldn't see what God was like. But when Jesus came to live on earth (uncover the picture) they could see that God was very kind, because Jesus was always very kind. What is he doing in this picture? He is making someone better. Jesus hated to see people suffering and being poorly, and often he would make them better. Today we are going to hear about a child who was very ill at the time Jesus was living on earth.

Unroll a bed mat (this can be a blanket) and explain that this is the kind of bed that people slept on in those days. The child was feeling very, very ill, and her mummy put her to bed. (Have one of the children to lie on the bed.) Just like you, when you are ill, her mummy and daddy probably stroked her face, wiped her hot head with nice, cool water, and gave her water to drink. (Do these things as you speak.) Her daddy and mummy were worried about their daughter, because instead of getting better, as usually happens, she got more and more ill.

Then they heard from a friend that Jesus was walking to their town. They had heard that Jesus was very kind, and that he could make people better, and they badly wanted their daughter better, because they loved her so much. But before Jesus got to the town, their daughter died, and everyone was very sad. 'Well,' said the girl's daddy, 'I'm still going to ask him to come!', and he got up and ran out of the house towards Jesus. 'Jesus!' he said, 'my daughter has just died! But if you come and touch her with your hand I'm sure she will live again!'

Jesus felt very sorry for this man and his family. He wanted to help them, and said that of course he would come. When they got to the house everyone was crying and making a lot of noise. Jesus told them to go away. 'The child is not dead,' he said. 'She is only asleep.' The people laughed at that, but they went out and left Jesus with the little girl and her mummy and daddy. He went to where she was lying and held her hand. The little girl started to open her eyes! She looked at Jesus and smiled. She looked at her mummy and daddy and smiled. Then she got up from her bed mat. 'Thank you, Jesus!' she said. 'I feel better than I have for ages!' And they all hugged one another and cried again – but this time because they were so happy.

Praying

Jesus, you are kind; Jesus, you are loving.
You made people happy and you made people well.
Jesus, you are kind; Jesus, you are loving –
so God is kind and loving, I can tell.

Activities

On the sheet there is a picture of a child, ill in bed, and they can draw in the things that might make them feel better. They can also colour, cut out and put in the right order the pictures of today's story. Provide them with strips of coloured paper to stick the pictures on to, then fold the strip of paper to make a zigzag book.

Print worksheet *Sunday between 5 and 11 June (A)* from CD-ROM.

For parents to pray with your child

Jesus you are kind, Jesus you are loving.
You made people happy and you made people well.
Jesus you are kind, Jesus you are loving-
So God is kind and loving, I can tell.

Sunday between 12 and 18 June

(if after Trinity Sunday)

Thought for the day

Jesus sends his ambassadors out to proclaim God's kingdom and bring hope and peace of mind to the harassed and lost in every age.

Readings

Exodus 19:2-8a
Psalm 100
Romans 5:1-8
Matthew 9:35–10:8 (9-23)

Aim

To know that Jesus chose twelve followers to teach, and to work with him.

Starter

As the children arrive, give them a piece of paper with their name written on it, which they can decorate. Then they all hold their names as they jump about to some music. When the music stops choose a name, and that child comes to stick their label on a poster titled 'We are the Pebbles'. Continue until everyone has been chosen, and the names are all stuck on the poster.

Teaching

Count to twelve with various things – leaves, stones, toys and crayons, for example. Then try counting to twelve together, using fingers of both hands and stamping each foot.

When Jesus was living on our earth he often taught crowds and crowds of people. They would all come out in the sunshine to the beach or the hills, and sit down to listen to what Jesus said. There were mums and dads, babies, toddlers, teenagers, uncles and aunties, grandmas and grandads. Jesus enjoyed teaching all the people and showing them God's love.

He didn't just talk to the crowds. He also chose some people to be his followers, so he could spend time with them and train them ready for when he had gone back to heaven. Can you guess how many people he chose? It was one, two, three, four, five, six, seven, eight, nine, ten, eleven, twelve! As you all count, place on the floor twelve paper shapes of people, based on the pictures below. They were all in Jesus' gang – they were like a class and Jesus was their teacher. As they walked along or sat around the fire in the evening eating their supper, Jesus would talk to them, and answer their questions. They were called disciples.

One day Jesus sent his one, two, three, four, five, six, seven, eight, nine, ten, eleven, twelve disciples out to try teaching the people in all the towns and villages round about, and making people better. They would be doing the kind of work Jesus usually did. Did he send them out with posh shoes? (Put a pair down.) No! Did he send them out with lots of spare clothes in a bag? (Put a bag down.) No! Did he send them out with lots of money to spend? (Put down a purse and cheque book.) No! He sent them out just as they were, with his blessing, and his prayers and his love.

Praying

Jesus chose
1 2 3 4 5 6 7 8 9 10 11 12 disciples
and told them all about God's love.
They told others, who told others,
who told others who told ME! So I know, too!
Thank you, Jesus.

Activities

If you have a set of Russian dolls, bring these along to show the children how the news gets passed on from person to person. Use a person shape cut from polystyrene so that the children can print twelve disciples in their places on the sheet. Make sure you protect clothing during the painting process.

Print worksheet *Sunday between 12 and 18 June (A)* from CD-ROM.

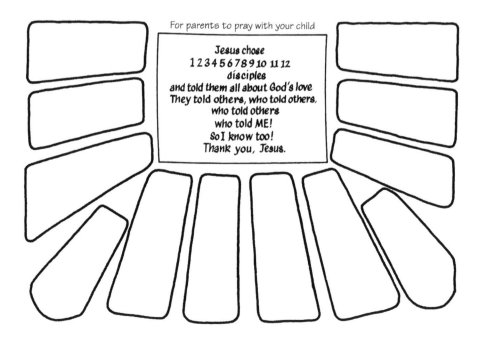

For parents to pray with your child

Jesus chose
1 2 3 4 5 6 7 8 9 10 11 12
disciples
and told them all about God's love
They told others, who told others,
who told others
who told ME!
So I know too!
Thank you, Jesus.

Sunday between
19 and 25 June

(if after Trinity Sunday)

Thought for the day

When we are willing to take up our cross with Jesus we will also know his risen life.

Readings

Jeremiah 20:7-13
Psalm 69:7-10 (11-15) 16-18
Romans 6:1b-11
Matthew 10:24-39

Aim

To be introduced to the idea of taking up something hard, and sometimes painful, out of love.

Starter

Play the singing game 'The princess slept for a hundred years', which includes the handsome prince cutting the forest with his sword in order to reach the beautiful princess.

Teaching

Tell the children this story, either reading it to them or preferably memorising the main points and telling it with your own character.

In Africa there was a village, and in the village there lived a girl called Eunice and her three brothers and her mother. Her father had to work in a big town a long way off, so he was not often at home. Every day Eunice and her little brothers went out with their mother, and all the other mothers, to fetch the water, because in their village there were no taps to get their water from. They walked quite a long way out of the village, until they came to a place where the water bubbled up out of the ground. The children played in the water while the mothers lifted down their heavy pots from their heads and filled them with water. Then the water pots were lifted high on to the heads of all the mothers, who were very strong, and everyone walked (more slowly, this time) back to the village, with enough water for the day.

One morning Eunice woke up to find that her mother was very ill. She was hot and shivery, and could not get up. One of the older women in the village came in to sit with her, but the family still needed the water to be fetched. Who could do that? Eunice thought to herself, 'I will get the water today for my mother.'

So she went down with her brothers and the other mothers, carrying the bucket, and when they got to the place where the water bubbled up out of the ground, she filled the bucket up to the brim. It was very heavy to carry, but Eunice kept thinking of her mother at home, and how happy she would be to have the water collected for the day, and somehow that made it easier to keep going. Some of Eunice's friends were playing together and they called out to her, 'Hey, Eunice, put that bucket down and come and play with us!' Eunice loved playing with her friends, but she knew that today it was more important to get the water home to give her mother a drink, and save her worrying. So she called back, 'Not today, I can't. I have the water to carry home.'

It seemed a very long walk back to the village, but at last Eunice reached the house, and carried the water inside. Her mother was lying there, weak and ill, but when she looked up and saw Eunice with the bucket full of water for the day, she smiled, and whispered, 'Well done, my child. God bless you for your kind heart!' Eunice ran and gave her a drink, and wiped her mother's head with some cool water. Suddenly it didn't matter that the bucket had been so heavy to carry, or that her muscles ached. She had carried it out of love.

Praying

Dear Jesus,
you gave up everything for us
because you love us.
Help us to do loving things
for one another
even if they are hard work.
Amen.

Activities

On the sheet there is a week's chart for them to fill in when they do something kind for someone else, and there are some pictures of ideas to help them. It would also be nice for the group to do something kind and thoughtful, such as gathering up the litter outside (or inside!) or preparing a song to sing for the rest of the congregation in church.

Print worksheet *Sunday between 19 and 25 June (A)* from CD-ROM.

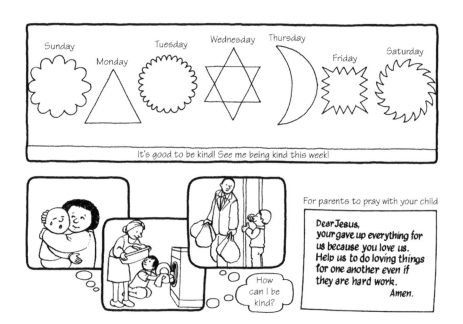

Sunday between 26 June and 2 July

Thought for the day

As Christ's people we are no longer slaves to sin, but available for righteousness.

Readings

Jeremiah 28:5-9
Psalm 89:1-4,15-18
Romans 6:12-23
Matthew 10:40-42

Aim

To know that we can use our bodies for good.

Starter

Draw some signs on separate pieces of card: eyes, ears, hands, mouth, feet and a whole body outline. When the whole body sign is shown, everyone dances around to some music. Whenever the music stops, one of the other signs is shown and everyone holds that bit of their body until the music starts again.

Teaching

Tell the children how God has made us with these lovely bodies that can do all sorts of things. Place the signs from the starter activity on the floor, face down, and uncover them one by one, as you talk together about all the things these parts of us can do. They can demonstrate some of them, too. Focus on all the positives, so that you are celebrating the way we can work in God's team for good.

Praying

Thank you, God, for this body of mine.
It can shout and help and play.
I like to use this body of mine
to show your love each day.
Amen.

Activities

On the sheet there is a picture of a person to which the children can add various parts by drawing them, or you could cut out the appropriate parts beforehand and the children can stick them on.

Print worksheet *Sunday between 26 June and 2 July (A)* from CD-ROM.

For parents to pray with your child

Thank you, God, for this
body of mine.
It can shout and help and play.
I like to use this
body of mine
to show your love each day.
Amen.

Draw yourself doing the loving you are thinking about

Draw or stick on the missing bits!

Sunday between 3 and 9 July

Thought for the day

To all who are weary with carrying heavy burdens in life, Jesus offers rest for our souls and unthreatening relief.

Readings

Zechariah 9:9-12
Psalm 145:8-14
Romans 7:15-25a
Matthew 11:16-19, 25-30

Aim

To know that we can tell Jesus all that weighs us down, and he will help us.

Starter

Bring along five or six items which the children can pick up as they choose which is the lightest and which is the heaviest. Make this fairly obvious weight-wise, except that the shapes and weights don't necessarily match up, so they might get a surprise when they expect a large item to be the heaviest and it isn't.

Teaching

Have one of the leaders struggling in with several bulky, heavy parcels. You greet them and comment on how weighed-down they look, and they agree, gratefully letting you unload them so they can feel better and sit down comfortably. They ask what we're doing today, and the children can tell them about choosing the heaviest and lightest parcel. Today we are thinking about carrying heavy loads.

Some loads we can see (like these parcels) but some we can't see – like when we are feeling very worried about something, and we carry our worry around with us and it feels quite heavy. (Pick up a parcel and hold it as you speak.) What kind of things do we sometimes worry about a lot? Ask the children to share their ideas about this, and share with them some of the things you worry about as well, so that you are all in it together.

The lovely thing about knowing Jesus is that we can tell him those worries, and ask him to help sort them out with us. (Have someone take the parcel from you.) And just talking it over with our friend Jesus makes it feel less worrying.

Another load we can't see is being frightened about something. (Pick up another load.) We carry that fear around with us and it can make us scared and sad. What kind of things are we scared and frightened about? Once again, share these together. Well, what's good about knowing Jesus is that we can tell him our fears, and ask him to help us be brave. (Have this load taken from you.) Jesus is never too busy to listen to us, and we can talk to him any time and anywhere. He will always be there for us because he loves us, and doesn't want us struggling along with heavy loads all the time – he wants us to be free to skip and run and play!

Praying

Heavy loads, heavy loads.
   (pretend to carry them)
'I'm worried!' and 'I'm scared!'
   (head in hands, then shake with fright)
'Come to me,' says Jesus,
   (beckon)
'and I will give you rest!'
   (arms out, palms up)
Thank you, thank you, Jesus!
   (jump up and down and clap hands)
You really are the best!
   (both hands up in air)

Activities

Give each child a stone to decorate with paint or stickers which they can put on the mat which they make from the sheet. Then they can use their 'worry stone' to remind them to talk things over each day with their friend Jesus.

Print worksheet *Sunday between 3 and 9 July (A)* from CD-ROM.

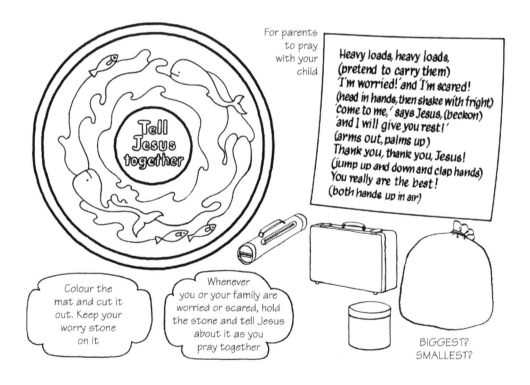

Sunday between 10 and 16 July

Thought for the day

Seed of God's word, sown in good soil, watered by his rain and warmed by his sunlight, produces a good crop of spiritual fruit.

Readings

Isaiah 55:10-13
Psalm 65:(1-8) 9-13
Romans 8:1-11
Matthew 13:1-9, 18-23

Aim

To know that God sends the rain to water the land and make things grow.

Starter

A rainy game. You will need either two tape recorders, so that you can play 'sunny' music from one and 'rainy' music from the other, or two different types of sounds, such as a rainstick and a xylophone. One of the leaders holds a large golfing umbrella. Play the sunny and the rainy music or sounds to the children. Whenever they hear the sunny sound, they skip about in the sunshine, and whenever they hear the rainy sound, they run to take shelter under the umbrella.

Teaching

Start with this puzzle song about water, the children joining in with the chorus. (See page 378 for the music.)

1. You can drink it, swim in it, cook and wash up in it, fish can breathe in it – what can it be?
   It's water! God has provided us water! Water of life.

2. It's as hard as rock, yet it flows down a mountain, and clouds drop drips of it – what can it be?

3. It's as light as snowflakes and heavy as hailstones, as small as dewdrops and big as the sea.

Show the children a large cut-out cloud, and talk with them about what it feels like to be out in the rain, and what they wear in the rain. What happens to the ground when it rains? Talk about puddles and sloppy mud. What happens to the plants and flowers when it rains? Show the children a daisy or buttercup, still attached to its root, and tell them how the plant drinks up the water through the roots, and that helps it to grow. After a long time without rain the grass looks all dry and brown, but after rain everywhere is lovely and green again.

God sends the rain so that everything can live and grow. We all need the rain – we couldn't live without it! Rain is one of the many ways God showers us with good gifts.

Praying

This is a water cycle prayer as it goes round and round!
Thank you, God, for sending rain,
pitter, patter, pitter, patter,
it makes the grass all green again,
pitter, patter, pitter, patter,
it makes the fruit and veggies grow,
pitter, patter, pitter, patter,
we all need water to live, and so . . .
pitter, patter, pitter, patter,
thank you, God, for sending rain!

Activities

Using the picture on the sheet the children can make a water cycle wheel. They will need to stick it on to thin card and poke a stick or pencil through the middle as shown. They can also have shiny paper raindrop shapes to tie on to string, so they can all come running and jumping into church as a refreshing shower of rain. (Arrange this with whoever is leading the worship in church.)

Print worksheet *Sunday between 10 and 16 July (A)* from CD-ROM.

Sunday between 17 and 23 July

Thought for the day

God's justice is always blended with mercy and loving kindness, so that we have real hope.

Readings

Wisdom of Solomon 12:13,16-19 or Isaiah 44:6-8
Psalm 86:11-17
Romans 8:12-25
Matthew 13:24-30, 36-43

Aim

To know that God is fair and kind.

Starter

Split an apple or a bar of chocolate up among everyone so that it is exactly fair, and everyone gets a piece if they want it. In a time of news-sharing, go round the circle in order, so that no one is left out and all are asked if they would like to share some of their news. Don't let anyone get an extra go just because they are noisy or attention-seeking.

Teaching

You will need four puppets, or you can make your own from old socks or wooden spoons. You don't need four hands, though – just pick up the one which is talking at any one time. One puppet is baby-sitting, and trying to give out biscuits fairly, but two of the 'children' are so demanding and noisy that they end up getting more than the other. The third child complains that it isn't fair. Why should they get more just because they're noisy?

Stop the puppets and ask the children what they think should happen. Then have a nearly-action-replay with the baby-sitter telling the noisy ones that the biscuits will be shared out fairly, which means one each, and being noisy won't make any difference.

Now have the puppets being a parent and children buying an ice-cream each. The parent tells the children to be very careful not to drop them. One child does drop the ice-cream, and cries about it. The parent is sympathetic, and says, 'You can share mine!'

God is like a loving mum or dad who is always fair, but very kind as well, and helps us out when we make mistakes.

Praying

Jesus, I'm glad you are always fair.
You love us all, and don't leave anyone out.
And when we make mistakes
you help us put things right again.

Activities

They can give everyone in the picture on the sheet the same things, so it is fair. This can either be done by drawing the items in, or you could provide separate, pre-cut items which they stick on.

Print worksheet *Sunday between 17 and 23 July (A)* from CD-ROM.

For parents to pray with your child

Jesus, I'm glad you are always fair.
You love us all, and don't leave anyone out.
And when we make mistakes you help us put things right again.

Are there enough shoes for the feet?

Give each child

a hat

a lollipop

a pet cat

Well done for being fair!

Sunday between 24 and 30 July

Thought for the day

Jesus, the teacher, enables the ordinary, unlearned people to understand God's wisdom – the eternal laws of his Father's kingdom.

Readings

1 Kings 3:5-12
Psalm 119:129-136
Romans 8:26-39
Matthew 13:31-33, 44-52

Aim

To know that finding Jesus is like finding treasure.

Starter

Have a treasure hunt where each child experiences the hunting and the discovering. To do this, wrap each 'treasure' in paper tied with a different coloured piece of wool. Give each child a matching piece of wool and send them off to find their own treasure.

Teaching

Talk about what fun it was to find the treasure. Today we are going to hear a story about finding treasure. It is one of the stories that Jesus told.

There was once a man who was digging in a field. He had been digging for most of the morning when his spade hit something hard. At first he thought it was a big stone. He dug around to find the edge of the stone so that he could lift it out. But this hard stone was straight at the edges and very flat at the top. 'What a funny stone!' thought the man, and he bent down and started to scrape away the earth to uncover it. 'This isn't a stone at all!' said the man to himself. 'It's more of a strong box. Whoever would want to bury a box in the middle of a field? How very strange.'

Very carefully he dug all round the edges of the box and brushed away earth until he could get his spade right underneath it. Slowly the box started to come out of the ground. It was heavy work and the man was using all his strength. 'Nearly there!' he kept saying to himself. 'We're nearly there!'

Suddenly the last of the box popped out and the man fell over backwards and rolled over. 'Whoopsadaisy!' he said and crawled back on his hands and knees to see what he had dug up.

It was a strong wooden box with a clasp to hold it shut. The man opened it a tiny bit and peered inside. 'Slugs and earthworms, what have we here?' he gasped. Inside the box was a gleam of gold. It was full of shiny things and sparkling things. The man was so surprised that he slammed the box shut, and then, very slowly, he opened it again so that the sun shone down on all the treasure and the treasure shone and sparkled back at the sun. At first the man could hardly believe his eyes. But he blinked and the treasure was still there. He pinched himself and it hurt. 'Ouch! It must be real and this must be my lucky day!' shouted the man, and he did a little dance all by himself in the middle of the field.

'Now', thought the man, 'what I need to do is to buy this field, and then the treasure will be mine. But fields cost a lot of money, which I haven't got. Let's see . . . I could sell my table and chairs . . . and my old car . . . and my stamp collection . . . and . . . and . . .' The man worked very hard that afternoon. First he buried the box safely back in the field. Then he went home and got together everything he owned and had a car boot sale. He even sold the car boot – with the rest of the car thrown in for free! Then he went and bought the field.

Full of excitement, the man ran back to his field and started digging. It had been well worth getting rid of everything else. This time the box of sparkling treasure belonged to him, and he would be rich for the rest of his life!

Praying

Jesus, you are the treasure of my life!
With your love I am rich for ever and ever.

Activities

On the sheet there is a treasure chest for the children to fill with shiny, sparkling things. Have ready a selection of different coloured sparkling and shiny paper, and gold-sprayed pasta in different shapes, so that they can stick them into the chest.

Print worksheet *Sunday between 24 and 30 July (A)* from CD-ROM.

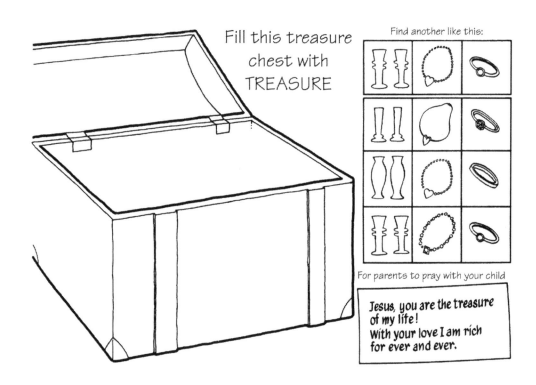

Fill this treasure chest with TREASURE

Find another like this:

For parents to pray with your child

Jesus, you are the treasure of my life!
With your love I am rich for ever and ever.

Sunday between
31 July and 6 August

Thought for the day

God feeds all who come to him hungry, and we, as the Church, are expected to share in that work.

Readings

Isaiah 55:1-5
Psalm 145:8-9, 14-21
Romans 9:1-5
Matthew 14:13-21

Aim

To know that Jesus fed a big crowd of people.

Starter

What's in my lunch box today? Have a lunch box, and a number of lunch items laid out on the floor. The children cover their eyes as you secretly choose a few things to put in the box. Then you ask, 'What's in my lunch box today?' Everyone tries to guess or work it out from the items that are now missing from the floor. When everyone has said what they think, reveal the true contents and take them out, ready to start again.

Teaching

Using the same lunch box, place inside it five little rolls and two sardines. (Be brave and go for real ones!) Set out a green bath towel on the floor, with a cut-out shiny blue lake laid on top of it. Tell the children how crowds and crowds of people wanted to be with Jesus all the time, because they could tell that he loved them. It's always nice to be with people who you know are very fond of you. The way they look at you and the way they talk to you makes you feel happy and safe. That's how Jesus makes people feel.

Well, they had heard that Jesus was going over the lake on a boat. (Make a toy boat go over the lake.) The people didn't have a boat, and they were on this side of the lake. So how could they reach Jesus? Yes, they could walk around the lake! So they did. It was quite a long walk but they were so keen to find Jesus that they didn't mind. Move the lunch box round the lake and put it down on the other side.

When Jesus saw them he was tired. He had actually come for a rest. So what do you think he said? 'Go away, I'm tired'? That doesn't sound like Jesus, does it, and he didn't say it. He made the people welcome, and healed the ones who were ill, and forgave the ones who wanted to put right bad things they had done, and he talked to them all in the sunshine.

By the evening they were still there, and they were all hungry. So what do you think Jesus did? He fed them. What with? Yes, one person said Jesus could use their lunch. What was the lunch? Open the box to see.

Jesus took what was offered (take it), thanked God for it (thank God), broke it all up (break it all up), and broke it all up . . . and broke it all up . . . and there was loads of food for everyone there, crowds and crowds and crowds of them! And they all shared it. (Share the food.)

Praying

Loving Father,
give us this day our daily bread.
Amen.

Activities

On the sheet they can hunt for the hidden loaves and fish in the picture, and model the loaves and fish from modelling clay or playdough to wrap in a small square of cloth (cut from an old sheet or shirt).

Here is a recipe for playdough:

Mix two teaspoons of cream of tartar, one cup of plain flour, half a cup of salt, one tablespoon of oil and one cup of water to form a smooth paste. Cook slowly in a saucepan until the dough comes away from the sides of the pan and forms a ball. When the dough is cool enough, take it out of the pan, add food colouring and knead for three or four minutes. (Store in an airtight container in the fridge.)

Print worksheet *Sunday between 31 July and 6 August (A)* from CD-ROM.

Sunday between 7 and 13 August

Thought for the day
God is faithful to us through all the storms of life, yet our faith in God is so very small.

Readings
1 Kings 19:9-18
Psalm 85:8-13
Romans 10:5-15
Matthew 14:22-33

Aim
To know that God can cope with our bad days as well as the good ones.

Starter
What's the time, Mr Wolf? The children creep up on Mr Wolf, who sometimes pleasantly tells them the time, and sometimes decides it's time to eat them.

Teaching
Use a few instruments – such as simple shakers and bells, saucepans and wooden spoons, and hand tapping and clapping – as you talk about the different moods of the weather. Sometimes it seems wild and cross, with the wind racing round and blowing everything over, and the rain lashing down. (Make the sounds.) Sometimes it seems in a quiet and gentle mood, perhaps when it's a bit hazy and misty, and there isn't any wind, or when the snow is quietly falling. (Make those sounds.) And sometimes the weather seems all happy and smiley, with the sun shining in a clear blue sky and just a little breeze, and everywhere warm and bright. (Make these sounds.) Sometimes it seems sad, with dark grey clouds and steady rain. (Make these sounds.)

It's the same with us. We have times when we feel all wild and cross, and we grumble and snap at everyone and make ourselves as horrid as possible. Sometimes we have quieter times, when we just want to sit and cuddle up to someone who loves us, and read a story, or watch television, or go to sleep. And sometimes we feel all sunny bright and happy, bouncing around with lots of energy and being friendly and helpful.

Which of those times do you think God loves you best? Answer with a simple 'No' to every suggestion until someone says that God loves us all the time, and celebrate that truth together. Sometimes what we do makes God sad, but he is loving us all the time, in all our different moods.

Praying

Sometimes the weather is wild and cross.
(shake fists and stamp feet)
Sometimes the weather is quiet.
(lie down still)
Sometimes the weather is sunshine happy.
(trace big sunshine smile)
Sometimes the weather is sad.
(make fingers into trickling rain)
Sometimes I feel wild and cross.
(shake fists and stamp feet)
Sometimes I feel quiet.
(lie down still)
Sometimes I feel sunshine happy.
(trace big sunshine smile)
Sometimes I feel sad.
(fingers make trickling tears down cheeks)
And ALL the time God loves me!
(stretch arms out in wide circle all around)
God loves me ALL the time!
(reverse the wide circle)

Activities

The sheet can be made into a weather chart for the children to set each day. They will each need a split pin, and you may like to make the pointers in advance, from different coloured paper. The chart can be strengthened by sticking it on to thin card.

Print worksheet *Sunday between 7 and 13 August (A)* from CD-ROM.

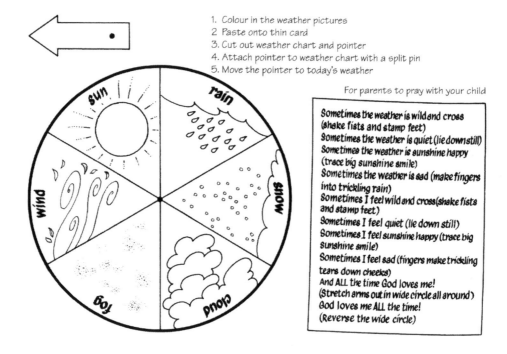

1. Colour in the weather pictures
2. Paste onto thin card
3. Cut out weather chart and pointer
4. Attach pointer to weather chart with a split pin
5. Move the pointer to today's weather

For parents to pray with your child

Sometimes the weather is wild and cross (shake fists and stamp feet)
Sometimes the weather is quiet (lie down still)
Sometimes the weather is sunshine happy (trace big sunshine smile)
Sometimes the weather is sad (make fingers into trickling rain)
Sometimes I feel wild and cross (shake fists and stamp feet)
Sometimes I feel quiet (lie down still)
Sometimes I feel sunshine happy (trace big sunshine smile)
Sometimes I feel sad (fingers make trickling tears down cheeks)
And ALL the time God loves me!
(Stretch arms out in wide circle all around)
God loves me ALL the time!
(Reverse the wide circle)

Sunday between 14 and 20 August

Thought for the day

The good news of salvation is not limited to a particular group or nation but available for the whole world.

Readings

Isaiah 56:1, 6-8
Psalm 67
Romans 11:1-2a, 29-32
Matthew 15:(10-20) 21-28

Aim

To know that God loves everyone in the whole world.

Starter

The world is turning. Make a circle and choose some children to be birds, some planes and some clouds. Walk round singing to the tune of *The wheels on the bus*:

The world is turning round and round,
round and round,
round and round.
The world is turning round and round
all year long.

As you sing it and walk around again, all the birds can fly around the moving earth. Then the planes can zoom around. Then the clouds can drift lightly around.

Teaching

Bring along either a large globe beach ball, or a globe, and spin it around, pointing out where on our planet earth we are. (Although this age group is too young to understand maps, they can begin to get an idea of living on a round world.)

Talk about the different places on our world where people live. Some children live where it is very hot all the time, and some where it is very cold all the time. Some children live where it rains and rains every day, and some where it hardly ever rains. Some children have never seen snow, and some live in snow all the year round. (Calendars are often a good source of pictures, or you can show them pictures from library books, or photographs you have taken.)

Some of the world is very flat, and some has high hills and mountains. Some children go to church by boat, and some by donkey. Lots of children all over the world walk to church and lots drive or cycle.

And all that goes on at the same time on our round, spinning world! (Spin the globe again.)

You know that God loves each of you? Well, he also loves each and every person living in the world. No one is left out.

You can sing the prayer today.

Praying

He's got the whole world in his hand,
he's got the whole wide world in his hand,
he's got the whole world in his hand,
he's got the whole world in his hand!

Activities

The children can make their sheet into a turning world. Beforehand use the land mass shapes as templates and cut these from green and white paper. Also cut out blue circles to fit the basic shape shown. The children can then stick these on. Punch a hole in the place shown so the children can thread a pipe-cleaner through it, and twist the ends together. They can then make the world turn by pushing it along a surface, holding the pipe-cleaner.

Print worksheet *Sunday between 14 July and 20 August (A)* from CD-ROM.

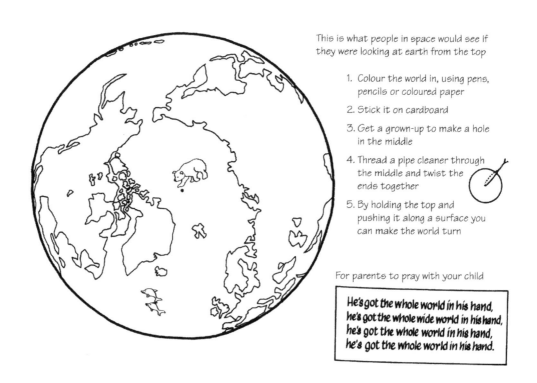

This is what people in space would see if they were looking at earth from the top

1. Colour the world in, using pens, pencils or coloured paper
2. Stick it on cardboard
3. Get a grown-up to make a hole in the middle
4. Thread a pipe cleaner through the middle and twist the ends together
5. By holding the top and pushing it along a surface you can make the world turn

For parents to pray with your child

He's got the whole world in his hand,
he's got the whole wide world in his hand,
he's got the whole world in his hand,
he's got the whole world in his hand.

Sunday between 21 and 27 August

Thought for the day

The Church is the Body of Christ, built on strong rock of faith and energised by the living Breath of God.

Readings

Isaiah 51:1-6
Psalm 138
Romans 12:1-8
Matthew 16:13-20

Aim

To know that the Church is made of people.

Starter

Who can it be? Have some large pictures of familiar things, people and places, and start with a picture completely covered up. Gradually uncover it. The children say what they think it is and can see if they're right when it is totally revealed.

Teaching

Have a picture of Jesus healing, or with the children. This could be an illustration in a children's Bible. Start with it fully covered, as in the starter activity, and tell the children that this picture is someone they have never seen, but who they know and love. As you talk, giving verbal clues, uncover the picture so they can see that it is Jesus. They are getting to know Jesus better and better as they hear more about him and as they talk with him in prayer.

Now show a large outline picture of a church. What do we do in church? We pray to God, we sing together to thank God and praise him, we give our money to God, we hear about Jesus, we share a meal, and we play in the children's corner.

What's inside our church? Coloured windows, an altar or table, candles, flowers, chairs and books. All those things are there to help us worship God, and to give him our best, as a thank-you for everything God has given us. There are people in church at the moment, and we are all here as well. And there are grown-ups and children all over the world in their churches today. They are all there to worship God and say thank you by giving him their best singing and their best living every day.

Praying

The Body of Christ needs eyes and legs
and feet and hands and mouth.
We are the Body of Christ on earth –
God's eyes and legs
and feet and hands and mouth!

Activities

On the sheet there are puppets to make which the children can work by pushing their fingers through the holes. They can also draw in the missing bits of body.

Print worksheet *Sunday between 21 and 27 August (A)* from CD-ROM.

Sunday between
28 August and 3 September

Thought for the day

As Jesus prepares for the necessary suffering of the cross, he is tempted, through well-meaning friendship, to avoid it.

Readings

Jeremiah 15:15-21
Psalm 26:1-8
Romans 12:9-21
Matthew 16:21-28

Aim

To know that Jesus is willing to suffer for us because he loves us.

Starter

Have ready some beanbags or rolled socks to throw about, and a basket or bag to put them in. Throughout the throwing activity, ask children by name to do things – 'Ben, will you give everyone a beanbag?' 'Noah, will you throw your beanbag as far as you can?' 'Julian, will you throw your bag as high as you can?' 'Eleanor, will you go round with the basket, and, everyone else, will you put your bag in the basket?' Give lots of praise, thanks and encouragement throughout. Catch them being good as much as possible, tactically ignoring the inappropriate behaviour as much as you can.

Teaching

Explain that the reason they all helped so well during that activity was that they were being kind. If they were selfish they wouldn't have done it. Being kind is doing things for other people, even when it isn't what we like doing best. Sometimes being kind is nice (Will you help me eat up these last biscuits so I can wash the tin?), and sometimes being kind is not so much fun (Can you help me by putting your toys away now?). Collect ideas about times they have been kind and celebrate these.

Tell the children that whenever they are kind they are being just like Jesus. He loves us so much that he was ready to give up everything for us, and put up with lots of hurts. Jesus was kind when he made people better, and when he made them feel safe and happy. He was kind because he helped people and set them free from worrying all the time. He was kind when they were sorry for what they had done wrong, and Jesus forgave them.

It is good to practise being kind, whether we are boys or girls, men or women, and when we do, it makes Jesus very happy.

Praying

Thank you, God, for those I love
and all they do for me.
Help me to be kind as well –
I really want to be!

Activities

On the sheet there are situations for them to look at and think how they could be kind here. They are also encouraged to celebrate the ways other people are kind to them. Also, the children can do something kind today, making some chocolate cornflake cakes to give away.

Print worksheet *Sunday between 28 August and 3 September (A)* from CD-ROM.

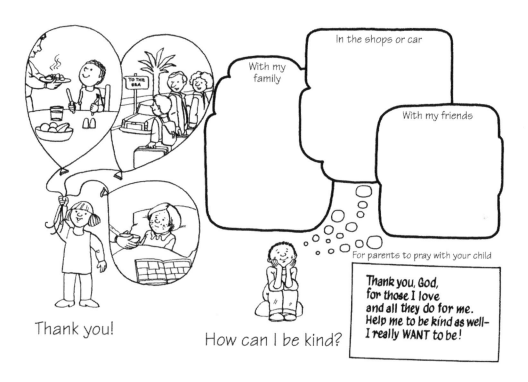

Sunday between
4 and 10 September

Thought for the day

It is our responsibility to encourage and uphold one another in living by the standard of real love.

Readings

Ezekiel 33:7-11
Psalm 119:33-40
Romans 13:8-14
Matthew 18:15-20

Aim

To know that God forgives us.

Starter

Provide enough potatoes and spoons for everyone, so that they can try getting from one end of the room to the other and back as quickly as possible, trying not to drop the potato. If the children are at the older end of the age-range you could make this into a race, but that isn't necessary, as it is the exercise in balance and sorting out mishaps which is important. Support those who are hesitant or timid, so they get used to picking the potato up and trying again when things go wrong.

Teaching

Talk about the potato and spoon runs, and how hard it was to manage without getting it wrong and dropping the potato. What did they do to put things right when their potato dropped? They didn't stand and do nothing and they didn't give up. They went after the runaway potato, picked it up and put it back in the spoon. Then they could carry on.

In our life we sometimes make mistakes. Sometimes we choose to do what we know is wrong. Both children and grown-ups sometimes choose to do what they know is wrong. We might have been told to stop drawing on the wall, but we choose to do it anyway. We might see our baby sister is asleep, and we choose to wake her up and make her cry. Lots of the time we choose to do the right thing, but what can we do to put things right when we have done what is wrong?

We can say sorry. Saying sorry means that we wish we hadn't been unkind or disobedient, and we want to put things right. We can say sorry to grown-ups, to our big brothers and sisters or our little brothers and sisters. We can say sorry to our friends. And we can say sorry to God. When we have said sorry, and meant it, God will help us to put things right, and then we can carry on happily with our life again.

Praying

Jesus, when people say to me, 'No!'
and I think, 'I'm still going to do it,
whatever they say',
I know that isn't good, and I'm sorry, Jesus.
Thank you for helping me put it right again.

Activities

On the sheet there are all kinds of things and people in the wrong places, and the children can try sorting out where they ought to be. They can also make a puzzle which can be put together wrongly, but they put it right.

Print worksheet *Sunday between 4 and 10 September (A)* from CD-ROM.

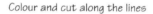

Colour and cut along the lines

For parents to pray with your child

Jesus, when people say to me,
'No!'
and I think 'I'm still going to
do it, whatever they say',
I know that isn't good, and I'm
sorry, Jesus.
Thank you for helping me put
it right again.

What's wrong here?

Sunday between 11 and 17 September

Thought for the day

Forgiving is a natural result of loving, so it is not an option for us but a command.

Readings

Genesis 50:15-21
Psalm 103:(1-7} 8-13
Romans 14:1-12
Matthew 18:21-35

Aim

To know that we are to love as God loves us.

Starter

Sit in a circle. One person does something and the next person does the same, then the next until everyone has done it. This might be standing up, turning round and sitting down again, clapping a rhythm or blinking twice. Everyone changes places, and then you start the round again with a different person and a different action.

Teaching

Tell the children that you are going to give them all a present, and that you want them to share the present they are given with everyone else. Make sure they are all clear about this expectation and then give every child a little pack of chocolate buttons, smarties, jelly babies or raisins. It's nice to have a variety, and only have a few sweets in each pack. Now play some music while the children can go round offering other children sweets from their packs. Encourage them to say 'thank you' for what they are given.

Sit in the circle again and talk about the fun of having things given to us, and the fun of giving to others which they have just enjoyed. God gives us his love all the time in so many ways, and we are to do the same – we are to be loving and giving.

Praying

Thank you, Father God,
for the love you give to me.
Teach me how to be like you,
happy to love and give.

Activities

There is space on the sheet for some printing, which passes on a picture all over the place from the master design, and so reinforces the generosity of God's giving. The children will need potato wedges cut into designs as shown, and some flat trays of thick paint mixed with a little washing-up liquid. Ensure their clothes are well protected and have washing-up bowls with warm soapy water and towels at the ready for afterwards.

Print worksheet *Sunday between 11 and 17 September (A)* from CD-ROM.

Potato printing

God loves giving again and again and again!

For parents to pray with your child

Thank you, Father God, for the love you give to me. Teach me how to be like you, happy to love and give.

Sunday between 18 and 24 September

Thought for the day
We have no right to be envious at the generosity and mercy God shows to others.

Readings
Jonah 3:10-4:11
Psalm 145:1-8
Philippians 1:21-30
Matthew 20:1-16

Aim
To know that God is generous, and when we are generous, we are being like him.

Starter
Play shops, with empty packets and cartons, play money and shopping bags and baskets.

Teaching
When we go out shopping we look out for things that are on special offer. (Show the children some things you have bought this week because there were two toilet rolls for the price of one, or because you got free chocolate bars with your tea bags.) The people who own the shop like to be generous and give things away sometimes so that we shoppers are happy and go back and buy more next time. They end up making more money if they are sometimes generous.

God is generous. He gives away free sunshine and free showers of rain. He gives us free sea and free clouds and free hills and rivers. He gives us life, so we can live in his lovely free earth and enjoy it. God doesn't give us all this because he makes money out of it. God doesn't make money at all. He generously gives us all this just because he loves us. He likes to see us enjoying his gifts, and there's something else he really likes to see.

God loves it when he sees his children being generous like him; when they share and give things away free, and are happy for their friends to have a nice time as well as having a nice time themselves.

When we are generous, we are being like God, and if we get good at giving, we'll end up much more happy than if we tried to keep everything for ourselves.

Praying

Father, you have given us a bright new day
and we would like to spend it
in the very best way.
Help us to be generous, giving it away,
helping one another in all we do and say.

Activities

The children can make rubbings of coins so that there is money in the drawn purse on the sheet, and they can make a posy of flowers to give away free.

Print worksheet *Sunday between 18 and 24 September (A)* from CD-ROM.

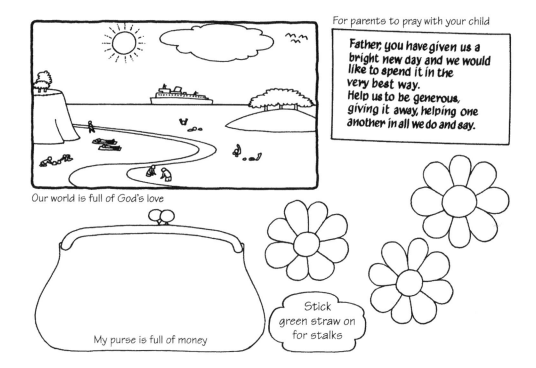

Our world is full of God's love

For parents to pray with your child

Father, you have given us a bright new day and we would like to spend it in the very best way.
Help us to be generous, giving it away, helping one another in all we do and say.

My purse is full of money

Stick green straw on for stalks

Sunday between
25 September and 1 October

Thought for the day

God longs for us to die to sin and live, but it has to be our choice, too.

Readings

Ezekiel 18:1-4, 25-32
Psalm 25:1-9
Philippians 2:1-13
Matthew 21:23-32

Aim

To know about making good choices.

Starter

Beforehand cut out blobs from different coloured paper and also a set of small blobs of the same colours. Have the small set laid out on a table at the side of the room and the others scattered all over the floor. Put on a praise tape and let the children all dance around. When the music stops they choose a colour to stand on. One child has been standing with her back to the others, facing the table of colours. She chooses one of the colours and the children standing on that colour blob get a sweet or a sticker. Then another child becomes the selector.

Teaching

Prepare a Y-shaped road junction from paper and lay it on the floor. In one direction have a full pot of honey hidden, and in the other direction an empty pot of honey. Introduce a bear who walks along the road until he comes to the fork junction. He says to himself, in a growly voice, 'Now which way shall I choose? I can go this way or that way. Now let me see.' Invite the children to help the bear choose. They can ask you where the roads go to, if that will help the bear to choose wisely.

When they ask, show them (but not the bear) that one way leads to a full pot of honey and the other way to an empty pot of honey. Now they can talk to the bear, giving him their help and advice. He talks back, wondering if they are really, really sure, and just supposing they are wrong...and having other misgivings that a bear might worry about. In the end the bear decides to take the children's advice and finds the full pot of honey, which makes him very happy.

When we have difficult things to choose, God will give us help and good advice. God is good, so what he tells us is always going to help us make a choice that is good.

Praying

Help us, dear God,
to choose the good
and loving way.
Amen.

Activities

On the sheet they can make their own road for a bear at home to try, drawing in something nice at one end of the road and something nasty at the other. They can also choose their favourite colours to decorate today's prayer.

Print worksheet *Sunday between 25 September and 1 October (A)* from CD-ROM.

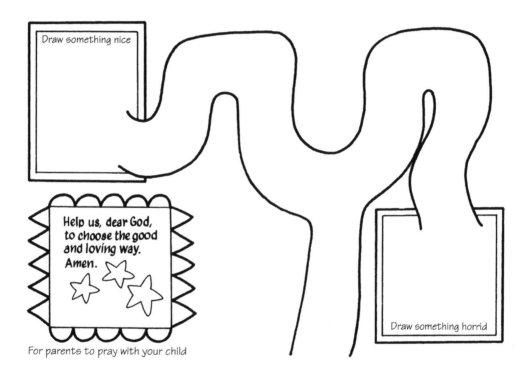

Sunday between
2 and 8 October

Thought for the day

God does everything possible for our spiritual growth and well-being, but still we can choose hostility and rejection.

Readings

Isaiah 5:1-7
Psalm 80:7-15
Philippians 3:4b-14
Matthew 21:33-46

Aim

To know that God helps us grow in all kinds of ways.

Starter

Plant some bulbs, either in pots to be flowering at Christmas time or outside to bloom next spring, brightening up a patch of ground near the church.

Teaching

Bring a selection of fruit and vegetables, preferably with a piece of the plant they came from, and let the children look, handle and smell them. You could also eat some. Talk about all the growing that had to go on before the plant gave us this fruit, and the hard work of the farmers or gardeners who looked after the plants so they had enough water, food and light.

We take quite a lot of careful looking after as well. All that eating and drinking we need, all those cuddles and games, all that washing and ironing, tooth-brushing, and comforting after nasty dreams.

God is in all the loving care that we get and give, and he hopes we will grow up to be:

- healthy and strong in our bodies, so we can work and play and help
- healthy and strong in our minds, so we can think sensibly and wisely
- healthy and strong in our souls, so we get to know God as our friend.

Praying

Dear God, thank you for making us grow
big and strong in your love
so that our lives are fruitful.

Activities

The children can make salads or fruit salad with the fruit and vegetables, and use some, such as cabbage and carrot and potato, to print a large picture which has the prayer stuck on to it.

Print worksheet *Sunday between 2 and 8 October (A)* from CD-ROM.

Sunday between 9 and 15 October

Thought for the day
We are all invited to God's wedding banquet; in accepting we must allow the rags of our old life to be exchanged for the freely given robes of holiness and right living.

Readings
Isaiah 25:1-9
Psalm 23
Philippians 4:1-9
Matthew 22:1-14

Aim
To know that God invites us to his party.

Starter
Either make party hats as shown (*right*) or decorate the room with streamers and balloons.

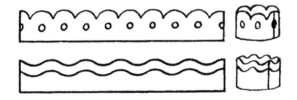

Teaching
Talk about the kind of things they like about parties, and then gather all these things into the happiness of enjoying ourselves together. God's kingdom is like being invited to God's party. He's invited us because he likes us, loves us and wants us to be there with him and all his other friends. Being in God's party is lovely because we are all together with God, enjoying ourselves.

Put on a praise tape, give out some instruments and streamers, and all enjoy worshipping God in a praise party, wearing our party hats.

Praying
Dear Father God,
thank you for inviting me
to your party.
Yes, please, I want to come!

Activities
On the sheet there is a picture of a party to colour, with some hidden things to look for, and a party game to play – putting the tail on the donkey with your eyes closed.

Print worksheet *Sunday between 9 and 15 October (A)* from CD-ROM.

Sunday between 16 and 22 October

Thought for the day

All leaders and rulers are subject to the ultimate authority and power of God, the living truth.

Readings

Isaiah 45:1-7
Psalm 96:1-9 (10-13)
1 Thessalonians 1:1-10
Matthew 22:15-22

Aim

To celebrate that God's in charge.

Starter

In a circle have a 'news time', passing round a coin, so that whoever holds it is allowed to speak without interruption.

Teaching

Tell the children this story.

'Here she is!' shouted Ali. She was looking out of the window, and could see the baby-sitter walking up to the front door. 'Ding, dong!' went the door bell. Mum opened the door.

'Hello, Vicky,' said Mum. 'They've had their baths, and they know they have to go to bed once this programme ends. Oh, and I've left the mugs for a drink. Sometimes they like hot chocolate, but Jonathan may want a cold drink. Don't let them eat anything after they've brushed their teeth.'

'Vicky, come and see the dead mouse that Molly brought in today,' said Jonathan.

'Sounds great,' said Vicky. 'Hi, everyone! Did your cold get better, Ali?'

'Yep,' nodded Ali. 'But I've got a plaster on my knee. Look!'

'Right, my loves, I have to go now,' said Mum. 'Where did I leave my car keys?'

'You're holding them,' said Jonathan. 'When will you get back?'

'Quarter to eleven,' said Mum. 'Now remember, Vicky's in charge. Look after her and give her a nice evening. Show her where those chocolate gingers are in case she wants some with her coffee. And don't you bring that dead mouse inside again or there'll be trouble! Must go. Love you lots! Bye, everyone, and thanks, Vicky.' Mum hugged and kissed Ali and Jonathan, and Vicky took them upstairs so they could wave from the window.

They watched Mum unlock the car and climb in. She waved back to them and then Vicky helped them make a drink each. Vicky had coffee with one sugar. Ali had hot chocolate and spilt a bit on the cat, who licked it off. Jonathan had apple juice. And they all had chocolate ginger biscuits.

Talk about people being in charge, and how we can help those who are in charge of us, and how they can help us. God is in charge of the whole universe, and he loves us, and looks after us.

Praying

Lord Jesus,
bless us and keep us safe
now and for ever.
Amen.

Activities

On the sheet there is space for the children to draw those who are in charge of them, and instructions for making an orb – the world with a cross on it. Each child will need an orange or apple, two sticks and a wire bag fastener.

Print worksheet *Sunday between 16 and 22 October (A)* from CD-ROM.

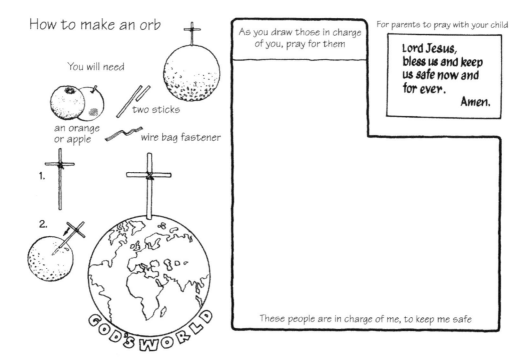

Sunday between 23 and 29 October

Thought for the day
We are to love God with our whole being, and love others as much as we love ourselves.

Readings
Leviticus 19:1-2,15-18
Psalm 1
1 Thessalonians 2:1-8
Matthew 22:34-46

Aim
To know the summary of the law: Love God, love one another.

Starter
Play 'Here we go round the mulberry bush'. It is a 'looking after yourself' kind of song, so you could have such verses as these: brush our teeth, take a shower, eat a pizza, and wrap up warm.

Teaching
As we sang in the song, we are good at looking after ourselves and caring for our bodies. Our arms are like big machines that we train to pick things up for us and take them over to our mouths. (They can try this with some crisps.) We love ourselves, and that's why we make sure we are comfortable and well fed.

In the Bible we are told two rules:

1. Love God.
2. Love others as much as you love yourself.

When we love others as much as we love ourselves, we look out for *their* needs as well as ours, and want *them* to be happy and comfortable as well as us.

Praying
Dear God,
you have given us life – thank you!
You have given us a lovely world
to live in – thank you!
You have given us people
to look after us – thank you!
You have given us friends – thank you!
You have given us two rules to help us:

'Love God' and 'Love one another'.
Thank you, God!

Activities

Get a drum beat going (a biscuit tin and wooden spoon works well) and clap hands to it. Over this, chant the words: 'Love God; love one another!' until it has become second nature and the children know it off by heart. Then they can colour the two arm or ankle bands drawn on the sheet, and either cut them out themselves or have help with this. Fix them round their wrists or ankles and try the chant again.

Print worksheet *Sunday between 23 and 29 October (A)* from CD-ROM.

All Saints' Day
Sunday between 30 October and 5 November

Thought for the day
Lives that have shone with God's love on earth are filled with joy as they see their Lord face to face.

Readings
Revelation 7:9-17
Psalm 34:1-10
1 John 3:1-3
Matthew 5:1-12

Aim
To know that saints are Jesus' friends and followers.

Starter
Sing *Oh when the saints go marching in*, marching around the room together.

Teaching
Bring along a family or parish photo album and look through the pictures together, recognising some and hearing about others. (This is my grandad who shouted at me when I climbed the cherry tree, and who loved his old dog called Judy. Here's the Brownies at the May Fair, with Mrs Phillips who sells birthday cards after church sometimes. This is Timothy's dad when he'd broken his leg playing football with the youth club.)

All these people are part of the big family of God. We're all God's friends.

Now look with them through another photo album, made up in advance from an enlarged Pebbles worksheet. These saints are all part of the family, too, who have lived good lives as specially good friends of God. Talk about them as you did about the family and parish people, without any 'holy language' reserved for saints.

Praying
Thank you, God,
for all the saints, your good friends.
Thank you for being my friend, too.

Activities
The pictures on the sheet can be made into a book of saints, and the cover made from a piece of coloured paper with tissue stuck into it as shown, so that they hold it up to the light and see the light shining through.

Print worksheet *All Saints' Day (A)* from CD-ROM.

For parents to pray with your child

Thank you, God, for all the saints, your good friends. Thank you for being my friend, too.

Saint Mary was Jesus' mother

Saint Joseph was Mary's husband

Saint Peter was a fisherman

Saint Francis looked after ill people and loved all God's created world

Saint Nicholas (Santa Claus) loved giving, to help people. He was a bishop

Saint Clare was a rich girl, but gave it up to live a simple life with God. She was Francis' friend

FRONT BACK — Stick piece of coloured tissue paper

Fourth Sunday before Advent
Sunday between 30 October and 5 November

For use if the Feast of All Saints was celebrated on
1 November and alternative propers are needed.

Thought for the day

With God's light and truth to guide us, we shall be brought safely through to the end of time.

Readings

Micah 3:5-12
Psalm 43
1 Thessalonians 2:9-13
Matthew 24:1-14

Aim

To know that God guides us through the bad times.

Starter

Set up chairs and tables and boxes as an obstacle course, and lead everyone through it together, helping them along.

Teaching

Put down on the floor some happy yellow sunshine shapes and some sad, grey cloud shapes. Let a soft toy walk about, sometimes going on to the happy times and sometimes the sad ones. Talk about how we sometimes go through happy times (share examples), and sometimes things go wrong for us and we are sad (share examples of things that have made them and you sad). Is God there with us in just the happy times? No. Just the sad, bad times? No! God is there with us all the time and helps us through.

And if they are in the middle of a bad time, like having chicken pox or saying goodbye to Granny, remember that Jesus shares the sadness, and it won't be sad for ever. It will stop, and then they will be happy again.

Praying

Sometimes life is sparkly and happy
  (open and close fingers and smile)
and, Jesus, you are there.
  (nod)
Sometimes life is dark and scary
  (close eyes and shake)
and, Jesus, you are there.
  (nod)

Sometimes life is exciting and busy
(run on the spot)
and, Jesus, you are there.
(nod)
Sometimes life is sad and lonely
(rest chin in hands)
and, Jesus, you are always there!
(turn around with arms stretched out)

Activities

On the worksheet there are pictures of people who may be in danger, and the children can warn them about it. And the prayer is illustrated this week so they can colour it, cut it out and mount it as shown to have at home.

Print worksheet *Fourth Sunday before Advent (A)* from CD-ROM.

Third Sunday before Advent
Sunday between 6 and 12 November

Thought for the day

We need to keep ourselves awake and prepared so that the Day of the Lord does not come to us as darkness rather than light.

Readings

Amos 5:18-24 or Wisdom of Solomon 6:12-16
Psalm 70 or Wisdom of Solomon 6:17-20
1 Thessalonians 4:13-18
Matthew 25:1-13

Aim

To know that we are called to shine like lights in the darkness.

Starter

Close the curtains, if practical, and give two children torches so that they can help the others to find some hidden milk bottle tops around the room.

Teaching

Point out how useful it is to have some shining lights when we have lost things in the dark. Show the children an oil lamp, fill it with oil and light it. We can shine like lights in the darkness, when we are kind and friendly, thoughtful and generous, when we tell the truth and help each other, when we cheer one another up. That makes the world a happier place for everyone to live in. Like this lamp, we need to be soaked with God's love so that we burn brightly.

Praying

Jesus, keep us shining
like lamps in the darkness,
shining with your love
in the world.

Activities

The sheet can be made into a lantern. Provide shiny red paper for the children to push inside so that it shows through the slits.

Print worksheet *Third Sunday before Advent (A)* from CD-ROM.

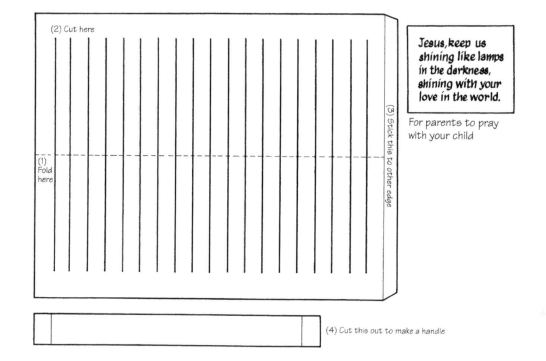

(2) Cut here

(1)
Fold
here

(3) Stick this to other edge

Jesus, keep us
shining like lamps
in the darkness,
shining with your
love in the world.

For parents to pray
with your child

(4) Cut this out to make a handle

Second Sunday before Advent
Sunday between 13 and 19 November

Thought for the day

The Day of the Lord will hold terror for the wicked and unprepared, but rejoicing for those living in God's light.

Readings

Zephaniah 1:7,12-18
Psalm 90:1-8 (9-11), 12 1
Thessalonians 5:1-11
Matthew 25:14-30

Aim

To know that God enjoys giving us gifts and wants us to enjoy them too.

Starter

Pass the parcel. Pack it with a sticker at each layer and make sure that everyone receives a gift.

Teaching

When do we give presents to people? Talk about birthday, Christmas and 'just because' presents that we give to people we love. What makes us happy is seeing they enjoy what we have chosen for them, and enjoy using it.

That's what it's like with God. God loves giving, and he enjoyed giving us the things we are good at. Some people are good at being friendly, or playing football, or cheering people up, or saving their money, or listening, or painting, or learning. Go round the group with the children saying, 'I'm happy that God made me good at . . . ' God is happy to see us making the most of the gifts he has given us, and enjoying using them. We can all use these gifts to make the world a better and happier place.

Praying

Thank you, God,
for making us good at things.
Help us to use these gifts
to make people happy.

Activities

There is space on the worksheet for the children to draw themselves doing whatever they are good at, and God smiling to see them enjoying the gift he has given them. They can also fill in the card to give someone else, to encourage them.

Print worksheet *Second Sunday before Advent (A)* from CD-ROM.

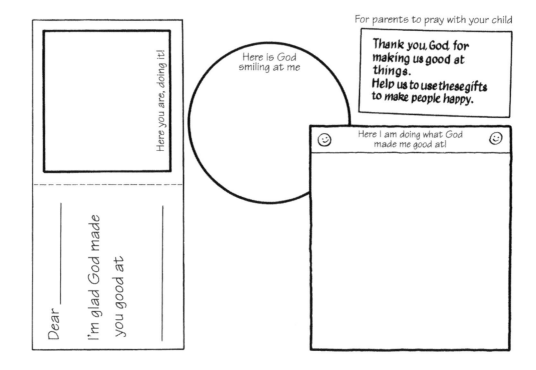

Christ the King
Sunday between 20 and 26 November

Thought for the day

In total humility, at one with the least of his people, Jesus, the Messiah or Christ, reigns as King, with full authority and honour for eternity.

Readings

Ezekiel 34:11-16, 20-24
Psalm 95:1-7a
Ephesians 1:15-23
Matthew 25:31-46

Aim

To know that Jesus is the greatest King of all.

Starter

Pass the crown. When the music stops, whoever is wearing the crown sits still while everyone stands up and bows or curtsies to them.

Teaching

Take along a globe and point out where you all live, and a few other places they might have heard of, such as the USA and Africa. Show the children a picture of our Queen and some other heads of state. These are all very important people. But there is one King who is over everyone who has ever been alive and who will ever live. His kingdom is not a place on a globe. Who can this important King be? It's our friend Jesus! We are friends with the most important King ever.

Then you can all sing *Who's the king of the jungle?*

Praying

Jesus, you are my friend
and you are my King.
You are the King of love.
I want to serve you for ever.

Activities

On the sheet there are instructions for making a flag to wave. Each child will need a stick to fix it on. There is also a picture of Jesus washing his disciples' feet, and the children can spot the hidden crowns.

Print worksheet *Christ the King (A)* from CD-ROM.

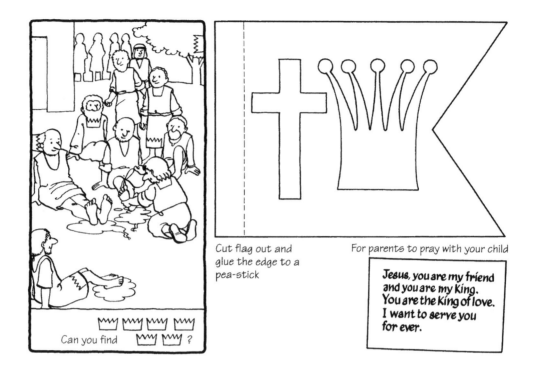

Cut flag out and
glue the edge to a
pea-stick

For parents to pray with your child

Jesus, you are my friend
and you are my King.
You are the King of love.
I want to serve you
for ever.

Can you find ?

YEAR B

First Sunday of Advent

Thought for the day
Be alert and watchful; keep yourselves ready.

Readings
Isaiah 64:1-9
Psalm 80:1-7, 17-19
1 Corinthians 1:3-9
Mark 13:24-37

Aim
To think about getting ready for Jesus.

Starter
Have three different types of music available, such as a drum, some bells, and a children's praise tape. Whenever they hear the drum they stomp about, whenever they hear the bells they run about silently on tiptoes, and whenever they hear the praise tape they dance. They will need to be ready and alert.

Teaching
Explain that today we are starting Advent which is 'getting ready' time because it means 'coming'. What's coming? Christmas! Who came to us as a baby at Christmas? Jesus!

Tell the children this rescue story.

Jake was a fisherman. When the tide came in he set off from the slipway and started the engine on his boat. Then he chugged out between the green and red buoys which showed him where the deep water was, until he reached the open sea. And there he fished and ate his sandwiches and drank his hot tea from a flask and fished some more. Jake enjoyed fishing. So did his dog, Sprat.

One day, when Jake was just halfway down his mug of hot tea, the sky got darker and darker and the wind blew stronger and stronger. The boat rocked up and down, up and down, this way and that way, and the hot tea slopped over the side of the mug, even though Jake had drunk it halfway down. Sprat made growling noises at the wind, but the wind wasn't frightened. It blew even harder.

'Dear me,' said Jake. 'This isn't a good time to be sitting out here fishing. We'd better make for home.'

He tried to start the engine but the engine just went splutter, splutter, clunk. Sprat barked at it with one ear up, to encourage it, but the engine could only go splutter, splutter, clunk.

'This is serious, Sprat,' said Jake. 'We can't stay here and we can't go home. What we need is someone to come and rescue us.'

They waited. Jake ate his other sandwich (it was tuna and salad) and Sprat had a dog biscuit, noisily. The boat went up and down, and the wind blew and blew.

Suddenly Sprat pricked up both ears and his nose twitched. He could hear something which made his tail wag. That made Jake look up. A smile began to spread over his face and he stood up, waving both arms.

'It's Bert! Hello, Bert! Ahoy there, Bert!' yelled Jake across the wind and waves. Bert was a fisherman too, and here he was chugging over in his boat towards Jake and Sprat. 'Bert to the rescue,' he grinned.

It wasn't long before Jake had thrown a rope across from his boat to Bert's and Bert had made it fast. Jake hauled up the anchor and there they were, being towed home by Bert. It felt so good to be rescued!

When they got back to the slipway Sprat gave Bert one of his half-chewed biscuits to say thank you, and Jake treated Bert to a drink at the pub.

'We couldn't have made it home on our own, you know,' said Jake into his pint of bitter.

Bert nodded. 'Good job I came to the rescue then,' he said.

Sprat thumped his tail on the pub carpet, happy to be a rescued dog.

Talk with the children about Jake and Sprat waiting to be rescued. Long before Jesus came, the people knew they were in a mess and needed God to come to the rescue. For years and years they waited and hoped for rescue, and then Jesus came into the world. Jesus was the rescuer!

Praying

Thank you, Jesus, Son of God,
you have come to save us all.
Thank you, Jesus, Son of God,
you came because you love us all.
Amen.

Activities

During Advent the children will be making a Christmas landscape, adding to it week by week, so that it is ready to take home in time for Christmas.

The Activity Sheet for the Fourth Sunday of Advent shows what this might look like when finished.

This week the children are forming the base from crumpled paper on a shoebox lid which is covered with green paper (or painted green). There are instructions on the worksheet, together with pictures of situations in which they can be the rescuer, drawing in the badly needed help.

Print worksheet
First Sunday of Advent (B)
from CD-ROM.

Second Sunday of Advent

Thought for the day

John the Baptist prepares the way for the coming of the Messiah by helping the people to realign their lives.

Readings

Isaiah 40:1-11
Psalm 85:1-2, 8-13
2 Peter 3:8-15a
Mark 1:1-8

Aim

To continue getting ready for Jesus at the Christmas festival.

Starter

Involve the children in preparing a road for the game. Give each of them a longish piece of string, and help them add their piece to make a continuous winding road on the floor. Now give them a second piece of string to mark out the other side of the road in the same way. When the road is ready, choose different children to walk, hop or skip along the road.

Teaching

Point out how we all had to get the road ready before we could use it for walking, hopping and skipping along. Some of them might have seen a road being made or mended, and you can talk with them about how this has to be done very carefully so that everyone can drive and cycle on it safely.

Getting ourselves ready for Jesus is a bit like building a good road. If there are bumpy, rocky places of grumpiness and bad temper, we can start clearing them away. If there are holes in our road where we are unkind, or unfair to other people, we can fill those places up with God's love. (If you draw all this on a blackboard, then you can rub out and re-draw as you speak.)

In Advent, when we are opening the windows in our Advent calendars every day, we can get our own roads sorted out so that Jesus can walk straight into our lives without falling down holes made of our unkindness, or tripping over rocks made of our grumpiness and bad temper.

Put all kinds of boxes and 'holes' on their string road and let everyone help to clear it again. As they are clearing, comment on what they are doing: for example, 'Here's a great lump of selfishness – let's get rid of that; oh, and here's a few clumps of wanting our own way all the time – let's clear those away, too, so the road is better to walk along. That's much better, now; well done!'

Praying

Dear Jesus,
I am learning how to be kind and helpful,
I am building a good strong road of love.
Help me to build my good strong road
of kindness, goodness and truth.
Amen.

Activities

Today we are making the next stage of our Christmas landscape. We are adding the town of Bethlehem, and the road. Instructions are on the sheet, together with a picture of road building to colour.

Print worksheet *Second Sunday of Advent (B)* from CD-ROM.

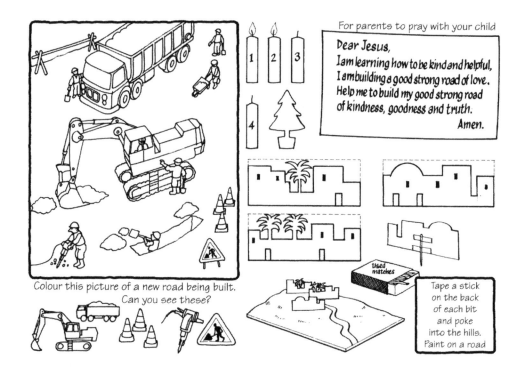

Third Sunday of Advent

Thought for the day
In Jesus, God will be fulfilling the Messianic prophecies about the promised Saviour.

Readings
Isaiah 61:1-4, 8-11
Psalm 126 or Canticle: Magnificat
1 Thessalonians 5:16-24
John 1:6-8, 19-28

Aim
To get ready for Christmas, and for Jesus.

Starter
Play some taped music which the children dance around to. Whenever the music stops, call out something for them to mime getting ready for, such as eating dinner (wash hands), driving a car (turn the ignition key), climbing a mountain (pull on boots), being a film star (put on make-up), and having a swim (changing clothes).

Teaching
Tell the children this story about waiting for someone and recognising them when they arrive.

One day the postman delivered a letter to the house where Hari and Meera lived. The envelope was pale blue, and it had a red and blue pattern all round the edge. (Hold an airmail letter as you speak.) 'That's an airmail letter,' said Hari. 'It's come from far away.'

Mum opened the letter, and read it. 'Who's it from?' asked Meera.

'It's from my brother, your uncle,' said Mum, 'and he says that he's coming to visit us. He'll be flying into Heathrow airport next month.' She was smiling and very excited.

Hari and Meera were excited too. They had never met Uncle Satich, but they had heard lots of stories about him. He sounded good fun and very kind. He never forgot their birthdays or Christmas, either.

A month seemed ages to wait for him to come. Meera kept counting the days left on the calendar until Uncle Satich was due to arrive. They all helped get Hari's room changed round, as Uncle Satich would be sleeping there as well for a few weeks. Dad borrowed a put-you-up bed from the next-door neighbours, and carried it up to the bedroom. The children picked some flowers and put them on the bookcase next to the bed. They did want him to feel welcome and happy in their home.

At last it was time to drive to the airport to meet him. The airport was full of people. 'How shall we know which is Uncle Satich?' asked Hari. 'We might miss him,' said Meera.

'Well, I shall know him, because he's my brother!' laughed Mum. 'But you will know him because he will look just like the photo he sent us at Christmas, and if I know Satich, he'll be smiling. Oh, and he'll probably tell me how much like Mother I look!'

They all stood around waiting for the passengers to come in from India. Everyone was pushing trolleys with luggage on, or carrying bags and parcels. There were families with tired children, old men, young men, old women and young women. The children looked at each person to see if they were anything like the Christmas photo, and if they were smiling.

Suddenly, there was a man coming with a big smile on his face, looking quite like that photo, but wearing different clothes. He came straight up to Mum and Dad, dumped his cases down and gave them a big hug. 'Oh, you look so much like Mother!' he said to Mum. So then Hari and Meera knew for certain that this was Uncle Satich.

Uncle Satich had stopped hugging Mum and Dad, and now he turned to the children, and knelt down so he was the same height as them. 'Hello, you must be Hari, and you Meera! I am very, very happy to meet you both!' he said. And they all hugged.

Talk about how the children were looking forward to their uncle coming even though they had never met him in person, because they knew their mum and dad loved him, and that he was kind. Talk about how they knew which person was their uncle. They knew what to look out for.

Before the first Christmas no one knew exactly what Jesus would be like, but they were looking forward to him coming because they knew he would be loving and fair and good. They knew they would be able to recognise him because he would be comforting those who were sad and setting people free to live good lives.

Praying

Lord Jesus,
as we get ready for Christmas
help us to know who you are
so we can welcome you
into our lives.
Amen.

Activities

The Christmas landscape continues. Today we are making the star, and fixing it above the house they choose in Bethlehem. Instructions and outlines are on the sheet. The children will need glue and glitter, two lengths of stick and some cotton each.

Print worksheet
Third Sunday of Advent (B)
from CD-ROM.

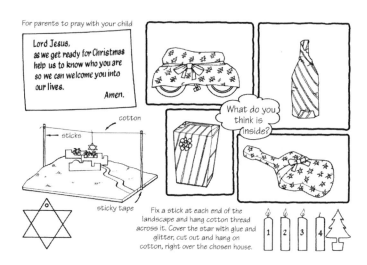

Fourth Sunday of Advent

Thought for the day

God's promised kingdom, announced both to King David in ancient times and to Mary by the angel Gabriel, will go on for ever.

Readings

2 Samuel 7, 1-11, 16
Canticle: Magnificat or Psalm 89:1-4, 19-26
Romans 16:25-27
Luke 1:26-38

Aim

To prepare for King Jesus coming into the world.

Starter

Have a cardboard crown and put it on one of the children who then leads the others to do whatever they do (follow my leader). Swap the crown over till everyone who wants to has a turn at being king or queen.

Teaching

Put the crown on one child's head, and a kingly robe round their shoulders. Once there was a famous king of Israel called King David. He loved God and was a very good king. King David had been born in a city you might have heard of. It was the city of Bethlehem! King David was not brought up in a palace. (Take out a toy sheep and hold it.) He was brought up as a shepherd boy on the hills near Bethlehem, where he helped to look after the sheep. He grew up strong and good, and looking after the people as their king.

(Get out a shiny star, and take the crown from King David. Place the star, the crown and the sheep on the floor together.) Many years later another baby was born in the city of Bethlehem who would grow up to be a king and a shepherd. Do you know what his name was? It was Jesus! (Place a Christmas card or picture showing the Nativity on the floor with the other things.) And as we get ready for Christmas we are getting ready to welcome Jesus, the baby king, who was born into our world at King David's city of Bethlehem.

Praying

Lord Jesus, my King,
  (bow head)
to you I will bring
  (kneel down)
my living, my loving,
  (arms out, palms up, then hands on heart)
and every good thing!
  (arms stretched up, hands open)

Activities

Today we complete the Christmas landscape, putting sheep on the hill and a title round the edge: 'Happy Birthday, Jesus!' Instructions are on the sheet. There is also a picture of King David on which to stick a crown and a robe.

Print worksheet *Fourth Sunday of Advent (B)* from CD-ROM.

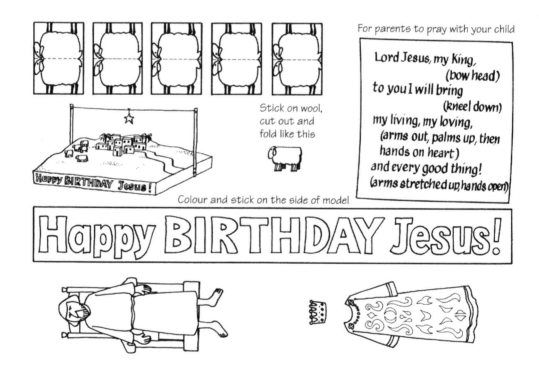

Christmas Day

Thought for the day

Jesus Christ, the world's Saviour, is here with us, born as a human baby.

Readings

Isaiah 62:6-12
Psalm 97
Titus 3:4-7
Luke 2:(1-7) 8-20

Activities

Christmas Day is very much a time for all God's children to worship together.

Involve all the children in the singing and playing of carols, and in the other ministries of welcoming, serving, collection of gifts and so on. Have nativity toys for the very young to play with, such as knitted Mary, Joseph and Jesus, sheep and shepherds.

I have included a drawing and colouring activity for today so that the children in church can work at this during the sermon.

Print worksheet *Christmas Day (B)* from CD-ROM.

PEBBLES

First Sunday of Christmas

Thought for the day

Just as the angels said, a Saviour has been born for us.

Readings

Isaiah 61:10–62:3
Psalm 148
Galatians 4:4-7
Luke 2:15-21

Aim

To know that when Jesus was born the shepherds came to welcome him.

Starter

Put stickers of different colours on the children, so that there are at least two of each colour used. They dance and jump around until the music stops. Call out a colour, and those wearing that colour sticker come and shake hands, and greet one another by name – 'Hi, Mazin', 'Wotcha, Will!' Then back to the dancing.

Teaching

Have a crib scene set up somewhere in the room, and dress one child up as an angel. Talk about going to visit people at Christmas – perhaps some of them got in a car or went on a bus or train to visit family or friends, or perhaps some of them had visitors coming to see them. Were there any babies in the places they went?

Today we are going to look at some of the visitors the baby Jesus had, soon after he was born.

In a circle, pretend you are all shepherds, sitting out on the hills under the night sky, round a warm fire. Wrap your cloaks around you, and warm your hands at the fire, getting nice and close to keep cosy. All around us the sheep are bleating. (All make some faraway and nearby bleats.) Look up at all the stars and try to count them . . . oh, there are too many to count, but isn't it beautiful to see the stars shining!

But what's that light in the sky? It's so bright, and it seems to be all around us! (All shrink away from the light, putting your hands up to shield your eyes.) And there's an angel, here on our ordinary hillside! (The child dressed as an angel comes and stands near the group, arms raised.)

The angel said to the shepherds, 'Don't be afraid!' (The angel says, 'Don't be afraid!') All start to relax a bit and get ready to listen to the angel's message. Go into narrative mode and explain that the angel told the shepherds that he had some wonderful news to tell them. A Saviour has just been born in their town of Bethlehem, and they are invited to go and visit him. They'll find him easily because he's wrapped up and lying in the straw in a stable.

The shepherds all look at one another with their eyes open wide in surprise. Just then lots of other angels fill the sky all around them (all look up and point at them), and they're all singing God's praises for all they're worth! (We could all join in – 'Glory to God, glory to God, glory to the Father.')

Then the brightness started to fade away, and the shepherds were sitting in the starry night, rubbing their eyes to make sure they weren't dreaming. But they all remembered the light and the angels and the singing, didn't they? (All look at one another, agreeing.)

Now you're back to being a shepherd again. Suggest that you all go and see if you can find this baby who is God's Son. In a stable in Bethlehem, didn't the angel say? Are we ready, then? (Lead the group of shepherds across to the crib and kneel around it.)

Praying

Jesus, like the shepherds,
we want to welcome you
and thank you for being born.
We love you, Jesus!
Amen.

Activities

On the sheet there is the stable in Bethlehem and the shepherds' hillside to colour in. The children can then draw in a winding road (following the dots, or with these blanked out as you wish) and walk their fingers from the hills to the stable.

Print worksheet *First Sunday of Christmas (B)* from CD-ROM.

Second Sunday of Christmas

Thought for the day

The Word made flesh at Christmas was always with God, always expressing his creative love.

Readings

Jeremiah 31:7-14 or Ecclesiasticus 24:1-12
Psalm 147:12-20 or Canticle: Wisdom of Solomon 10:15-21
Ephesians 1:3-14
John 1:(1-9) 10-18

Aim

To know that Jesus is God saying, 'I love you!'

Starter

Collect some model cars and trucks (sized to suit the children in your group) and sit everyone down, spread out. Let them whizz the cars from one to another across the spaces.

Teaching

Talk about how we can send a car off to reach a friend (demonstrate with one car to a child on the other side of the circle) and they can send it back to us. We do the same thing with messages. I can think to myself, 'Mmm, I'd like to thank the children for putting the cars away so nicely', and all I have to do is say the words out loud (say them out loud) and the message races across to your ears! Hands up if you caught the message. Clever, isn't it?

(You could have one or two children sending out a message, and the rest of you catching the spoken message with your ears.)

You can't see those messages, can you? But you can hear them. Some messages you can see. What's this one? (Show the road sign for a school.) And this? (Show a green man sign.) That time you caught the message with your eyes.

At Christmas God sent us a very important message. The message looked like this. (Show a picture of the Nativity.) And it meant this. (Show a red heart with the words 'I love you' on it, and read them out.)

Jesus is God's message of love. Jesus is God saying, 'I love you!' (All join in.)

Praying

Dear God, I am glad
that you love us so much.
It makes me happy!
Amen.

Activities

On the sheet they can match the messages and send a loving one to someone. Provide envelopes for the messages.

Print worksheet *Second Sunday of Christmas (B)* from CD-ROM.

The Epiphany

Thought for the day

Jesus, the promised Messiah, is shown to the Gentile world.

Readings

Isaiah 60:1-6
Psalm 72:(1-9) 10-15
Ephesians 3:1-12
Matthew 2:1-12

Aim

To know that the wise men brought presents to Jesus.

Starter

Fix a star on to a stick and give it to one of the children. Wherever this child goes with the star, the others follow. If the star stops, everyone stops. Swap the star around until everyone who wants to lead has had a go.

Teaching

On a long strip of lining paper or wallpaper draw some hills and a starry sky, based on the picture below. Lay the sheet out in front of the children, and have at the ready a shiny star and a cut-out picture of the wise men. The smaller you make these the longer the journey will look.

Who do we know who followed a star? Yes, it was the wise men from many miles away. They followed a great bright star in the sky which was moving, night by night. (Move the star as you speak, and then make the wise men walk after it to catch it up.) The star went on like this for nights and nights, until at last it stopped. (Stop the star over the town of Bethlehem.) And the wise men followed it all the way to a town called Bethlehem. Who did they find at Bethlehem? They found Jesus there. (Place a Christmas card of Joseph, Mary and Jesus on the city of Bethlehem.)

What did they do when they found Jesus? (Swap the Christmas card for one showing the wise men giving their presents.) They treated Jesus as if he was a little king. They bowed and knelt in front of him, and gave him the presents they had brought.

What were the presents? There was gold (lay down something gold – preferably real gold if practical! If you are wearing a gold ring you can take it off and place it down, which says a lot about real giving without a word spoken) . . . frankincense (again the real thing is ideal, so they can smell what it's like) . . . and myrrh (the Body Shop sells it, or use any spicy ointment and let them rub a bit into their skin if they want to).

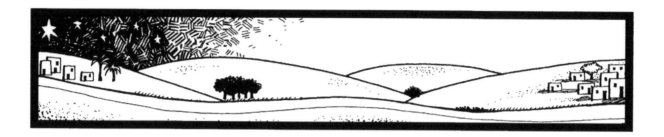

Praying

Jesus, can you guess
(pretend to hide a present behind your back)
what I have brought to give you?
It's ME!
(bring hands out and hold them up and out, as you jump forward)

Activities

There is an activity to match objects with their silhouettes, and a picture to colour of the wise men giving their presents.

Print worksheet *The Epiphany (B)* from CD-ROM.

Match the toy with its shadow

For parents to pray with your child

Jesus, can you guess what I have brought to give you? [pretend to hide a present behind your back]

It's **ME!** [bring hands out and hold them up and out, as you jump forward]

You can colour this picture of the wise men giving Jesus their presents

The Baptism of Christ
First Sunday of Epiphany

Thought for the day

Through the Holy Spirit, Jesus is affirmed at his Baptism as God's beloved Son, and we too are given the Spirit of God which affirms us as God's adopted daughters and sons.

Readings

Genesis 1:1-5
Psalm 29
Acts 19:1-7
Mark 1:4-11

Aim

To know what baptism is.

Starter

Have a time of water play. To cut down on mess, protect the floor with plastic sheeting (plastic tablecloths are good for this job) and have several washing-up bowls with a lowish level of water in them. Gather an assortment of containers, tea strainers and funnels to play with.

Teaching

Talk about playing in the water at a swimming pool, on the beach or by a river, and what the water looks, sounds and feels like. What is it like under the water? What happens to dirty things when they're washed in water?

When people promise to spend their life following Jesus, they are washed in water in church, and given their name. It's called being baptised, or Christened. (Talk about the font in your church, and any baptisms they remember, and show some pictures of people being baptised.)

Today we remember when Jesus was baptised in the river Jordan. He waded into the water and John the Baptist (who was Jesus' cousin) dipped him right under the water. When he came up, all wet, he heard God, his Father, saying to him, 'You are my Son and I love you. I am very pleased with you.'

Praying

Lord God,
I am one of your children.
I belong to you!
Amen.

Activities

Have some strips of blue and silver wool, paper or cloth which the children can stick on to the picture of Jesus' baptism for the water in the river Jordan. A reminder of their own baptism can be made using the outline provided, and more water-coloured wool or string.

Print worksheet *First Sunday of Epiphany (B)* from CD-ROM.

Stick on wool, cellophane or cloth to be the water.

For parents to pray with your child

Lord God,
I am one of
your children.
I belong to you!
Amen.

• Colour yourself in.
• Thread blue and silver wool through the holes and fix with tape.

Second Sunday of Epiphany

Thought for the day
Jesus, the Christ, unlocks the mysteries of God.

Readings
1 Samuel 3:1-10 (11-20)
Psalm 139:1-6, 13-18
Revelation 5:1-10
John 1:43-51

Aim
To know that Jesus shows us what God is like.

Starter
Cut up a magic painting book and supply clean water and brushes, so the children can watch a coloured picture emerging. Alternatively, draw simple pictures (like a sun or a house) on white paper with a candle and let the children paint a colour wash over them to reveal the pictures.

Teaching
Talk about how we couldn't at first see the colours or the pictures, but they were there, hidden, waiting for us to find them.

We can't see God, either. That doesn't mean God isn't there; it means he is there hidden from our sight. We can look around us, up into the sky and down into the deep seas, and know God must be very clever and important to make all this.

But the one who most explains to us what God is like is Jesus.

What is Jesus like? He loves people, whoever they are, however poor or rich they are, and however young or old they are. He helps them, makes them better and chats with them. He is a good friend. He never lets anyone down. He forgives people even when they are really nasty to him.

The more we get to know Jesus, the more we will be finding out about what God is like.

Praying
Thank you, Jesus,
for showing us
what God is like.

Activities
On the sheet there is space for the children to draw an invisible picture with a candle or a white crayon. They can then take this home for someone else to make visible by painting. Also there are some pictures which help them state what they know about God.

Print worksheet *Second Sunday of Epiphany (B)* from CD-ROM.

1. Draw an invisible picture here!

Thank you, Jesus, for showing us what God is like.

Jesus shows us what God is like

What do I know about God

2. Paint a colour wash over here to see the hidden picture!

Third Sunday of Epiphany

Thought for the day
Signs of glory lead us to believe in Jesus as Lord and Saviour.

Readings
Genesis 14:17-20
Psalm 128
Revelation 19:6-10
John 2:1-11

Aim
To know we can follow the signs to find out who God is.

Starter
A treasure trail in pictures. Prepare simple drawings of different places in the room and number them. Keep number 1 yourself, and place number 2 in the place shown on number 1. Continue placing all the pictures until at the last place (pictured in the previous number) you put the treasure – enough sweets/stickers/crayons for everyone. Start off by showing everyone the first picture, which sends them off to where the second one is lurking, and so on until they are led to the treasure.

Teaching
Talk about how we were led to the treasure bit by bit, and not straight away. Each clue led us a little closer.

What things can help us to find out who Jesus is?

Have a candle, some water and a toy sheep all hidden separately under cloths or tea towels. Explain that hidden here we've got some things which can lead us to find out who Jesus is and what he is like.

Uncover the candle. What can a candle tell us about Jesus? Light the candle as you explain that a candle is a living flame of light in the darkness; it helps us see, so we don't trip over things, and it shows things up clearly. And that's what Jesus does. He is the light of love and goodness shining in the darkness of all that is wrong and bad. He helps us see the right way to live so we don't waste our lives hating and spoiling.

Uncover the water. What can water tell us about Jesus? Water is clear and clean, it washes, and when we are thirsty it takes our thirst away. And that's what Jesus does. We can always trust him because he is always honest with us, he forgives us when we are sorry for making others unhappy, and he is like a drink when you're thirsty – very nice!

Uncover the sheep. What can a sheep tell us about Jesus? Sheep need a shepherd, and so do we. Jesus is like a good shepherd who looks after us and leads us safely through our whole life.

Praying

Left, right, left, right,
we are walking your way, Jesus.
Left, right, left, right,
that's the way to go!
Left, right, left, right,
we are walking your way, Jesus.
Left, right, left, right,
Let the loving show!

Activities

There is a tangled lines activity to discover which line leads them to the treasure, and instructions for making a shoe imprint on foil so they can match up the print with the sole of the shoe they are wearing. Each child will need a shoe-sized piece of foil, and the group will need newspaper, a folded cloth and either a normal damp patch of ground, snow or a damp washing-up bowl.

Print worksheet *Third Sunday of Epiphany (B)* from CD-ROM.

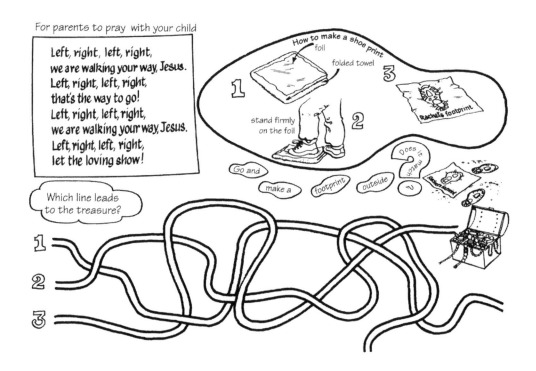

Fourth Sunday of Epiphany

Thought for the day

Jesus displays all the signs that mark him out to be God's chosen One.

Readings

Deuteronomy 18:15-20
Psalm 111
Revelation 12:1-5a
Mark 1:21-28

Aim

To explore the power and glory of God.

Starter

Take the children outside to look up at the sky and wonder at the clouds and the stars which are out there but which we can't see because the sun is shining. Draw their attention to the way they are breathing in the air that is all around them, and let them swish their arms around to feel it moving against them.

Teaching

Back inside, look at our hands and the skin on them which keeps our insides together, protects us so well and exactly fits us! All the things we have been looking at are the work of someone so amazing that our eyes can't even see him – we can only see the wonderful things he has made.

And his name is God. We are only alive here because God invented us. God invented the universe we live in. God sees everything that goes on. He is watching us now. He is listening to us now – not just to what we're saying, but to what we are all thinking as well! He hears us feeling sad when we're sad, grumpy when we're grumpy, and happy when we're happy. He knows when we try hard to be kind, even when we don't really want to. He knows when we feel sorry for someone and want to help them. He knows when we are being silly or unkind.

God knows each of us and every other person really well, even if we don't know that much about him yet. But as we get to know God more, we'll find out that he is completely good and completely loving as well as completely powerful.

Praying

Star maker, sky maker,
help me to see
that God who made everything
knows and loves ME!

Activities

Each child will need a large circle cut from half a black bin bag. There are instructions on the sheet for turning this into a prayer mat of the starry sky, using silver and gold tinsel, and silver foil. There is also a star-to-star picture to complete, and a picture to colour of some of the wonderful things God has thought of.

Print worksheet *Fourth Sunday of Epiphany (B)* from CD-ROM.

Sunday between 3 and 9 February

(if earlier than the Second Sunday before Lent)

Thought for the day

The good news about God is far too good to keep to ourselves.

Readings

Isaiah 40:12-31
Psalm 147:1-11, 20c
1 Corinthians 9:16-23
Mark 1:29-39

Aim

To look at how they can spread the good news of God's love.

Starter

Distribute the contents of a tube of Smarties around the group, or spread some slices of bread with butter and jam to make small sandwiches to give out at coffee time after church.

Teaching

Start with a news time, encouraging the children to share any good news they have, so that everyone can enjoy the good things with them.

The good news we all have to share is that our God is fantastic! Think together about some of the things about God which are wonderful and good.

Not everyone knows these things yet. Quite a lot of people don't know much about God at all, or they don't know how lovely and kind and loving he is. Point out that it seems a great pity that they don't yet know and we do – so how can we let them know our good news about God?

We can use our eyes (everyone points to their eyes) to notice when people need cheering up, or when they need some help, or when they need a hug, just as God notices our needs. We can use our ears (point to ears) to listen carefully, as God listens carefully to us. We can use our mouths (point to them) to speak words that are kind and friendly, and we can tell people about God. And we can use our hands (show them) to do things for people that are kind and loving and helpful.

Praying

I'm not going to keep it a secret – Shh!
I'M GOING TO SHOUT IT LOUD!
GOD IS REAL!
GOD'S THE ONE WHO MADE US ALL
AND GOD'S THE ONE WHO LOVES US ALL!

Activities

On the sheet there are pictures of different things to shout about, and they can work out what the good news is in each case. There is also a picture to colour of all kinds of people happy and dancing because they have just found out that God loves them all.

Print worksheet *Sunday between 3 and 9 February (B)* from CD-ROM.

Sunday between 10 and 16 February

(if earlier than the Second Sunday before Lent)

Thought for the day

Jesus wants to heal us to wholeness, and to him no one is untouchable.

Readings

2 Kings 5:1-14
Psalm 30
1 Corinthians 9:24-27
Mark 1:40-45

Aim

To know that God enjoys helping us and making us better.

Starter

Cut out a number of spots of different colours (about 30 centimetres across) and spread them out on the floor. All round the room are placed small spots of the same colours, and the children go round spotting the spots and placing them on the matching large spot on the floor.

Teaching

Sometimes we get spots when we're ill. Does anyone remember having spots? (With chicken pox, for instance.) Today we are going to meet someone whose skin was covered in white spots because he had a skin illness. The man's name was Naaman.

Spread out carpet tiles or a couple of large towels on the floor and tell the story from 2 Kings 5:1-14 in your own words, using cut-out pictures of the characters based on the drawings below.

Praying

Dear Father God,
we pray for all the people
who are ill,
and for those who are looking after them.
Amen.

Activities

Using the sheet the children can cut out a Naaman and dip him seven times in the river.
There is also a series of pictures of the story to place in order and colour in.

Print worksheet *Sunday between 10 and 16 February (B)* from CD-ROM.

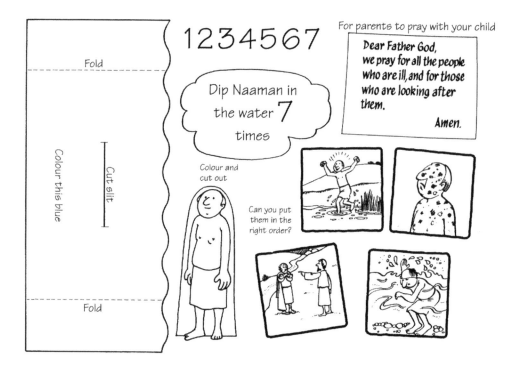

Sunday between
17 and 23 February

(if earlier than the Second Sunday before Lent)

Thought for the day

The Son of Man has authority on earth to forgive sins.

Readings

Isaiah 43:18-25
Psalm 41
2 Corinthians 1:18-22
Mark 2:1-12

Aim

To know the story of the man let down through the roof.

Starter

Construct a pulley as shown in the diagram (*right*), and let everyone help load the bricks that are on the top of our building down to the ground, taking it in turns to do the winding.

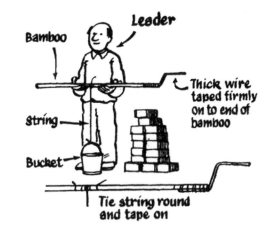

Teaching

In our story today, four friends were lowering something down from the roof on to the ground below –like we were, but it wasn't bricks!

Use a prototype model from the worksheet, made from a shoe box as shown, and tell the children the story of today's Gospel as you act it out with the working model.

Praying

Thank you for the friends
who brought us to you, Jesus.
And thank you for legs to run with!
    (*Run*)
Amen.

Activities

Each child will need a cardboard box to make the model of the house. Have the hole in the roof already cut. They will also need some tape or wool to place under the man to lower him down through the roof, and modelling clay to make the man.

Print worksheet *Sunday between 17 and 23 February (B)* from CD-ROM.

3. Colour the people, cut them out and stick them in the house

in the house

in the house

1. Make the man who can't move out of plasticine

2. Cut out this bed. Stick tape here and here

on the roof

on the roof

You can lower the man down through the roof

For parents to pray with your child

Thank you for the friends who brought us to you, Jesus. And thank you for legs to run with! (Run)   Amen.

Second Sunday before Lent

Thought for the day
Christ is the image of the unseen God.

Readings
Proverbs 8:1, 22-31
Psalm 104:24-35
Colossians 1:15-20
John 1:1-14

Aim
To delight, like God's wisdom, in all creation.

Starter
Prepare a selection of smells and textures for the children to sample. Here are some suggestions:

- incense sticks or essential oils of different fragrances
- primroses and daffodils
- fruits and vegetables
- bark, new and crackly leaves, shells, feathers and stones
- different textured fabrics

Teaching
Gather round all the objects and talk with the children about the ones they specially like, enjoying the variety. We have all been born into this beautiful world, with all its colours and shapes to look at and enjoy. Go through different categories of what there is, so that they can think of examples of them all (for example, round, red, yellow, prickly, shiny, rough and smooth, quiet and loud, quick and slow, little and big, and things that are invisible and hidden). What a loving God it must be who thought of all this and gave us such a lovely planet to live on!

Praying
All that we can hear and everything we can see, including me,
we all of us spring from God,
who cares for each of us unendingly.
Let the whole earth sing of his love!

Activities

Have ready plenty of glue, and an assortment of small examples of things that are shiny, colourful, tasty, soft and round, so that they can choose things to stick on to the appropriate spaces on the sheet. There is music to go with today's prayer (see page 379), which the children can sing as they hold up their finished 'samplers'.

Print worksheet *Second Sunday before Lent (B)* from CD-ROM.

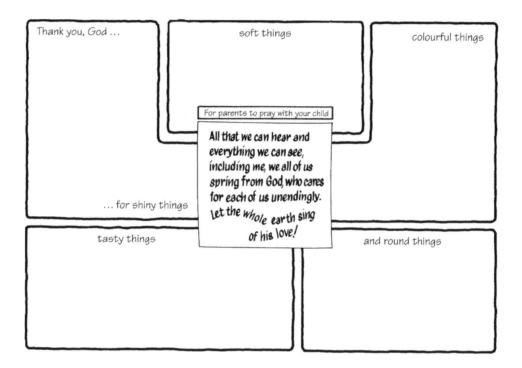

Sunday next before Lent

Thought for the day
God's glory shows.

Readings
2 Kings 2:1-12
Psalm 50:1-6
2 Corinthians 4:3-6
Mark 9:2-9

Aim
To sense God's glory and holiness.

Starter
Use a set of Christmas tree lights, strung across a notice board or round a door frame. If you haven't access to any fairy lights, bring a couple of bedside lamps and a multi-socket, so you can turn them all on and off from one switch. Everyone jumps and dances around the room, but whenever the lights go on they stop and face them, standing completely still.

Teaching
When everyone is sitting in a circle, turn on the fairy lights, make the room as dark as possible and light some candles, standing them on a mirror or some foil so that the lights are reflected. As you light the candles have some quiet music playing, and talk about how good light is, and how beautiful. Draw the children's attention to the colour of the flames, and the bright reflections. Remind everyone that God is here with us, and he loves us and our families very much. For a short while, encourage everyone to sit here very still in the candlelight with the music playing, in God's company. Then explain how we often think of God as being like light, because he is so full of goodness and loveliness. The prayer can be sung (to the tune of *See-saw, Marjorie Daw*) as you sit around the candles.

Praying
Jesus, Jesus,
Lord of earth and heaven,
Jesus, Jesus,
Lord of earth and heaven!

Activities

The sheet can be turned into a stained glass window by colouring the outline with wax crayons, and then sponging a little cooking oil over it. Leave to dry out, and the paper will have become translucent.

Print worksheet *Sunday next before Lent (B)* from CD-ROM.

First Sunday of Lent

Thought for the day

After his Baptism Jesus is led by the Spirit into the wilderness before returning to proclaim God's kingdom.

Readings

Genesis 9:8-17
Psalm 25:1-10
1 Peter 3:18-22
Mark 1:9-15

Aim

To know the story of Noah, the flood and the rainbow.

Starter

Put stickers of different colours on the children and stand in a circle, holding hands to make archways. When you hold up a colour, the child wearing that colour sticker runs in and out of the archways, round the circle and back to their place. Whenever you hold up a picture of a rainbow, the whole circle joins hands and comes in to the middle and out again, shouting, 'God loves us!'

Teaching

Spread out carpet tiles or a large sheet on the ground and sit around it. Use cut-outs, based on the pictures below to tell the story of Noah and the flood. Animals can be models if you prefer. The children can help move the characters around. Bring out the way God rescued Noah and his family and kept them safe, and how the rainbow is a sign of God's love that will never let us down.

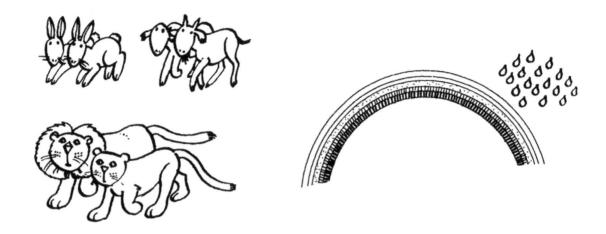

Praying

(This can be sung to the tune of One, two, three four five, once I caught a fish alive)

Violet, indigo and blue –
God loves me, that's always true.
Green, yellow, orange, red –
that is what the rainbow said!

Activities

The sheet can be turned into a rainbow mobile. The children will need lengths of different coloured wool, glue sticks and cotton, and you may prefer to copy the sheet on to thicker paper than usual.

Print worksheet *First Sunday of Lent (B)* from CD-ROM.

Second Sunday of Lent

Thought for the day
A commitment of faith has far-reaching implications.

Readings
Genesis 17:1-7, 15-16
Psalm 22:23-31
Romans 4:13-25
Mark 8:31-38

Aim
To know that we can trust God.

Starter
Sit in a circle and show the children the items mentioned as you ask them to decide which of the two they would trust:

- Which would you trust to sit on – a chair or a balloon?
- Which would you trust to build a house with – bricks or sponges?
- Which would you trust to swing on – cotton or a rope?
- Which would you choose to carry your packed lunch in – an airtight box or an envelope?

Teaching
We trust things that we think will work well – things that won't let us down. And we trust people who love us, because we know they will be wanting us to be safe and happy. We can't trust strangers, because we don't know if they are wanting us to be safe and happy or not. Use a parent and a child puppet to act this out. First the child is scared of riding a new bike, but the parent reassures them that they will be holding them so they will be safe. The child agrees to try, as the parent has promised to make sure they don't fall. Then the child wants to ride on the main road, but the parent explains they can't because it's too dangerous. The child reluctantly agrees, knowing that the parent is wanting them to be safe because they are loved.

God is like a loving parent to all of us – God loves us and wants us to be safe and happy for always, in this life and after we die. So we can trust God completely. He will never do anything bad or wrong. He will never let us down. He is always there, watching over us and loving us.

Praying

Jesus, we know we can trust you –
you love us
and will never let us down.
Amen.

Activities

The teaching on trust is continued on the sheet, with some thinking to do about what we are prepared to trust and why. There is also a picture of some people in dangerous places, and they can experience being on the caring end by noticing needs and providing the necessary help by drawing it in.

Print worksheet *Second Sunday of Lent (B)* from CD-ROM.

Third Sunday of Lent

Thought for the day

God's wisdom may shock us. Jesus, obedient to God's Law and fulfilling it, dies a death which, according to the Law, makes him cursed.

Readings

Exodus 20:1-17
Psalm 19
1 Corinthians 1:18-25
John 2:13-22

Aim

To know Jesus' summary of the Law.

Starter

Traffic lights. Prepare three coloured circles – red, amber and green. Explain that to play this game we have to obey the rules. When the green is shown, everyone jumps and dances around the room. When amber (or yellow) is shown, everyone gets ready to stop. When red is shown, everyone stops quite still. When red and amber are shown together, everyone gets ready to move again.

Teaching

Praise them for obeying the rules so well. That meant we could all enjoy playing the game together. It's very useful to have rules. Some rules are there to keep us safe (like not playing in the road), and some are to make sure that things are done fairly (like queuing up for rides at a theme park).

Jesus gave us two good rules to help us live our lives really well, and we're going to learn them today. As we've got two hands each we can use our hands to help us learn the rules.

Demonstrate raising one hand to heaven as you say, 'Love God', and then stretching the other hand out, palm up, as you say, 'Love one another'. Then everyone can try it a couple of times. The rules can also be written on two balloons with an OHP pen, and the balloons inflated. Any of the children who now think they can say the two rules on their own can do that in front of the others. (Everyone will benefit from the reinforcement, and the children enjoy being able to do it well.)

Now we've learnt God's two rules, all we have to do is live by them! Each day we can think over what we've done and ask ourselves, 'How have we been loving God today? And how have we been loving one another today?' And the next day we can try and do it even better!

Praying

(Say the prayer with actions.)

Love God, love one another,
That's the way to live.
Love God, love one another,
happy to forgive.

Activities

There is a picture on the sheet with children and adults of all ages. The children can pick out all the loving God and loving one another that is going on. Part of the sheet can be made into wrist bands with the two rules on, which the children can decorate and wear.

Print worksheet *Third Sunday of Lent (B)* from CD-ROM.

Fourth Sunday of Lent
Mothering Sunday

Thought for the day

God provides comfort in all our troubles and sufferings.

Readings

Exodus 2:1-10 or 1 Samuel 1:20-28
Psalm 34:11-20 or Psalm 127:1-4
2 Corinthians 1:3-7 or Colossians 3:12-17
Luke 2:33-35 or John 19:25-27

Activities

Today is not one for learning separately but for celebrating and learning together. Involve the children and young people in the music group or choir, as servers, welcomers, collectors for the offering, and so on. Provide shakers and bells for the younger ones to play during one or two hymns, and streamers to wave. Gather the children round the altar for the eucharistic prayer and choose hymns where the language is accessible.

Have materials for making flowers available for the younger children. The activity sheet should be enlarged to A3 size if possible.

Print worksheet *Fourth Sunday of Lent (B)* from CD-ROM.

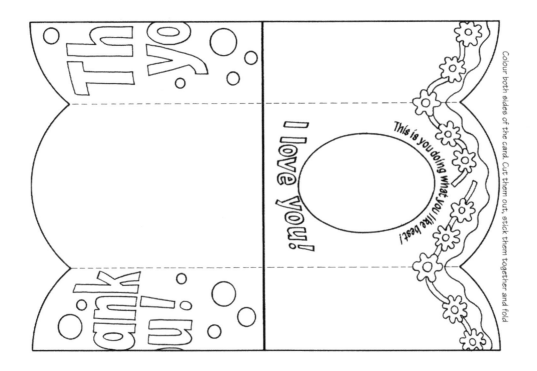

PEBBLES

Fifth Sunday of Lent

Thought for the day

Through Christ's death, full life would come to people of all nations and generations.

Readings

Jeremiah 31:31-34
Psalm 51:1-12 or Psalm 119:9-16
Hebrews 5:5-10
John 12:20-33

Aim

To know that Jesus loves us enough to help us even when it hurts.

Starter

Play shops, with cartons, fruit and vegetables for sale and toy money, so that they get the idea of there being cost and payment.

Teaching

Talk about their shopping, and bring out a carrier bag from a local supermarket, with some cheap and expensive items in it. Talk together about which don't cost very much, and which cost a lot. Mention other things which cost lots and lots of money, like houses and holidays. We have to save up for things like that. Sometimes we see a toy or a game we would like, but we don't think it's worth all the money, so we choose not to get it. (Or Mum and Dad say that!)

There was something that Jesus wanted very, very much. It wasn't a toy, and it wasn't something to eat or wear. What Jesus really wanted was to save the world. He wanted us all to be happy and free. But how much would it cost? It couldn't be bought with money. It could only be bought with his life.

Jesus thought about it. He wondered if it was really worth giving up his life so we could be happy and free. He knew that giving up his life would hurt. A lot.

But remember, Jesus loves us very much. He loves us so much that he decided he was even willing to give up his life so we could be free and happy. He thought it was worth the cost of all that hurt. So he did it, and that's why we can be happy and free!

Praying

(Sing this to the tune of *Frère Jacques*, with the children echoing the leader's words and actions.)

I am dancing, **I am dancing,**
   (dance)
'Thank you, God!' **'Thank you, God!'**
   (clap hands)
I am singing, **I am singing,**
   (sway)
'Thank you, God!' **'Thank you, God!'**
   (clap hands)

Activities

On the sheet there is a purse full of pictures, and some other things which 'cost' the items in the purse. The children choose what they would be willing to give up for the experiences 'on offer'. There is also a 'thank you, Jesus!' hat to make and wear. Have a selection of sparkly and shiny things to decorate it with.

Print worksheet *Fifth Sunday of Lent (B)* from CD-ROM.

Palm Sunday

Thought for the day

As the Messiah, Jesus enters Jerusalem, knowing that he rides towards rejection and death in order to save his people.

Readings

Liturgy of the Palms:
Mark 11:1-11 or John 12:12-16
Psalm 118:1-2, 19-24

Liturgy of the Passion:
Isaiah 50:4-9a
Psalm 31:9-16
Philippians 2:5-11
Mark 14:1-15:47 or Mark 15:1-39 (40-47)

Aim

To know that Jesus came into Jerusalem, welcomed and cheered by all the people.

Starter

If possible, let the children join in with the all-age procession, playing their instruments, dancing and singing as they go. Or gather all the age groups and take them on a Palm Sunday procession, preferably outside. Take a portable tape player so they can all sing along with the songs.

Teaching

Show a picture or a model of a donkey. There's a donkey in our story today. He was just an ordinary donkey, and a young one, but he was given a very important job to do.

Tell the children the story of Jesus' entry into Jerusalem from the donkey's point of view. Bring in what the donkey saw and heard and felt and smelt, and how pleased and proud he felt to have his friend Jesus riding on his back. If you prefer to have a 'script', Nan Goodall's classic, *Donkey's glory* (Mowbray, 1980) includes this special journey.

Praying

(Jingle some keys or bottle tops during this prayer.)

Donkey riding, donkey riding,
hear the children sing!
Donkey riding, donkey riding,
'JESUS IS OUR KING!'

Activities

Pin the tail on the donkey. Use the picture of a donkey and make a tail from some wool, with sticky tack on the top end. The children shut their eyes (or have them blindfolded) and fix the tail where they reckon it belongs. Using an old sock and some wool they can make a donkey puppet to remind them of today's teaching. (If you don't have any old socks, try the charity shops, or a jumble sale.)

Print worksheet *Palm Sunday (B)* from CD-ROM.

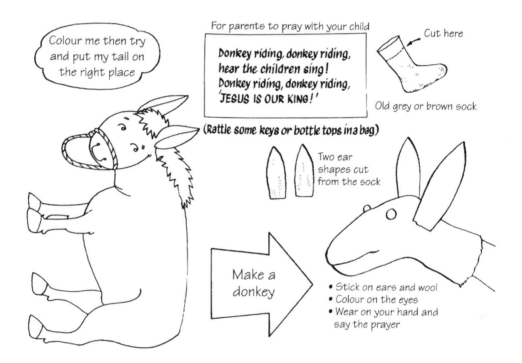

Easter Day

If possible, it is recommended that the children and young people are in church with the other age groups today. Involve the young people in some of the music and in the cleaning and decorating of the church.

Thought for the day
Jesus is alive; Love has won the victory over sin and death.

Readings
Acts 10:34-43 or Isaiah 25:6-9
Psalm 118:1-2, 14-24
1 Corinthians 15:1-11 or Acts 10:34-43
John 20:1-18 or Mark 16:1-8

Aim
To know that Jesus died and is alive again for ever.

Starter
Hide some Easter eggs (outside if possible) and have an Easter egg hunt before distributing them fairly among the children.

Teaching
Look together at some hens' eggs and pictures of chicks, birds and dinosaurs, all coming from eggs. Talk about the springtime and all the signs of new life around at the moment.

Today is Easter Day. It's very special because it's the day we remember Jesus coming to life for ever. Jesus went around doing good and loving people, making them better and helping them get to know what God is like. But some people wanted Jesus out of the way, and he was killed – they nailed him to a big cross. It was very sad, but Jesus went on loving and forgiving even then.

When some of his friends went to the grave on the Sunday morning, they couldn't find his dead body; it wasn't there. Why? Because Jesus wasn't dead any more – he was alive! He would never die again. Jesus is alive for ever! (You could all sing *Jesus' love is very wonderful* to celebrate.)

Praying
Did Jesus die? YES!
Is Jesus dead? NO!
Is he alive again? YES, YES, YES!
JESUS IS ALIVE!

Activities

On the sheet there are pictures of a chick being hatched to put in sequence, and a picture of the Easter garden to colour. This can be stuck on a folded piece of coloured paper and given as an Easter card to the family.

Print worksheet *Easter Day (B)* from CD-ROM.

Second Sunday of Easter

Thought for the day

Our faith in the risen Christ is bound to affect the way we live.

Readings

Acts 4:32-35
Psalm 133
1 John 1:1-2:2
John 20:19-31

Aim

To know that Jesus is with us now.

Starter

Have four different sounds, such as a bell, a drum, a rattle and a whistle. When the children hear the sounds they do the appropriate actions. The bell means 'now clap', the drum 'now jump up and down', the rattle 'now sit', and the whistle 'now smile'.

Teaching

Talk about what we are all doing now. This might be sitting in a circle, listening, folding our arms, breathing, and thinking. Some things, like breathing, we do all the time, and hardly notice. Take a few breaths to notice what goes on day and night, when we're awake and when we're asleep, so that we stay alive. So there's lots going on now just in our own body.

What's going on now as well as us sitting in a circle in St Martin's, East Ham? Lots of other groups of Pebbles are sitting in their circles in other churches! (Why not pray for them now – they will be praying for you!) What else is going on now? Think about what is happening at the moment on the roads and in hospitals, and in other countries, where some people are fast asleep and others are going to bed.

We only see our little bit of now, but God sees all of it! Jesus is here now for all the people and all the places!

Praying

(Loudly) Tick tock, tick tock,
Jesus you are with us NOW!
(Softly) Tick tock, tick tock,
(Very softly) Jesus . . . you are here.

Activities

On the sheet there are pictures of Jesus with us while we're playing, eating, travelling, working. It helps children to have it pictured for them, and then they have no problem in understanding that Jesus is with us even though we can't actually see him. They can colour the pictures and put them around the house at appropriate places to remind them. There is also a 'Jesus is my friend' badge to make.

Print worksheet *Second Sunday of Easter (B)* from CD-ROM.

Third Sunday of Easter

Thought for the day

Having redeemed us by his death, Jesus can offer us the forgiveness of our sin, which sets us free to live.

Readings

Acts 3:12-19
Psalm 4
1 John 3:1-7
Luke 24:36b-48

Aim

To know that Jesus calms our fears when we're scared.

Starter

What's the time, Mr Wolf? The children creep up on Mr Wolf, asking him the time, and he replies with different times. If he says, 'Dinner time!' the children turn and run as Mr Wolf tries to catch someone.

Teaching

Talk about how mums and dads make us feel safe when we're scared or frightened. Sometimes they make us laugh and show us that we don't need to be frightened. (Like Dad pretending to wear a bib, so the baby sees it as funny instead of scary.) Sometimes they explain so we aren't scared any more because we understand it better. (Like barking being a dog's way of saying hello.) And if something really is frightening, mums and dads make us feel safer just by holding us close to them, or just being there. (You can use parent and baby soft toys to act out these situations.)

Now explain that God is like that with us all. When his disciples were all scared, on the first Easter Day, Jesus came and comforted them. Jesus knows when we're scared, and we can tell him all about it. He will help us to be brave. He works through other people to look after us, and he works through us to look after other people who are scared. So whenever we make someone feel better, or calm their fears, we are working on God's team!

Praying

I will lie down in peace and sleep;
it is you, Lord,
who keeps me safe.
Amen.

Activities

On the sheet there are some pictures of people who need some help to stop them being frightened, and the children can draw in the things or people they need. The prayer can be hung up in the bedroom to use as a night prayer.

Print worksheet *Third Sunday of Easter (B)* from CD-ROM.

Fourth Sunday of Easter

Thought for the day

'I am the Good Shepherd and I lay down my life for the sheep.'

Readings

Acts 4:5-12
Psalm 23
1 John 3:16-24
John 10:11-18

Aim

To know that Jesus is our Good Shepherd.

Starter

Hunt the sheep. Use a soft toy sheep and take it in turns to hide it while everyone closes their eyes. Then everyone looks for it until it's found again.

Teaching

The children can help you make a landscape of hills, using a large towel draped over some upturned pots and basins, and arranging a few pot plants on it. Wind a long blue scarf between the hills as a stream of water. Place some sheep on the hills. These can either be model or toy ones, or they can be made from the pattern (*right*).

Move the sheep around (the children can make all the sheep and lamb bleating noises) as you tell them how a good shepherd looks after the sheep, taking them to places where there is plenty of grass to eat, leading them to the water so they can drink, and making sure they are safe from howling wolves and growling bears. A good shepherd loves his sheep and knows each of them by name, and he'll never leave them in danger, even if it means getting hurt himself.

Explain that Jesus talks about himself as being like our Good Shepherd. (Move the sheep around as you talk about God's care of us.) He looks after us and loves us, and knows each of us by name. (Mention each of the children and leaders' names.)

Praying

The Lord is my Shepherd,
(hold each finger in turn, so the ring finger is held on 'my')
there is nothing else I need.
(keep holding ring finger and shake head)

Activities

Today's prayer, from Psalm 23, can be learnt by heart, using the actions as a memory aid. Encourage the children to pray this whenever they feel frightened, holding on to their ring finger to remember that Jesus, the Good Shepherd, knows and loves them by name, and they belong to him. This teaching is reinforced on the sheet and the children can make a sheep, with their own name on it.

Print worksheet *Fourth Sunday of Easter (B)* from CD-ROM.

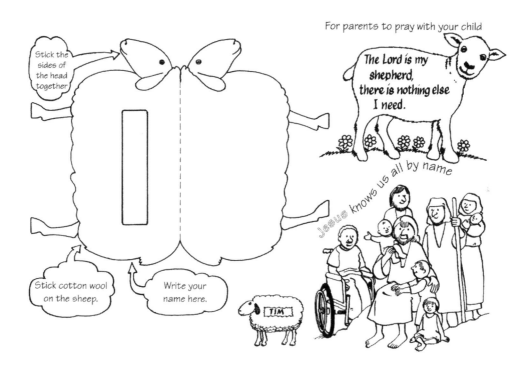

Fifth Sunday of Easter

Thought for the day

To produce fruit we need to be joined on to the true vine.

Readings

Acts 8:26-40
Psalm 22:25-31
1 John 4:7-21
John 15:1-8

Aim

To know they can be generous at passing on Jesus' love.

Starter

If you have access to a garden or patch of grass, give the children containers which you fill with water so they can go and water the plants. They can get a refill when their container is empty. Otherwise, play inside with water in washing-up bowls, funnels and containers.

Teaching

Talk about the way we were able to pour the water out on to the plants or into other pots because we had the water to use. What do we do at home if we need water to make a drink, or wash, or brush our teeth? We go and turn on the tap and out comes the water. If we get thirsty again, or need another bath after playing and being busy all day, we can go back to the tap and there's some more water waiting for us to use!

Have a bowl of water and a dry sponge. God's love goes on and on, and there's always plenty of it for us. Whenever we settle down with our friend Jesus (place the sponge in the water), we can't help soaking up some of his love, so we get more loving, just as this sponge is getting more wet by soaking up the water.

We can go back to soak ourselves in God's love every day, so that we are people filled with love. Then we can spread God's love around to other people and make the world a happy place.

Praying

Jesus, fill me up with your love
so I can spread love around
wherever it's needed!
Amen.

Activities

Each child will need an empty plastic pot. The children are going to decorate them with the picture and prayer which is on the sheet. There is also a picture to colour, of a gardener looking after a vine with grapes on it.

Print worksheet *Fifth Sunday of Easter (B)* from CD-ROM.

Sixth Sunday of Easter

Thought for the day

We are to love one another as Jesus loves us.

Readings

Acts 10:44-48
Psalm 98
1 John 5:1-6
John 15:9-17

Aim

To know that Jesus thinks of us as his friends.

Starter

Have an assortment of toys to play with, so that everyone can enjoy playing together as friends.

Teaching

Talk together about friends. Friends play together, giggle together and chat together. Friends stick up for one another and share things. Friends like being with each other. What do some of the children like about their friends? (Pass a soft toy around. This is held by the person who is talking, and the others listen.)

We are friends of Jesus. Jesus likes being with us and chatting with us, listening to our news and all the sad as well as the happy things. And he's always there for us – he doesn't suddenly go off us and not like us any more.

What do friends of Jesus do? They love one another, just as Jesus loves them.

Praying

Jesus, you are our friend and we are yours.
In all we think and speak and do
    (point to head, mouth and then open hands)
help us to love one another.
    (spread arms wide)
Amen.

Activities

On the sheet there are some pictures of people behaving like friends to tick, and some to cross out where people are not behaving lovingly at all. They can make a picture for Jesus to say 'thank you' for something in their life.

Print worksheet *Sixth Sunday of Easter (B)* from CD-ROM.

Tick the pictures of people being friends

Jesus, you are our friend
and we are yours.
In all we think and speak
and do (point to head, mouth,
then open hands) help us
to love one another.
(Spread arms wide)
Amen.

For parents to pray with your child

For my friend Jesus

Stick all kinds of things on to make a picture for Jesus
or draw the people you want to thank God for.
Thank you, Jesus

Ascension Day

Thought for the day

Having bought back our freedom with the giving of his life, Jesus enters into the full glory to which he is entitled.

Readings

Acts 1:1-11 or Daniel 7:9-14
Psalm 47 or Psalm 93
Ephesians 1:15-23 or Acts 1:1-11
Luke 24:44-53

Activities

It is likely that Ascension Day services for schools will not need a separate programme for children. However, I have included a drawing and colouring activity for today so that children in church can work at this during the sermon.

Print worksheet *Ascension Day (B)* from CD-ROM.

PEBBLES

Seventh Sunday of Easter
Sunday after Ascension Day

Thought for the day

Although now hidden from our sight, Jesus lives for ever, and in him we can live the Resurrection life even while we are on earth.

Readings

Acts 1:15-17, 21-26
Psalm 1
1 John 5:9-13
John 17:6-19

Aim

To hear about Jesus going back to heaven.

Starter

Hello, goodbye. As the music plays, the children skip and jump about. When it stops, they find another person, shake hands and say, 'Hello'. As the music starts again, they wave and say, 'Goodbye', before skipping and jumping off somewhere else.

Teaching

Our lives are full of hellos and goodbyes. Share some of the times we say hello and goodbye. Sometimes the goodbyes can be sad, if we've been with a special friend, or grandparents, and have to say goodbye to them. We know that means we won't be seeing them for a while.

Jesus' friends had got used to him being there to talk and laugh with. They loved being with Jesus. Even when Jesus had risen from the dead he would spend time with them sometimes. But now Jesus took his friends out to a hill and told them it was time to say goodbye. They wouldn't be seeing him any more as it was time for him to go back to heaven.

But Jesus wasn't going to leave his friends all alone. He loved them! He promised that in a few days he would send them a special present. When the present came they would be able to feel Jesus there with them all the time. That made the friends happy. They watched as a cloud took Jesus up out of their sight, and then they went back to Jerusalem to wait for the special present.

Praying

Be near me, Lord Jesus, I ask thee to stay close by me for ever and love me, I pray. Bless all the dear children in thy tender care, and fit us for heaven to live with thee there.

Activities

The pictures of clouds and a crown can be coloured and hung together as a mobile. Or you can use the outlines as templates for white and gold thin card. The prayer can be stuck to one of the clouds.

Print worksheet *Seventh Sunday of Easter (B)* from CD-ROM.

JESUS

Stick on cotton wool

Stick on cotton wool

Stick on cotton wool

For parents to pray with your child

Be near me, Lord Jesus,
I ask thee to stay
close by me for ever
and love me, I pray.
Bless all the dear children
in thy tender care,
and fit us for heaven
to live with thee there.

Day of Pentecost
Whit Sunday

Thought for the day
The Holy Spirit of God is poured out in power on the expectant disciples, just as Jesus promised.

Readings
Acts 2:1-21 or Ezekiel 37:1-14
Psalm 104:24-34, 35b
Romans 8:22-27 or Acts 2:1-21
John 15:26-27; 16:4b-15

Aim
To celebrate the Church's birthday.

Starter
Pass the parcel. Beforehand prepare an outline picture based on the one on the right.

Cut flame shapes from coloured paper to fit exactly over the flames in the picture. Pack the flames into the layers of the parcel and the silhouettes of the disciples' heads in the 'prize' place. You can add a sweet if you wish! As each flame is unwrapped the child sticks it on to the right space, until the group has collectively completed the whole picture.

Teaching
Today we are celebrating! It's rather like the birthday of the Church, because today we remember how Jesus sent the Holy Spirit on his friends so they would be filled with God's love and power.

What did the Holy Spirit sound like? It sounded like a strong wind, blowing round the house. (All make the sound.)

What did the Holy Spirit look like? It looked like flames of fire. (Light twelve tea-light candles.)

What did the Holy Spirit feel like? It felt like being happy and excited and peaceful all at once, and wanting to tell everyone about how lovely it is to be loved by God.

Praying

Come, Holy Spirit,
and fill me up with God's love.
I may be small
and not very tall
but I can be BIG with God's love!
  (Make yourself as big as possible)

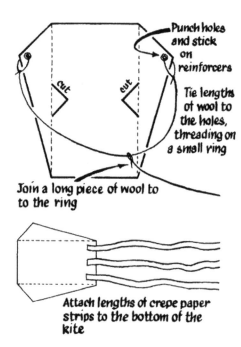

Activities

The sheet can be made into a simple kite to fly. Each child will also need some cotton. Put reinforcers on the punched holes and staple the kites like this.

The kites should fly even in a very light breeze if the children run with them.

Print worksheet *Day of Pentecost (B)* from CD-ROM.

Trinity Sunday

Thought for the day

The mysterious and holy nature of the one true God is beyond our understanding, but it is both communal harmony and individual personality, Father, Son and Holy Spirit.

Readings

Isaiah 6:1-8
Psalm 29
8:12-17
John 3:1-17

Aim

To learn about God from the wind.

Starter

Go outside and feel the wind. Work out where it's coming from, and watch what it does to such things as a piece of thread, a balloon, our clothes, and blown bubbles.

Teaching

Come back inside and sit in a circle, talking about the wind. What did it feel like on our skin? What did it do? Was the wind real? Could we see it? No! The wind and air are invisible, but we know they are very real. How? Because we can feel the wind and see what it does.

The wind is very useful because it can teach us about God. Like the wind, God's love and closeness to us can't be seen, but it is very, very real. We can feel that God loves us. We can see all around us the beautiful world God has made. Like the wind, we can see the good things God does.

Praying

I can't see the wind
but I can feel it's there.
I can't see you, Lord God,
but I can feel your love!

Activities

Using the sheet they can make a prayer wheel to hang in the wind, and there is a windy day picture for them to look at and colour, spotting the things the invisible wind is doing.

Print worksheet *Trinity Sunday (B)* from CD-ROM.

Sunday between
29 May and 4 June

(if after Trinity Sunday)

Thought for the day

Jesus has the words of eternal life – he sheds light on a right attitude to the Law.

Readings

1 Samuel 3:1-10 (11-20) or Deuteronomy 5:12-15
Psalm 139:1-6, 13-18 or Psalm 81:1-10
2 Corinthians 4:5-12
Mark 2:23-3:6

Aim

To know that we are like clay pots holding God's treasure.

Starter

Have a number of boxes, pots and tins with a different thing in each. Name one of the objects and let the children guess which container it's in. Open each one to look until you find the right one. With the next object they may have seen it already, so memory as well as guesswork comes into the choosing. Continue till all the objects have been found inside their containers.

Teaching

Talk about how all those ordinary containers held different treasures. We've got some more containers here in Pebbles today. Count round the number of people present – we've got that number of treasure pots sitting here!

Each of us is like one of those ordinary pots, with secret treasure inside. The treasure is God's great love for us. (Gradually open up a huge red heart of paper.) Wherever we go and whatever we're doing, we know that God loves us, and that treasure makes us very special pots indeed! It means that we can be loving and kind, happy and strong because we haven't just got our loving in us – we've got God's as well.

Praying

I am filled with the love of Jesus –
love in my seeing,
    (point to eyes)
love in all I do.
    (open hands)
Thank you, Jesus,
    (raise arms)
love in my speaking,
    (point to mouth)
your love is ENORMOUS!
    (stretch arms in huge circle)

Activities

Give each child a really big piece of paper cut into a heart shape. With paints or crayons they can make it very beautiful, as it is God's love they are drawing. Then help them to fold it up really small, so it will fit into the envelope made from the sheet, on which they draw themselves.

Print worksheet *Sunday Between 29 May and 4 June (B)* from CD-ROM.

Sunday between 5 and 11 June

(if after Trinity Sunday)

Thought for the day

Anyone who does God's will is considered a close family member of Jesus.

Readings

1 Samuel 8:4-11(12-15) 16-20 (11:14-15) or Genesis 3:8-15
Psalm 138 or Psalm 130
2 Corinthians 4:13-5:1
Mark 3:20-35

Aim

To know that Jesus thinks of us as family when we do God's will.

Starter

Part of the family. Stand in a circle. Tell each group in turn the way to move in the circle, like this: 'If you are a brother, run in the circle; if you are a sister, skip round the circle; if you have an uncle, stand still in the circle; if you have a grandma, walk about in the circle.'

Teaching

Talk about the way we look a bit like other people in our family, and look for family likenesses in children from the same family, or with families everyone in the group knows well. Sometimes we are alike in the way we look and sometimes in how we walk, fiddle with our fingers, or laugh. Sometimes we are like other people in our family in being quiet or noisy, losing our temper or liking music.

One day Jesus was sitting talking to a circle of his friends, rather like we are sitting now. Someone told him that his mother, brothers and sisters were outside. Jesus looked around at all the people and told them he thought of everyone living God's way as part of his close family!

So that means us as well. We are part of Jesus' family, and when we are living God's way we're showing the family likeness.

Praying

(To the tune of *Twinkle, twinkle, little star*)

Jesus, Jesus, can I be
in your loving family?
When I live the loving way,
loving others every day,
Jesus, Jesus, I can be
in your loving family!

Activities

On the sheet there is a picture of Jesus sitting in a house surrounded by people who are listening to him. They add themselves to the group, and other people who are living as Jesus' friends. Also there is a praying space in which they can draw someone who doesn't know Jesus yet. As they draw this person meeting Jesus, they will be thinking of them and that is very real prayer.

Print worksheet *Sunday Between 5 and 11 June (B)* from CD-ROM.

Sunday between 12 and 18 June

(if after Trinity Sunday)

Thought for the day

From small beginnings, and by God's power, the kingdom of heaven grows.

Readings

1 Samuel 15:34-16:13 or Ezekiel 17:22-24
Psalm 20 or Psalm 92:1-4,12-15
2 Corinthians 5:6-10 (11-13) 14-17
Mark 4:26-34

Aim

To know that God's love grows and grows in his people.

Starter

Play with very soapy water, making bubbles by blowing through your hands. (Ordinary bubble mix is the rather boring substitute!) As you play, talk about the bubbles growing bigger and bigger, and see who can make the biggest.

Teaching

How did we make our bubbles grow? We had to blow very carefully and gently. Show the children some little seeds and pictures of what they grow into. Show them some real 'grown' examples as well if this is practical. In the story of Jack and the beanstalk, the beans grew up overnight into a huge plant, but usually the growing goes on bit by bit, day by day, until instead of a tiny seed you find a big tall plant, or even a tree.

Bubbles and plants aren't the only things which grow. We grow too! Let them stand up as tall as they can and remember when they were only very short. In the world God has made, there is lots and lots of growing that goes on.

Jesus told his friends one day that, just like the other things that grow, the kingdom of heaven grows and grows. Bit by bit God's love and goodness is growing and spreading. Once there were just a few of Jesus' followers, but now there are friends of Jesus all over the place. We know a few of them, because they are with us in our church. (Name some of them.) Then there are Jesus' friends in all the other churches, not just in this country, but all over the world.

Praying

Pray for each other by name:
Lord Jesus, bless . . .
Let your love in her/him grow and grow
a bit more every day of her/his life.

Activities

When they have coloured and cut out the plant on the sheet, they can fold it as shown so that they can make it 'grow' like Jesus' love in us. They can also match the seed to the tree pictures.

Print worksheet *Sunday Between 12 and 18 June (B)* from CD-ROM.

Sunday between 19 and 25 June

(if after Trinity Sunday)

Thought for the day

What kind of person is this? Even the wind and waves obey him.

Readings

1 Samuel 17:(1a, 4-11,19-23) 32-49 or1 Samuel 17:57-18:5, 10-16 or Job 38:1-11
Psalm 9:9-20 or Psalm 133 or Psalm 107:1-3, 23-32
2 Corinthians 6:1-13
Mark 4:35-41

Aim

To know that Jesus calms our fears.

Starter

Bring either a small parachute or a large sheet and stand everyone around the outside, holding the edge. They can now make a flat calm, then build up through very gentle ripples to a full-blown storm, before making it die down again, ending with a gentle peace.

Teaching

Talk about what happens when we're frightened and about the people who calm us down and make us feel better. Also talk about any people and pets we calm down and comfort, when they're feeling frightened or worried.

Jesus is like that. When we are frightened or scared or upset, whether we're children or grown-ups, we can all come to Jesus and he will help to calm us down and comfort us. He may do that through your family, and he may use your words and arms to comfort other people or other creatures!

Sometimes you will find that as you ask Jesus to help you calm down, you will suddenly feel inside like our sheet was at the end of our pretend storm – all gentle and peaceful. Jesus is very good at bringing us peace, and all we have to do is ask for his help.

Praying

Give me your peace,
O Jesus Christ, my brother,
give me your peace,
O Jesus Christ, my Lord!

Activities

On the sheet there are pictures of a storm and a calm sea, children fighting and the same children playing together. Use these for spotting the differences, not just in the detail, but in what's going on. There is also space for them to draw in the calmed version of the pictured panic zone. Actively drawing the peace will help them work through the next conflict, Jesus' way.

Print worksheet *Sunday Between 19 and 25 June (B)* from CD-ROM.

Sunday between 26 June and 2 July

Thought for the day

God's power can reach even into death and draw out life.

Readings

2 Samuel 1:1, 17-27
or Wisdom of Solomon 1:13-15; 2:23-24
Psalm 130 or Psalm 30 or Lamentations 3:23-33
2 Corinthians 8:7-15
Mark 5:21-43

Aim

To know that Jesus is never too busy to bother with them.

Starter

Play the singing game *Here we go round the mulberry bush*, with lots of busy verses, such as 'This is the way we clean the car/carry the shopping/hoover the hall/make the packed lunches'.

Teaching

Talk together about being busy, and all the things that need to be done each day and each week. Sometimes we have to wait to tell our news or talk over a worry we have because people are too busy to listen straight away. They might say, 'Just wait till I've got the dinner on', or 'till I've driven round this roundabout', or 'till we've paid at the checkout'.

But Jesus is always ready to listen to us, because he isn't stuck in time like us. He can give us his full attention straight away, wherever we are. He never rushes us or tells us to wait. He's always ready to listen to our worries and fears, and enjoy our news and jokes with us.

Praying

Thank you, Jesus,
for listening when we pray.
You're never too busy to hear what we say.

Activities

There are pictures of some very busy animal life – ants, birds, bees and spiders – to talk about, with an observation activity. There is also someone telling some news, and they draw in a friend who is really listening to what she's saying. This discussion of what good listening involves will help the children become better at the skill themselves, as well as helping them understand that Jesus is the very best listener ever.

Print worksheet *Sunday Between 26 June and 2 July (B)* from CD-ROM.

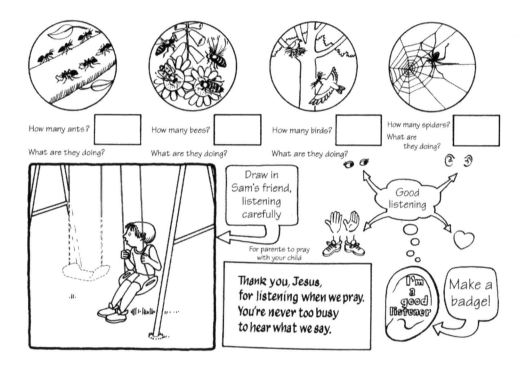

Sunday between 3 and 9 July

Thought for the day

If we are not ready to listen to the truth, we will not hear it.

Readings

2 Samuel 5:1-5, 9-10 or Ezekiel 2:1-5
Psalm 48 or Psalm 123
2 Corinthians 12:2-10
Mark 6:1-13

Aim

To know that God talks to us and teaches us, and to learn about listening.

Starter

Explain that you are going to do a spot of listening today. Give out to the children pictures or models of different animals. Ask them all to shout to you the name of their animal or the noise it makes, and you will listen to what they are telling you. Finding that very hard, ask them instead to tell you one by one, so that you can hear them better.

Teaching

Point out how much easier it is to listen when we are quiet and still, without lots of other noises going on. One of the ways we pray to God is by making ourselves very quiet and still, so that we can listen to God's love, and feel him close to us.

Try being very quiet and still and listening for a pin to drop. Then try being still and quiet, with eyes closed (they can lie face down for this if they like), while you read this to them:

Imagine you are walking along beside a high wall and you see a little door in it. Over the door there is a picture of you and your name is written there. You turn the handle and the door opens. You walk inside and find a sunny day with soft green grass under your feet, and flowers growing there. You feel happy and safe in this place, and take off your shoes and run across the grass, enjoying the coloured flowers and the butterflies. You come to a sandy beach, and the sea is lapping against it, so you sit down and listen to the waves. Although you can't see him, you know that Jesus is here with you, and you sit quietly in the sunshine together by the sea, with the seagulls calling.

After a while you get up and walk back across the beach and the grass, put on your shoes and make your way to the door. As you go out of the door you know that you can come back to this garden of prayer whenever you like.

(Put on some very quiet music as you tell the children to sit up slowly and open their eyes. Pray today's prayer together while the music plays.)

Praying

O Jesus, we love to be with you!
Thank you so much for being our special friend,
always here with us and always loving us.
Amen.

Activities

On the sheet there are lots of sounds 'pictured'. They look at the pictures and make the sounds. There is a checklist for top listeners – what do our eyes, ears, hands, brains, feet and heart do when we are really listening? They can also draw their own garden of prayer with Jesus there.

Print worksheet *Sunday Between 3 and 9 July (B)* from CD-ROM.

Sunday between 10 and 16 July

Thought for the day

Those who speak out God's will are bound to be vulnerable to rejection and abuse.

Readings

2 Samuel 6:1-5, 12b-19 or Amos 7:7-15
Psalm 24 or Psalm 85:8-13
Ephesians 1:3-14
Mark 6:14-29

Aim

To know that in Jesus they can stand up tall and upright for what is right in God's eyes.

Starter

Choose three different sounds (such as a bell, a shaker and a drum), and a grand, regal piece of music on tape such as *Land of hope and glory*. They move in a different way for each sound – such as crawling, jumping and bunny-hopping – but when the grand music plays they stand up tall and strong, like a good king or queen.

Teaching

Talk together about behaving well and being good (both adults and children), so that the children are telling you all they know about this. In voicing these good and noble things they will be reinforcing their own expectations of behaviour and beginning to own those values. Don't make any comments which contrast any of this with unacceptable behaviour, or the times we don't do it – we are simply celebrating the good we know about. Talk about how we behave well in different situations, such as in the car, at meal times, when playing with friends, when doing jobs at home. Help them to see that what they are describing is loving behaviour, thinking of other people and being kind and generous, honest and brave. It's Jesus behaviour, and it makes God very happy to see us doing it.

Praying

In your love, Lord Jesus, I can stand up tall –
do what's right,
do what's good,
live the way I know I should.
In your love, Lord Jesus,
I can stand up tall!
Amen.

Activities

On the sheet there is a person to colour, cut out and fold so they stand happy and upright, living Jesus' way in the world. The whole sheet ends up being a landscape. Some of the children will need help with the cutting, and it's a good idea to have completed one sheet beforehand to show them what theirs will look like.

Print worksheet *Sunday Between 10 and 16 July (B)* from CD-ROM.

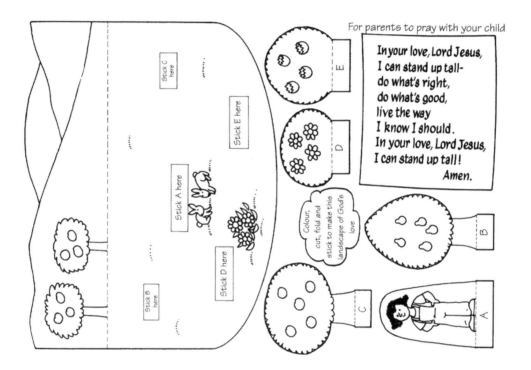

215

Sunday between
17 and 23 July

Thought for the day

Like a good shepherd, Jesus sees the needs of his people and always responds with love.

Readings

2 Samuel 7:1-14a or Jeremiah 23:1-6
Psalm 89:20-37 or Psalm 23
Ephesians 2:11-22
Mark 6:30-34, 53-56

Aim

To know that Jesus likes them, enjoys their company and knows their needs.

Starter

Talk about how our mums and dads often seem to know when we're feeling a bit sad, when we're thirsty, or when we are frightened. That's because they love us. God loves all of us, and so he knows all about the times we feel happy and sad, excited or frightened. He is like a good, kind, strong shepherd and we are like his lambs and sheep.

Starter

Have a selection of toys and construction bricks (or boxes) to play with, and enjoy a time of playing together or alongside each other, while quiet music is playing.

Teaching

Talk about how lovely it is to enjoy time playing together, knowing we are safe and in God's good care. We didn't have to talk to each other – it was nice just to be there in the Pebbles group.

God enjoys spending time with us. It makes him really happy when we want to be in his company, when we chat to him about our ideas and when we sing our songs of praise to him. (You could sing one now.)

Talk about how our mums and dads often seem to know when we're feeling a bit sad, when we're thirsty, or when we are frightened. That's because they love us. God loves all of us, and so he knows all about the times we feel happy and sad, excited or frightened. He is like a good, kind, strong shepherd and we are like his lambs and sheep.

Praying

Sing this to the tune in the song of thanksgiving after the storm from Beethoven's Pastoral Symphony. (The melody line is given below.)

Jesus, you love me,
you love me very much;
I love you, Jesus,
I love you very much!
Amen.

Activities

On the sheet there is a picture of Jesus with space for the children to draw in themselves, playing in Jesus' company. There are also pictures of different times of day with speech bubbles of prayers the children are chatting to God. These can be cut out and hung on lengths of wool ready to be put up all over the place at home.

Je - sus, you love me, you love me ve - ry much;
I love you, Je - sus, I love you ve - ry much!

Theme from Beethoven's 'Pastoral Symphony', arr. Kate Gallaher
This arrangement © Copyright 1999 Kevin Mayhew Ltd.

Print worksheet *Sunday Between 17 and 23 July (B)* from CD-ROM.

Sunday between 24 and 30 July

Thought for the day

Out of God's riches, a great crowd is fed and satisfied from a small offering of food.

Readings

2 Samuel 11:1-15 or 2 Kings 4:42-44
Psalm 14 or Psalm 145:10-18
Ephesians 3:14-21
John 6:1-21

Aim

To know the story of the feeding of the crowd of people.

Starter

Prepare enough different coloured paper shapes for each child in the group to have one of each. There need to be as many different categories as there are children. Give each child a pile of a particular coloured shape so that everyone has a pile. (They can set up their own 'base', or have their shapes in a yoghurt pot.) All the children go round sharing the shapes out until they end up with a pile of different ones. These are arranged into a pattern on the floor in front of them.

Teaching

Admire everyone's patterns and talk about how we have all been sharing what we were given so that we could all make our lovely pictures. Today we are going to hear about a child who offered to share his lunch with Jesus.

Spread out a sheet or bath towel on the floor and sit around it. Place on it some blue material or paper to be a lake, and stand a few plants in pots around as bushes and trees. Place a model boat on the lake. Talk about the landscape you are making as you add the items, and let the children help.

One day Jesus and his friends went over the lake in a boat. All the crowds of people walked round the side of the lake (everyone finger walks), so they could be there when the boat arrived. Jesus climbed out of the boat and taught the people, telling them stories to help them understand how much God loved them.

Soon they were all very hungry, but they were a long way from their homes. One boy had some packed lunch with him. (Produce a packed lunch box.) He could have just sat and eaten it, but he knew the others were hungry too, and he heard Jesus talking to his friends about how to feed all these people.

So he went up to Andrew, one of Jesus' friends.

'Excuse me,' he said, 'but is this any use? There's five barley loaves and two small fish.'

Andrew took the boy and his lunch to Jesus, and Jesus looked very happy and thanked the boy very much for offering to share his food. 'Because you've been so kind, you've given enough here for everyone!' Jesus whispered to the boy. 'Watch carefully!'

Everyone sat down on the grass and Jesus gave thanks for the little lunch; he thanked God for providing enough for everyone, but the boy couldn't think how there would be enough. Jesus started breaking up the bread and the fish, and his friends kept taking it to the groups of people. Somehow the food went on and on, until everyone had eaten as much as they needed. And there was even some left over!

Praying

(This can be prayed before we eat.)

Thank you, God, for food we eat,
that keeps us strong and healthy.
Amen.

Activities

The Pebbles are going to make sandwiches, which can be cut up and shared with the rest of the congregation. If you want to be authentic you can have tuna or sardine sandwiches, but other fillings would be fine! On the sheet there is also a dot-to-dot picture of the boy's lunch, and a map for them to walk round with their fingers.

Print worksheet *Sunday Between 24 and 30 July (B)* from CD-ROM.

For parents to pray with your child
Thank you, God, for food we eat, that keeps us strong and healthy. Amen.

Join the dots to see what the boy had for lunch

Can you see the lake?
Walk your fingers from the village to the picnic spot.

Picnic place

Sunday between
31 July and 6 August

Thought for the day

Jesus is the Bread of Life who satisfies our hunger and sustains us on our journey to heaven.

Readings

2 Samuel 11:26-12:13a or Exodus 16:2-4, 9-15
Psalm 51:1-12 or Psalm 78:23-29
Ephesians 4:1-16
John 6:24-35

Aim

To know that God gave the people of Israel food in the desert.

Starter

Manna? – What is it? Teach the children some Hebrew - that 'manna?' means 'what is it?' and then show them some items, mostly hidden in a bag or by a cloth. As you draw out a bit of a teddy, a jumper or an orange, you say to them, 'Manna?' so they can give the answer – 'It's a teddy!' Then a child can be the person who asks, 'Manna?'

Teaching

Remind the children, using a Moses basket, a crown, a whip of plaited string and a piece of blue cloth, that Moses was the baby who had been put in a basket and floated down the river to keep him safe when all God's people were slaves in Egypt. He was brought up by Pharaoh's daughter in the palace. When he grew up he had seen how his own people were badly treated as slaves. God used Moses to lead his people out of slavery. They had crossed through the middle of the Red Sea on dry land and now they were travelling in the desert, with Moses leading them.

And they got very hungry, so they all started grumbling. (Perhaps they start grumbling when they're hungry as well.) They said, 'It's not fair, Moses! If we were back in Egypt we could be eating nice stews and casseroles.' And they all got very grouchy with Moses.

Moses went off to talk with God about it. 'Lord, they're all moaning and grumbling about not having any food to eat,' he said. 'What should I do?'

God told Moses to let the people know that God knew they needed food and would be getting them some, so the people waited to see what would happen. That evening a flock of quails flew over. Some of the birds couldn't manage to fly any further, and they fell down dead on the ground. So the people picked them up and made a kind of chicken stew with them, and everybody enjoyed it very much.

Next morning there were white flakes all over the ground (scatter some pieces of white paper all over the floor). The people didn't know what it was, so they said to Moses, 'Manna? Manna?' And Moses said, 'This is the food God promised you!' So all the people took bowls (give out little pots) and gathered the white flakes. (The children go and gather it up in their bowls. When they've finished, they sit down again in the story circle.) Explain that our white flakes are just pieces of paper, but the flakes the people gathered up were food which tasted sweet – a bit like honey. And because no one knew what it was really called, they all called it 'manna'.

Praying

Thank you, God,
for giving us food each day.
Thank you for the farmers who grew it,
the shops that sell it,
and the people who cook it for us!
Amen.

Activities

Using a paper plate the children can make a plate of their favourite food out of playdough. Prepare some brown, green, yellow, red and white – most food can be made from roughly those colours! On the sheet there is a place mat to make for them to use at home.

Here is a recipe for playdough. Mix two teaspoons of cream of tartar, one cup of plain flour, half a cup of salt, one tablespoon of oil and one cup of water to form a smooth paste. Cook slowly in a saucepan until the dough comes away from the sides of the pan and forms a ball. When the dough is cool enough, take it out of the pan, add food colouring and knead for three or four minutes. (Store in an airtight container in the fridge.)

Print worksheet *Sunday Between 31 July and 6 August (B)* from CD-ROM.

Sunday between 7 and 13 August

Thought for the day

Just as bread is the visible form of life-giving nourishment, so Jesus is the visible form of God's life-giving love.

Readings

2 Samuel 18:5-9, 15, 31-33 or 1 Kings 19:4-8
Psalm 130 or Psalm 34:1-8
Ephesians 4:25-5:2
John 6:35, 41-51

Aim

To see God in the ordinary.

Starter

Share some ordinary things and look at them carefully. For example, bring a rosehip, break it open and look at all the seeds inside, a peapod with its neatly arranged peas, a selection of bright colours in feathers, flowers, stones and shells. Look up at the huge sky and the clouds, or the rain or shadows. Feel some wool, our hair. Work out how many sunrises there have been since they were born.

Teaching

Everything that we know and make, here in our exciting and beautiful universe, comes from something God has made. If we look carefully we can see God's love all around us in the things he has made. Look at all the objects again, helping the children to see how the great big sky over all of us is like the great big love God has for all of us. In the rosehip and the peapod we can see the loving way that God is careful with all the little things as well as the huge things. Each tiny seed and pea, each tiny baby, young child and little old woman is important to God.

God's love shines in our lives and warms our hearts, just as the sun shines on our bodies and warms us. The rain shows us how God showers us with blessings and happiness, without checking up first on how good we have been. And just as the sun rises day after day after day, so God is faithful and reliable, and we know we can trust him.

Praying

Your love is deeper than the sea
and wider than the sky.
You shower us with love
like you shower us with your rain –
lots and lots and lots of it!
The warm sun is just like
the warmth of your love.
And day after day after day you forgive us
again and again and again!
Amen.

Activities

Provide some tubes for the children to look down, so they can focus on signs of God's love. They can also look through a magnifying glass at various things. On the sheet there is a magnified butterfly wing to colour in (or use collage), and they are encouraged to be observant, both physically and spiritually, in the 'What can you see?' activity.

Print worksheet *Sunday Between 7 and 13 August (B)* from CD-ROM.

Sunday between
14 and 20 August

Thought for the day
God's wisdom may appear foolishness without the God-given grace to understand.

Readings
1 Kings 2:10-12; 3:3-14 or Proverbs 9:1-6
Psalm 111 or Psalm 34:9-14
Ephesians 5:15-20
John 6:51-58

Aim
To know that God helps us understand, and that he understands everything.

Starter
Have a time of sharing news, or let different children share with the others something they have learnt how to do.

Teaching
Spread all the pieces from a jigsaw puzzle over the floor in the circle, but don't show a picture of the completed puzzle. Talk about how we can put it together. First we can look for pieces with straight edges as they will make the edge of the picture. (Do this in turns.) Point out how much easier it would be if we had a picture to help us.

There are lots of things in life which are a big puzzle to us, and we find them very hard to understand. Perhaps we don't understand how dogs bark, why grown-ups talk so long on the phone, what makes heavy planes stay up in the sky, why Mum was cross with us that time, why Dad wasn't cross with us last week, how some people can be cruel to animals, why some people have asthma, why some people are very rich and others very poor.

Our life is full of puzzles. And we are always trying to work the puzzles out.

God understands all the puzzles, and knows why everything is as it is, and how. It's as if God holds the finished picture. So when we're puzzled about anything at all in life, we can ask God to help us understand. (Produce the jigsaw picture.) Bit by bit, if we keep working with God and with each other (talk as you work together on the puzzle), we'll start to understand some of those puzzles, even before we get to heaven!

Praying

Over the earth is a mat of green
over the green is dew,
over the dew are the arching trees, over the trees, the blue.
Across the blue are scudding clouds, over the clouds, the sun,
over it all is the love of God, blessing us every one.

By Ruth Brown from *Children Praising*.
Reproduced by permission of Oxford University Press. All rights reserved.

Activities

The sheet can be made into a hanging model of today's prayer. Each child will need a circle of green paper stuck on thin card. The prayer is stuck on to this and the other layers made into circles as shown and fastened together with wool.

Print worksheet *Sunday Between 14 and 20 August (B)* from CD-ROM.

Sunday between 21 and 27 August

Thought for the day

'To whom else could we go? You alone have the words of eternal life.'

Readings

1 Kings 8:(1, 6, 10-11) 22-30, 41-43 or Joshua 24:1-2a, 14-18
Psalm 84 or Psalm 34:15-22
Ephesians 6:10-20
John 6:56-69

Aim

To know that God gives us spiritual armour to protect us from evil.

Starter

Give the children lots of rolled-up balls of newspaper as snowballs and have either a leader or a child who volunteers to be the one everyone is trying to hit with the paper. However, this person is given a tray as a shield, to protect themselves.

Teaching

Talk about how much better it was to have the tray as a shield. It really helped to protect the person being pelted with snowballs! Have a look at some other things we use to protect ourselves – overalls and aprons protect our clothes from paint and glue, umbrellas and wet weather clothes protect us from getting 'too soaked, sunglasses protect our eyes from the glaring sun. If possible, have a look at some toy Roman armour, or a picture of a Roman soldier.

God knows that it isn't always easy to be loving and good, honest and kind. And he knows that sometimes people are hurt by bad things that happen, like wars, or someone being nasty to them, or frightening them, or making them feel silly. God hates to see any of his children getting hurt by any kind of evil, or hurting others. So he gives us armour to protect us from evil.

The armour is God's love, and if we imagine ourselves getting dressed in God's love every day, we'll be wearing his special armour to help us live God's way and fight against evil.

Praying

I am wearing the armour of God
to help me fight against evil.
I am carrying the shield of faith
'cos God wants me to be safe.
Yes, God wants me to be safe and strong,
and I belong to him!

Activities

On the sheet there is a picture of a Roman soldier and the children can dress him up in his armour by sticking on the cut-out sections. Talk with them about God's armour of love, goodness and faith as they work.

Print worksheet *Sunday Between 21 and 27 August (B)* from CD-ROM.

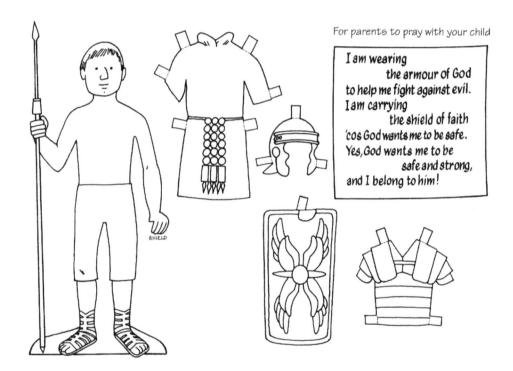

Sunday between 28 August and 3 September

Thought for the day

We need to be careful never to replace the timeless commands of God with man-made traditions.

Readings

Song of Solomon 2:8-13 or Deuteronomy 4:1-2, 6-9
Psalm 45:1-2, 6-9 or Psalm 15
James 1:17-27
Mark 7:1-8,14-15, 21-23

Aim

To look at how we can say 'thank you' to God with our lives as well as our voices.

Starter

Sit in a circle and pass round a paper plate or a broom stick. Each person mimes with the object to show what it is. (Examples might be a steering wheel or a fishing rod.)

Teaching

Point out how we managed to say what the plate or stick was, using not words but actions. In the circle try out some more telling actions, such as showing by our faces that we're pleased or grumpy, interested or scared.'

Today we are going to look at some of the ways we can say 'thank you' to God for making us and such a lovely world, for forgiving us and looking after us.

We can say our thanks to God. Go round the circle with the children who want to thank God for different things.

We can silently say our thanks to God. Suggest everyone shuts their eyes and puts their hands together, as we all thank God silently for something or someone special to us.

We can sing and shout and dance our thanks to God! Play and sing a favourite praise song, with the children singing along, dancing and playing instruments.

So we can tell God our thanks by saying aloud, saying silently, singing, shouting, dancing and playing ... and by living our thanks.

How do we live our thanks?

Well, if we want to tell God how happy we are that he has made a lovely world, we can show him our thanks by being careful to look after it. (Chat together about ways this might be done.)

If we want to tell God how happy we are that he has given us loving people to look after us, we can show him our thanks by being helpful to those people. (Again, talk over examples.)

If we want to tell God how happy we are that he forgives us when we do things wrong, we can show him our thanks by forgiving other people.

Praying

Father God, we want to thank you
for your loving kindness,
and to show you that we thank you
we will live our thanks each day.
Watch our living and you will see
how loving and kind we'll try to be!
Amen.

Activities

On the sheet there are pictures to discuss and colour in of two friends of Jesus whose lives said a big 'thank you' to God. They are Saint Francis and Saint Clare, looking after the lepers, enjoying the lovely world and living simply.

Print worksheet *Sunday Between 28 August and 3 September (B)* from CD-ROM.

Sunday between
4 and 10 September

Thought for the day

Jesus comes fulfilling the hope of healing to wholeness; he shows that mercy has triumphed over judgement.

Readings

Proverbs 22:1-2, 8-9, 22-23 or Isaiah 35:4-7a
Psalm 125 or Psalm 146
James 2:1-10 (11-13) 14-17
Mark 7:24-37

Aim

To know that God loves everyone whatever they look like and however rich or poor they are.

Starter

Have enough small gifts as prizes for each child to have one. Keep these hidden. Put some folded pieces of paper in a hat and tell the children that whoever picks the piece of paper with a smiley face on it will be able to have a prize! Hype this up a bit so they are all really hoping to be the lucky one. Pass round the hat, and tell each child to pick a piece of paper but not to open it until you say. When everyone has their paper, let them all open them up and discover that they have all won a prize. Give out the prizes with love from the church.

Teaching

Talk about what it feels like to be left out, and how it feels when we are the chosen ones. With our God no one is ever left out and we are all special to him, even though we are all different. God doesn't just love those with long hair in bunches, because God loves everyone! He doesn't just love those who are wearing stripes, because God loves everyone! Or those who eat without making a mess, because God loves everyone! He doesn't just love those who go to our church, or those on television. Why not? Because God loves everyone! He doesn't just love those who are good at football, or those who live with both Mum and Dad. Why not? Because God loves everyone! He doesn't just love nice people. He doesn't just love good people. Do you know why? Because *God loves everyone!*

Praying

Every person I can see
is loved by Jesus, just like me!
Whoever I am, whatever I do,
you love me, Jesus! And that's true.

Activities

On the sheet there is a picture of the earth with people all over it. The children can work out which ones Jesus loves by following a wiggly line with their finger. They can also make fingerprint pictures with their own special fingerprints that no one else has.

Print worksheet *Sunday Between 4 and 10 September (B)* from CD-ROM.

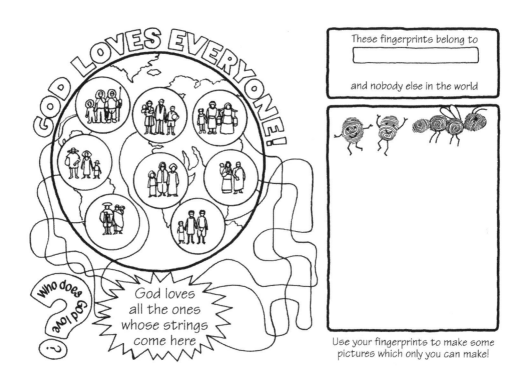

Sunday between 11 and 17 September

Thought for the day

Loving obedience to God is shown by Jesus to be a quality rich in courage and wisdom, a quality to be highly respected.

Readings

Proverbs 1:20-33 or Isaiah 50:4-9a
Psalm 19 or Wisdom of Solomon 7:26-8:1 or Psalm 116:1-9
James 3:1-12
Mark 8:27-38

Aim

To look at how we can use our tongues to speak for good.

Starter

Tongue twisters. Try saying some of these: 'She sells sea shells on the sea shore'; 'red lorry, yellow lorry'; 'thirty thousand feathers on a thrush's throat'.

Teaching

Our tongues are very useful for talking. There are lots of sounds we can only make if we use our tongues – like dudd, ttt, nnn, ng, kkk, lll, sss. They can try making these sounds, noticing where their tongues go. Talking is a wonderful skill to have, and we start learning how to do it as soon as we are born. (Perhaps some of them have baby brothers and sisters who are just beginning to say the odd word.)

So now that we have learnt how to use our tongues for talking, what can we do with our talking? We can ask for exactly what we want or need, instead of crying and hoping someone will understand. We can tell other people what we are thinking. We can tell jokes. We can chat to our friends and we can pray to Jesus. We can cheer people up. We can help other people by telling them how to do something. (They can think of examples for all of these.) Put down a happy face and point out that we can use our tongues for saying all kinds of good and useful things.

Is that the only way we can use our tongues in talking? No, we could choose to use our tongues to say nasty, unkind things, or to be rude and disobedient, or to tell lies, or make someone cry. (Show an unhappy face.) But what a waste of a good tongue that would be. God has given us a wonderful gift of speaking. Let's use that gift to make the world a happier place.

Praying

Chatter, chatter, chatter,
thank you, God, for tongues to talk with,
tongues to tell the truth with,
tongues to speak kind words with,
tongues to pray and tongues to say,
chatter, chatter, chatter!

Activities

There are pictures on the sheet for the children to 'read' the sound effects, and also some situations with empty speech bubbles, where the children can work out what words could be said there.

Print worksheet *Sunday Between 11 and 17 September (B)* from CD-ROM.

Sunday between 18 and 24 September

Thought for the day

The truly great in God's eyes are those who are prepared to be last of all and servant of all.

Readings

Proverbs 31:10-31 or Wisdom of Solomon 1:16-2:1, 12-22 or Jeremiah 11:18-20
Psalm 1 or Psalm 54
James 3:13-4:3, 7-8a
Mark 9:30-37

Aim

To know that God loves to see us looking after one another's needs.

Starter

Think of someone in the church community who would appreciate receiving a special 'get well soon' card from the Pebbles group (or whatever the need is). Explain this to the children and bring a suitable card along. Give each child a small piece of paper on which to draw a message, write the children's names on their drawings and stick them all into the card. The children can help put the card into its envelope and see it addressed and stamped.

Teaching

The Pebbles have done a very kind thing this morning, and that card will certainly cheer someone up. God loves to see us looking after one another's needs like that. It makes him very happy indeed!

Jesus always noticed what people were wanting, and went out of his way to help them. If he saw that someone was sad and lonely he would go and talk to them. When people came to him with their legs or backs not working, Jesus loved to mend their bodies and put them right. Jesus calls all his followers (and that's us!) to do the same thing – to look after one another's needs.

So how can we do that? What kind things could we do? Talk over their ideas and write them down. (It doesn't matter that they can't read them; they can see that you think they are important.) Read the list of suggestions back to them and give each of them a secret sign on their hand and your own (draw a smiley face) to remind you all of the kind things you and God are planning to do together. Suggest they do them as a secret between them and God.

Praying

Father God, we want to pray
for those who are sad or lonely,
for those who are ill,
for those who are very busy
and get tired from all their jobs.
Please help us to help them.
Amen.

Activities

The children can do another kind thing by making a scrap book of pictures and prayers to be passed around among those who would enjoy such a book. Provide a scrap book and some pictures for the children to cut out and stick in, and scribe for each child so that their prayers are also included. The pictures on the sheet can be coloured and added to the book.

Print worksheet *Sunday Between 18 and 24 September (B)* from CD-ROM.

For parents to pray with your child

Father God, we want to pray
for those who are sad or lonely,
for those who are ill,
for those who are very busy and
get tired from all their jobs.
Please help us to help them.
Amen.

Sunday between 25 September and 1 October

Thought for the day

Don't let your body lead you into sin and risk exchanging eternal life for eternal punishment.

Readings

Esther 7:1-6, 9-10; 9:20-22 or Numbers 11:4-6, 10-16, 24-29
Psalm 124 or Psalm 19:7-14
James 5:13-20
Mark 9:38-50

Aim

To know that it's good to pray for one another.

Starter

Prepare a prayer area which looks beautiful and special, with lights and flowers, pictures and a cross. It might include a mirror lying flat so that everything is reflected. Have quiet music playing and gather the children to sit round, to sing a quiet worship song such as *Jesus, reign in me* or *Jesus, I adore you*.

Then all pray for each of the children in turn by name, like this:

Jesus, we ask you to bless Sean
with your love in his life.
We thank you for his funny jokes
and the way he cheers us up.
We ask you to help him and his family
as they get ready to move house soon.
Be with Sean every day of his life.
Amen.

The other children can stretch one hand up to God and the other towards the child being prayed for to remind them 'in body' that they are being channels of God's love as they pray.

Teaching

It's good to pray for one another. It's good to know that other Christians are praying for us. Praying is the way that God helps us look after one another and deepen our love for one another. Today we're going to learn a bit more about how to pray.

Show the children a walking stick, zimmer frame or crutches, and talk with them about who uses these and why. Imagine together what it must be like just to need help walking, and to be in pain, let alone losing the use of your legs. When we pray for people, we need to imagine what it's like for them, and feel sorry for them. Then we ask our lovely Jesus to help those people. (Do this.) Jesus has lots of ways of helping someone. Sometimes he helps by making their legs strong again so they work. Sometimes he makes the person happy and peaceful even though their legs still don't work. Whatever is best and right, Jesus will do when we pray, trusting him.

Show the children a watering can, with water inside. When we pray, Jesus can pour out his love through us so that it reaches other people who don't pray. (Pour out the water so it sprinkles over a plant.) When we pray we are like channels of God's love. We reach up to God (reach up one hand), letting him fill us with his love, and send it out over the places and people in the world who need it (stretch out other hand). As they are in this position ask them to close their eyes and think of God's love coming into them and them pouring that love over the people who are sad at the moment, all over the world. 'Jesus, fill us now with your love. Let that love pour out over all the people who are sad, so that they feel your love and peace instead of their sadness. Amen.'

You can tell them that children are specially good at praying because they are so good at trusting God. God enjoys working with children of their age – they don't have to wait until they're older.

Now they can practise, talking about people they feel need praying for, and all the children praying together in their own words, for this person or situation. Thank God for answering all our prayers and letting us work with him to spread his love and peace.

Praying

Jesus, show me
who to pray for
and what to pray for.
Thank you for having me
on your prayer team.
Amen.

Activities

The sheet can be made into a prayer corner for their bedroom. They will need thin card to strengthen it and a hole punch and some cord or wool to fasten it.

Print worksheet *Sunday Between 25 September and 1 October (B)* from CD-ROM.

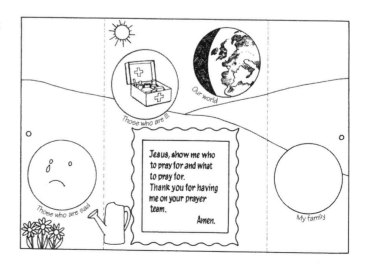

Sunday between 2 and 8 October

Thought for the day

Human beings are made responsible for the care of creation but are subject to God in all aspects of their lives.

Readings

Job 1:1; 2:1-10 or Genesis 2:18-24
Psalm 26 or Psalm 8
Hebrews 1:1-4; 2:5-12
Mark 10:2-16

Aim

To know that God wants us to look after the world.

Starter

Scatter around some fallen leaves. The children gather them up one at a time and bring them to place them on brown, red, orange, yellow or green paper, matching the leaf to the approximate colour of the paper.

Teaching

Talk about the lovely colours of our world in all the different seasons, and show them different coloured pieces of paper. What do the colours remind them of? (The blue of sky and sea and forget-me-nots, the pink of sunsets and roses, and so on.) Celebrate the colourful world God has made.

When God made people, he gave us an important job to do. We are to look after this world, and all the universe, as carefully as we possibly can. We are to look after the ground (place down a chunk of rock) and all the minerals of our planet like gold and silver, iron and copper, calcium and sulphur. We are to look after all the growing plants (place down a potted plant) like rain forests and cactus, fruits, flowers and herbs. We are to look after all the animals (place down a book of animals and turn through some of the pages) like horses, fish, birds, spiders and worms.

And we are to look after one another (place down a book with pictures of people from all different parts of the world and flick through it), sharing so that everyone has enough to eat, and taking care of one another.

Are there any Pebbles who are ready to help God look after the world? That's good! Could we start today? How? Talk over their ideas and do your best to put into practice any that are practical. (What about giving each child a bag to collect litter in and cleaning up this patch of the world together? Or recycling their newspapers, bottles, stamps and cans?) Scribe the ideas and put them in the church magazine.

Praying

Father God, we love this world
that you have made.
We are old enough to help look after it
and we're going to start by ...

Activities

Use the leaves from the starter activity to stick on the sheet and make leaf pictures. There is also a picture of a rain forest so they can go on safari, hunting for hidden plants, fruit and creatures.

Print worksheet *Sunday Between 2 and 8 October (B)* from CD-ROM.

What can you see in the rain forest?

For parents to pray with your child

Father God, we love this world that you have made. We are old enough to help look after it and we're going to start by
....

This is my picture made of leaves

Sunday between 9 and 15 October

Thought for the day

The word of God is living and active, piercing right to the heart; only with God is it possible to be saved.

Readings

Job 23:1-9, 16-17 or Amos 5:6-7,10-15
Psalm 22:1-15 or Psalm 90:12-17
Hebrews 4:12-16
Mark 10:17-31

Aim

To know that we are to seek God and find him, and help others to do the same.

Starter

Set up an edible treasure hunt, leading the children from one numbered box to the next. Spread the boxes around the edges of the room. Give them each a length of string, with a twiglet tied to one end. (This stops them losing the other things off the end.) In numerical order they thread on an object from each box. They should each end up with their strings looking identically threaded. Box one contains hula hoops (the edible sort) box two has polos, box three has jelly rings and box four has biscuits with a hole in the middle. Those with the right order on the string can eat their necklace.

Teaching

Talk about our funny treasure hunt. We had to seek for the right number on the box, and get that right. Then we had to do something with what we found. That led us on to the next thing to seek – we found the treasure as we went along, didn't we? And it was treasure that tasted good.

   The Bible tells us that we are to seek God as we live our lives. It's a bit like our treasure hunt. We seek, or search, for God by looking out for his love, just as we looked out for the numbers on the boxes. We might find God's love in helping someone, being friendly, enjoying God's beautiful world or talking over our fears and worries with God. There are lots of different ways we can find God's love around, just as there were lots of different tasty things to thread on our string. Our strings were filled up with all sorts of tasty things, and our lives will be filled up with the love of God as we seek him.

   Seeking God will help us to know what is right and good, and that will make us happy as Jesus' friends.

   Ask if any of them helped someone to find any of the boxes. Thank them for doing that. God wants us to help others to seek him as well. We could lend them one of our favourite Bible stories, and we can pray for them. That way we will be helping them to get to know our lovely God.

Praying

As I get to know you, Jesus,
I love you more and more.
You're kind and good,
you're strong and brave,
and I'm glad you are my friend.

Activities

On the sheet there are pictures of children who are seeking God in different ways, and they can circle the ones they do as well, or want to start doing. There is space for them to draw a person they want to help to seek God.

Print worksheet *Sunday Between 9 and 15 October (B)* from CD-ROM.

Sunday between 16 and 22 October

Thought for the day

Even the Son of Man himself came not to be served but to serve, and to give his life as a ransom for many.

Readings

Job 38:1-7 (34-41) or Isaiah 53:4-12
Psalm 104:1-9,24, 35c or Psalm 91:9-16
Hebrews 5:1-10
Mark 10:35-45

Aim

To know that Jesus is a Servant King.

Starter

Yes, your majesty. You will need a small handbell. One child is the king (or queen) and wears a crown. The others are all the king's servants, and they do all the work at the palace. Whenever the king rings his bell, the servants have to run up to where he is and bow or curtsey. Then the king gives his command (with the leader's help) and the servants rush about doing what he says. A leader takes the king to different parts of the palace for ringing the bell. Commands are household jobs, such as 'Sweep the floor!', 'Make the bed!', 'Clean the windows!' and 'Peel the potatoes!'

Teaching

Put down the crown, and a dustpan and brush. Hold the appropriate symbol as you refer to kings and servants. What is a king? A king is the person who rules over a land and is in charge of it. (We're thinking about traditional, storybook kings here, as this is in keeping with the imagery Jesus uses.) He's the one who gives the orders and tells everyone else what to do. He knows he is powerful and expects everyone to bow or curtsey to him, and say, 'Yes, your majesty!' to him. (The children can try that out, with another child wearing the crown and strutting about importantly.)

What is a servant? They are the ones who do the work, looking after the king and his family, and making sure he has all the things he needs. The servants cook and clean, and do the washing, and tidy up, and buy the food, and weed the garden, and clean out the gerbils, and put out the rubbish, and polish the tables, and scrape mud off the shoes . . . ! (The children can try all these out in quick succession, till everyone is out of breath.)

Who would they rather be – the king or a servant?

Now Jesus is our King, but he isn't anything like the sort of king we've been talking about, is he? It's true he is very important. It's true he is powerful and reigns over us all. But Jesus came into our world as a tiny baby, living in an ordinary family, like ours, without any palace or power. He worked as an ordinary carpenter, making things out of wood. In fact, Jesus is a king, but he behaves like a servant! He went around looking after people, making them better and cheering them up. He looks after us now, helping us wherever we need help.

(Put the crown over the dustpan and brush.) So Jesus is both a king and a servant, not bossing us around but caring for us all because he loves us.

Praying

Leader	We pray for kings and queens and presidents and everyone in charge.
All	Lord, make them wise and good.
Leader	We pray for those who clean and cook and everyone not in charge.
All	Lord, make them wise and good.
Leader	Our Servant King, we pray for each other.
All	Lord, make us wise and good.
	Amen.

Activities

On the sheet is a game to play with the king giving orders to the players who are the servants. They mime the jobs pictured when they land on those squares. The children can mount the sheet on thin card and make the pieces to play with from coloured playdough. Provide a plastic envelope for each complete game.

Print worksheet *Sunday Between 16 and 22 October (B)* from CD-ROM.

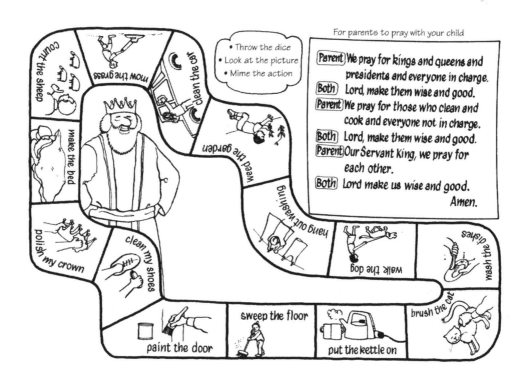

Sunday between 23 and 29 October

Thought for the day

In Jesus, God gathers his scattered people and opens their eyes to see.

Readings

Job 42:1-6, 10-17 or Jeremiah 31:7-9
Psalm 34:1-8, 19-22 or Psalm 126
Hebrews 7:23-28
Mark 10:46-52

Aim

To know that Jesus helped a blind man to see.

Starter

I spy with my little eye . . . using either colours, or letter sounds.

Teaching

Tell the story of Bartimaeus while you (or an assistant!) draw it on a black or white board, rubbing out and changing things as you go. Very simple drawings are fine, and most effective. The visuals are there to aid imagination, not replace it. Basically you'll be drawing Bartimaeus begging by the road, a crowd of people coming in a cloud of dust down the road, the disciples' cross faces, the disciples turning friendly, Bartimaeus meeting Jesus, and Bartimaeus happy and able to see.

Praying

With my eyes, Lord, I can see
all the love you have for me.
Help me spread your love to others,
friends and parents, sisters, brothers,
till the world is full of love.

Activities

On the sheet the children can make a face with closed eyes which open. There are also hidden things for them to use their eyes to find in the picture.

Print worksheet *Sunday Between 23 and 29 October (B)* from CD-ROM.

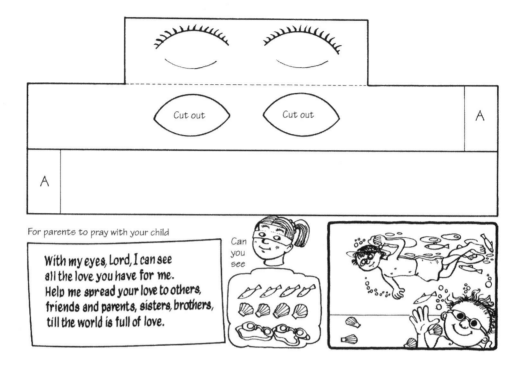

Cut out

Cut out

A

A

For parents to pray with your child

With my eyes, Lord, I can see
all the love you have for me.
Help me spread your love to others,
friends and parents, sisters, brothers,
till the world is full of love.

Can you see

All Saints' Day
Sunday between 30 October and 5 November

Thought for the day

Great is the rejoicing in heaven among the saints of God as they worship their Lord in glory.

Readings

Wisdom 3:1-9 or Isaiah 25:6-9
Psalm 24:1-6
Revelation 21:1-6a
John 11:32-44

Aim

To know that Jesus' friends get to party in heaven.

Starter

Party games. Give everyone a party hat and play a couple of party games such as animal statues. (You tell them which animal to be and when the music stops they freeze in this species. Then they become a new animal.)

Teaching

We're having quite a party today because we're joining in with all the saints in heaven.

When close friends of Jesus die, that isn't the end of their life. They are welcomed into heaven by Jesus and all the angels, who are very happy to see them. They may have come into heaven tired and worn out from doing lots of good and loving things on earth all through their life, but now all their tiredness goes away and they feel like dancing and singing! They might have known sadness on earth, but when they get to heaven, all their tears are wiped away, and they are filled with happiness and joy instead.

They are really happy to meet their friend Jesus face to face, and it's wonderful to be in all the light and beauty of heaven, where there is nothing nasty or evil, nothing selfish or unkind, but only all that is good and lovely.

All close friends of Jesus will get that welcome in heaven when they die. And the happiness is not just for an afternoon or a week. It lasts for ever and ever and ever!

Praying

Bless all the dear children in your tender care,
and fit us for heaven
to live with you there.

Activities

Continue the party with a few nibbles, and some singing and dancing, praising God. On the sheet there are instructions for making a musical instrument. Each child will need a plastic bottle, some dried peas and some lengths of crepe paper.

Print worksheet *All Saints' Day (B)* from CD-ROM.

Fourth Sunday before Advent
Sunday between 30 October and 5 November
For use if the Feast of All Saints was celebrated on
1 November and alternative propers are needed.

Thought for the day
To love the living God with heart, soul and strength, and to love our neighbour as ourselves means far more than any sacrificial offerings.

Readings
Deuteronomy 6:1-9
Psalm 119:1-8
Hebrews 9:11-14
Mark 12:28-34

Aim
To learn the summary of the law.

Starter
Have lots of building bricks or cartons for the children to play with, balancing one on another to construct towers and buildings.

Teaching
We were building on the good strong floor, and that helped us build good strong towers. The Bible tells us two good strong rules to build our lives on, and we're going to learn them off by heart, so that we'll always have them inside our minds, and won't lose them or drop them.

The first and most important is to love God (point up), with all our heart (hands on heart), with all our mind (hands hold head), and with all our strength (flex arm muscles). And the second is to love other people as we love ourselves.

Teach the children to sing this summary of the law to the tune of *London's burning*. The accompanying actions will help them to learn the words and understand them.

You shall love the
  (hands on heart)
Lord your God with
  (point upwards)
all your heart and
  (hands on heart)
all your mind and
  (hold head with hands)
all your strength! All your strength!
  (show biceps)

And love each other, and love each other.
(arms round one another's shoulders)

Read verse 7 in Deuteronomy 6 to them, explaining that grown-ups have been passing on this rule to their children and grandchildren and great-grand-children for thousands of years, and now you are passing it on to them. When they grow up and have children they are to pass it on to their children and their grandchildren to make sure that everybody knows it really well, and can live by God's love every day.

Praying

I love you, Lord God,
with all my heart and mind and strength!
Amen.

Activities

The children can decorate the summary of the law with stickers, printing or stencils. It can then be tied on to a chair or door at home to remind them of God's rule of love.

Print worksheet *Fourth Sunday before Advent (B)* from CD-ROM.

Third Sunday before Advent

Sunday between 6 and 12 November

Thought for the day

When we are called we need to respond with obedience so that many may be brought to repentance.

Readings

Jonah 3:1-5,10
Psalm 62:5-12
Hebrews 9:24-28
Mark 1:14-20

Aim

To know that Jesus called the fishermen to follow him.

Starter

Play the fishing game, using either a commercial version or a homemade one – coloured paper fish with paperclips, and pea-stick fishing rods with string lines and opened paperclip hooks. Use a (dry) paddling pool, scatter the fish in it and stand each rod in a wellie. The children can hook the fish and throw them back in.

Teaching

Jesus lived beside a big lake which had lots of fish in it. That meant there were fishing boats, and fishermen who went and caught fish to sell. Invite the children to be fishermen, and do all the actions of mending the nets so there aren't any big holes, and scrubbing the boat out to keep it clean. Then they have to push the boat off from the shore, wade out and climb in the boat, hoist the sail and steer the boat. They let down the anchor, throw the fishing nets out into the water and wait. Then when the net is full of fish they haul the heavy net in, tip the fish into baskets at the bottom of the boat and sail back to the shore. They jump out of the boat and haul it up the beach. Then they have to carry the baskets full of fish to sell in the market. After all that they can lie down and have a bit of a rest while they listen to a story!

One morning a man called Jesus was walking along the beach. He was looking for some people to help him in his work, and he saw the fishermen. Some of them were throwing their nets into the water. (And we know how to do that, don't we?) Some of them were sitting on the beach mending their nets. (And we know how to do that, don't we?)

And Jesus thought fishermen, who are good at catching fish, would be just the people he needed to reach people for God. Fishermen who mended their nets would be just the people he needed to mend people through God's love. So he called them to follow him. 'Follow me!' he said.

And the fishermen were happy to follow Jesus and work with him.

Praying

If I was a fisherman
(mime fishing)
and Jesus called me,
(cup hand to ear)
I'd throw down my fishing nets
(do that)
and run to his side.
(run on the spot)
I am a child and Jesus calls me.
(point to yourself, and cup hand to ear)
I say, 'Here I am!'
(shout it, waving at the same time)
and run to his side.
(run on the spot)

Activities

Each child will need a piece of old net fabric, about the size of a handkerchief. There are fish to colour and cut out on the sheet and these can be put in the net which is then tied up with a rubber band or length of string or wool.

Print worksheet *Third Sunday before Advent (B)* from CD-ROM.

Second Sunday before Advent
Sunday between 13 and 19 November

Thought for the day

We are to be on our guard; great anguish will accompany the last days, but all that is good and loving, wise and true will be saved and celebrated for ever.

Readings

Daniel 12:1-3
Psalm 16
Hebrews 10:11-14 (15-18) 19-25
Mark 13:1-8

Aim

To know that love lasts for ever and heaven is full of it.

Starter

Give out chocolate buttons to suck and see who can make theirs last the longest.

Teaching

Some things only last as long as a chocolate button. They are nice to suck but we know they won't last for ever. Bubbles don't last long either. (Blow a few and enjoy their colours and roundness, until they pop.) Lots of good things are with us for just a little while, so it's a good idea to really enjoy them while we have them.

Some things, like long journeys, or grown-up conversations, seem to go on for ages and ages! But they don't go on for ever. In the end, it's time to get out of the car, or the grown-ups say goodbye and we can carry on walking to the swings.

What will last for ever and ever and ever? To give them a clue, show them a red heart shape. It's love that will last for ever, and that's because our God is Love, and God lasts for ever and ever.

What kind of loving things do we do? (Share ideas.)

One day, at the end of everything, God will gather up all that goodness and love into his heaven, so it's safe for ever, and not one bit of it will be lost.

Praying

God of love, we thank you
for all the love in our world.
What a good thing that love
lasts for ever and never wears out!

Activities

On the sheet there is the shape of a heart. The children cover this with glue and then sprinkle glitter, sand or tiny off-cuts of shiny paper on to the page. At the moment they can't see what will stay and what won't, but when they shake their sheet, the thing that lasts is the love.

Print worksheet *Second Sunday before Advent (B)* from CD-ROM.

Christ the King
Sunday between 20 and 26 November

Thought for the day

Jesus Christ is the everlasting King whose kingdom is not of this world, but grows in the hearts of his people and lasts for ever.

Readings

Daniel 7:9-10, 13-14
Psalm 93
Revelation 1:4b-8
John 18:33-37

Aim

To celebrate Jesus as our King.

Starter

Everyone helps decorate the room with paper chains and gold crowns. Then sing and dance to some praise songs, using recorded music.

Teaching

Talk about the dreams we have, and then tell the children the vision of Daniel as a story, like this.

Long, long ago there lived a man called Daniel. Daniel worshipped God and tried his best to live God's way. In the days of King Belshazzar, king of Babylon, Daniel had a dream. It was such an amazing dream that he couldn't get it out of his head. Daniel kept thinking about his dream, and in the end he realised that the dream had been given to him by God. So Daniel thought to himself, 'If God has shown me these amazing things in my dream, I expect he wants me to tell all the others about it.'

So Daniel wrote his dream down, and this is it.

'As I looked, I saw a great throne put in its place, and God Almighty sat down on the throne. His clothes were as shining white as snow. His hair was white like sheep's wool. His throne was flaming with fire, blazing and glowing. From the throne there ran a river of fire, pouring out, and burning brightly. Thousands and thousands of people were standing before the throne, as if they were waiting for something. The books were opened.

'Then I saw in front of me what looked like a man. He was coming with the clouds of heaven, closer and closer to Almighty God, and they led him up to the throne. This man was made King over all the people in every place and every time. And as I looked I knew that he would be King for ever and ever and ever.'

That was the dream which Daniel dreamed long, long ago. Long before Jesus had been born. And yet God had shown Daniel a picture of heaven, and he had seen Jesus, coming into heaven and being made King for ever.

Praying

Jesus, you are my King.
Reign in me and my home,
in my life for ever.
Amen.

Activities

Together make a large collage picture of Daniel's dream. Have the outline drawn already (based on the picture, right) and bring some shiny flames of fire for the children to stick on to the throne and the fiery river. They can stick wool on to the clouds and coloured tissue paper to the rest of the picture. Call the picture: Daniel's dream about heaven.

On the sheet the same picture is there for them to colour or build with collage, and they can find the matching crowns and flames.

Print worksheet *Christ the King (B)* from CD-ROM.

YEAR C

First Sunday of Advent

Thought for the day

The gathered hopes of generations remind us to get ourselves ready, so that Christ's return will be a day of excitement and great joy.

Readings

Jeremiah 33:14-16
Psalm 25:1-10
1 Thessalonians 3:9-13
Luke 21:25-36

Aim

To help them understand getting ready for Christmas in terms of getting ready to meet Jesus in person.

Starter

Stop . . . Get ready . . . Go! Starting always from standing still in a space on their own, on the word 'Go!' the children do whatever the leader calls out (e.g. hop like rabbits, swim around like fish, slither like snakes). When the leader calls 'Stop!' the children stop and at 'Get ready!' they go to the starting position again.

Teaching

Draw their attention to the way they had to get ready for the game each time. Christmas is coming – whose birthday is it at Christmas? How are we going to get ready for Christmas?

Jesus told us that one day he would come back. We will be able to see him, either then or when we die, whichever happens first.

How can we get ready to meet Jesus? What would he like to see us doing?

During the discussion, make simple drawings of the way they think Jesus would like to see them living.

Praying

The children find a space on their own again. Taking the ideas they have come up with, lead the children to pray: 'Jesus, we want to be ready to meet you. Please help us to . . . (share our toys/forgive each other/be kind to our brothers and sisters, etc.)' and everyone mimes the activity. Then call out 'Stop!' and the children go back to their space for the next prayer.

Activities

Use the worksheet to reinforce the idea of getting ready for Christmas being linked with getting ready to meet Jesus.

Print worksheet *First Sunday of Advent (C)* from CD-ROM.

Here I am getting ready for Christmas.

Weeks to Christmas

Here I am getting ready for Jesus.

Jesus is coming

Get ready to paint!

We are starting to make a Christmas crib today.
You will need a box.

a brush

some brown paint

POSTER COLOUR

For parents and children together.
This week's prayer

Dear Jesus, thank you for loving us so much.
Amen.

Next week we will make the manger.

Second Sunday of Advent

Thought for the day

It had been prophesied that there would be a messenger to prepare the way for the coming of the Messiah. Now John the Baptist appears with his urgent message of repentance.

Readings

Malachi 3:1-4
Canticle: Benedictus
Philippians 1:3-11
Luke 3:1-6

Aim

To understand that John was the messenger helping people get ready for Jesus.

Starter

Call and change. Sit round in a circle. One person calls someone else's name and these two change places. The one who was called becomes the next caller. This game helps build the group together, and is an acting-out of what John the Baptist was doing.

Teaching

Find out if any of the children have cousins, and what their names are. Point out that they may not live with you but they are members of your family.

Tell them that one of Jesus' cousins was John. And God had a job he needed John to do. When John was grown up God asked him to go and get people ready for Jesus.

How could he do that? First he went off on his own to pray. Then he started talking to the people. He said to them, 'Listen, I've got a message for you!'

'A message for us?' asked the people. 'What message have you got for us?'

'Well,' said John, 'we all need to get ready. Soon God will be coming to us, and we aren't ready for him yet.'

'How exciting!' said the people. 'You are right, we must be ready to welcome him. But what can we do?'

John said, 'God will want to find that we are kind and loving and being fair to one another.'

'Oh dear!' said the people. 'I'm afraid we're not always like that. Some of us have bad tempers and some of us are greedy and some of us want our own way all the time. But we do want to be ready. Please help us get ready.'

'All you have to do,' said John, 'is to be sorry about those things and want to put them right.'

'We are sorry,' said the people. 'We don't want to be bad tempered and greedy and wanting our own way all the time. We want to make God happy when he comes.'

'In that case,' said John, 'I will wash you in the river as a sign that your bad temper and greediness and wanting your own way all the time are washed away and you are forgiven.'

The people felt happy and free. They went back home to enjoy loving and sharing and being fair. It would not be easy, but they were determined to do their best.

Praying

Ask the children to sit with their hands closed up as if they are hiding something inside. Imagine that one hand holds something for which you want to thank God that you are good at. As you open that hand, think of showing the thing you are good at to God. Everyone says, 'Thank you, God, for making me good at this.' Imagine that in the other hand you are holding something you would like to be better at (telling the truth / being a good friend / helping at home). As you open this hand, think of showing God and say, 'Please, God, help me to be better at this.'

Activities

Use the worksheet to continue getting the crib ready for Christmas – today is the manger – and reinforce the teaching about John the Baptist.

Print worksheet *Second Sunday of Advent (C)* from CD-ROM.

Jesus and John were cousins and played together.

'Your life is washed clean.'

Weeks to Christmas 4 (3) 2 1

John helps us to get ready

We are getting our Christmas crib ready. You will need

crayons   a box

• Colour the box brown
• Cut the paper into strips of hay and fill the manger   yellow paper

scissors

Parents and children together at home.

A prayer when you open each Advent calendar window.

Dear God, thank you for loving us so much. Amen.

Third Sunday of Advent

Thought for the day

Our period of preparation shifts from repentance and forgiveness to the freed exhilaration of hope, as the momentous truth of God's immanence begins to dawn on us.

Readings

Zephaniah 3:14-20
Canticle: Isaiah 12:2-6
Philippians 4:4-7
Luke 3:7-18

Aim

To celebrate looking forward to Christmas as a time of God's love being shown to us.

Starter

I'm thinking of someone . . . Everyone sits in a circle and tries to guess who you are thinking of. Start with something that could refer to lots of children (he's a boy/wearing a sweater) and gradually get more specific (his shoes have green dinosaurs on the bottom) until lots of children know who you mean. Everyone says, 'God made Jack and God loves Jack.'

Teaching

Beforehand, get a good quality picture of the Nativity (from a Christmas card) and put it in a box. Wrap the box in Christmas paper. We will use this during the teaching.

Get out some wrapping paper and scissors, and let the children guess what they are used for. Talk about why we give each other presents at Christmas, and establish that it isn't because we want something back but because we love the people and want them to see that we love them.

Now remind them of the starter activity and how God knows and loves each of us. Explain that at the first Christmas he gave the world the best Christmas present ever, not because he wanted anything back, but just because he loves us so much. Show the Christmas present. What was God's Christmas present to the world, to show he loves us? Open the present and let the children see that it is Jesus.

Praying

As you hold the Christmas present and then open it and hold up the picture, say this prayer together:

Thank you, God,
for loving the world so much
that you gave us Jesus
to be with us for ever.
Amen.

Activities

Use the worksheet to continue getting ready for Christmas by making the crib – this week it's Mary, Joseph and Jesus. The present-wrapping activity will need a variety of small pieces of Christmas paper.

Print worksheet *Third Sunday of Advent (C)* from CD-ROM.

Fourth Sunday of Advent

Thought for the day
When we co-operate with God amazing things happen.

Readings
Micah 5:2-5a
Canticle: Magnificat or Psalm 80:1-7
Hebrews 10:5-10
Luke 1:39-45 (46-55)

Aim
To understand that Mary was happy to work with God.

Starter
Working together. Ask the children to help you do various jobs as you get ready for the session. If you have access to a parachute, play some parachute games which need everyone to work together (such as 'mushroom', 'roll the ball' or tent making). Alternatively have everyone helping to make a 'Happy Christmas' frieze for the church.

Teaching
Point out how we all worked together in that activity. What jobs do they help with at home? Each time emphasise the co-operation that gets the job done well.

Use rag dolls or cut-out figures to tell the story.

God needed a very important job done. He needed someone to bring Jesus into our world and look after him. So he looked around and saw just the right person: Mary. He didn't choose her because she was rich or pretty or clever. He chose her because she was ready to work with God. She was already friends with him. She talked to him and listened to him in her prayers each day, and tried to live as God wanted her to. (How was that?)

So one day God told her he had chosen her to be the mother of Jesus. Mary was very surprised. It was such an important job, and she knew it would be a hard job to do well. What do you think – did she say yes or no?

Mary said 'Yes!' and went off to visit her cousin Elizabeth who lived in another town. Elizabeth was going to have a baby, too. You remember John the Baptist we met last week? Well, it was him, only he hadn't been born yet when Mary went to see his mother.

As soon as they met they hugged and kissed, and John started leaping about inside his mum because he was so excited! (Have you ever felt a baby moving about inside your mum? It's a funny feeling.)

Mary didn't need to tell Elizabeth her news. Elizabeth seemed to know already, and they sang and danced to praise God for being so wonderful.

Praying

Leader	Dear God,
	when you want us to be kind, help us to say
All	Yes!
Leader	When you want us to be honest, help us to say
All	Yes!
Leader	When you want us to help someone, help us to say
All	Yes!

Activities

The worksheet helps the children to complete their Christmas crib today, so these can be blessed in church and taken home. They are also going over the main points of today's story.

Print worksheet *Fourth Sunday of Advent (C)* from CD-ROM.

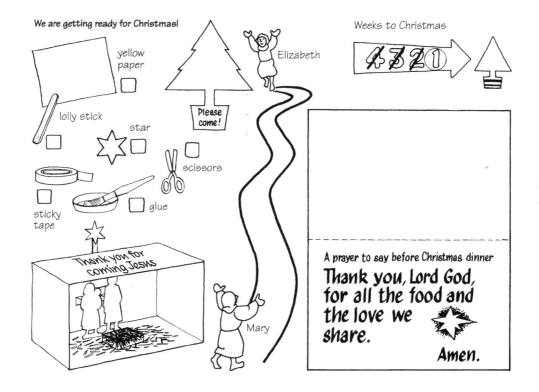

Christmas Day

Thought for the day

Emmanuel – 'God with us' – is born at Bethlehem into the human family. Now we will be able to understand, in human terms, what God is really like.

Readings

Isaiah 9:2-7
Psalm 96
Titus 2:11-14
Luke 2:1-14 (15-20)

Activities

Christmas Day is very much a time for all God's children to worship together.

Involve all the children in the singing and playing of carols, decorating the church, and in the other ministries of welcoming, serving, collection of gifts and so on. Have nativity toys for the very young to play with, such as knitted Mary, Joseph and Jesus, sheep and shepherds.

A colouring activity for today is provided.

Print worksheet *Christmas Day (C)* from CD-ROM.

PEBBLES

First Sunday of Christmas

Thought for the day

Jesus' perception and understanding of his purpose and work begins to take shape throughout his childhood.

Readings

1 Samuel 2.18-20, 26
Psalm 148
Colossians 3:12-17
Luke 2:41-52

Aim

To get to know the story of Jesus being lost and found.

Starter

Play hide and seek in small groups so that everyone gets the chance both to hide and be found.

Teaching

Talk about how it felt to be looking for the hidden children and how it felt to find them. Today's story is about a time when Mary and Joseph went looking for Jesus.

Using the 'carpet tiles and cut outs' method tell the story of the visit to Jerusalem with all the mums and dads and children and uncles and aunties and grandparents and cousins. Jesus was twelve years old. Give all the children a cut-out donkey or camel to add to the trail of visitors going up to Jerusalem. Pictures to use in the story are given with the worksheet.

When everyone sets off for home all the trail of animals can be turned over to face the other way, and then Mary and Joseph's donkey will turn back again to find Jesus, before finally joining the others.

Praying

When we are sitting still
    (sit still):
we know you are with us, Jesus.
When we are walking along
    (walk along):
we know you are with us, Jesus.
When we are playing
    (play):
we know you are with us, Jesus.
When we are helping
    (pretend to help clean or tidy up):
we know you are with us, Jesus.
Amen.

Activities

The worksheet has a searching to find activity and consolidates the main points of the story. The children can also talk over what to do if they ever lose their mum or dad when they are out shopping.

Print worksheet *First Sunday of Christmas (C)* from CD-ROM.

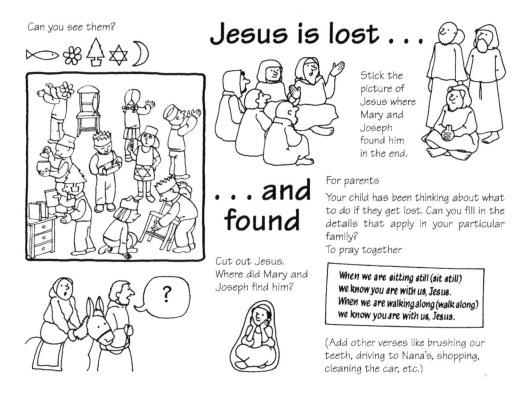

Can you see them?

Jesus is lost . . .

Stick the picture of Jesus where Mary and Joseph found him in the end.

. . . and found

Cut out Jesus. Where did Mary and Joseph find him?

For parents

Your child has been thinking about what to do if they get lost. Can you fill in the details that apply in your particular family?

To pray together

When we are sitting still (sit still)
we know you are with us, Jesus.
When we are walking along (walk along)
we know you are with us, Jesus.

(Add other verses like brushing our teeth, driving to Nana's, shopping, cleaning the car, etc.)

Second Sunday of Christmas

Thought for the day

Christ is the way God tells people about himself.

Readings

Jeremiah 31:7-14
Psalm 147:12-20
Ephesians 1:3-14
John 1:(1-9) 10-18

Aim

To help them understand that God shows us he loves us by coming to live with us.

Starter

Have some raisins or chocolate buttons which you hand round to each child in turn, by name. Point out that you are fond of them, and wanted to show them by giving them a little something. God loves each of us by name, and he had a very good idea for showing us his love.

Teaching

One day God was looking at all the world he had made. He smelt the roses, laughed at the monkeys playing in the trees, smiled to himself as a child helped his baby brother to play football, and enjoyed the beautiful sunset. It was a very good world.

Then he got sad as he watched an owner hitting a dog, two children fighting, and a grown-up stealing some money. God had made people able to choose right or wrong, and lots of them were choosing wrong instead of right, even though God knew it would make them happier to choose right.

The trouble was that although he was there, the people couldn't see him. No one can see God. And God longed to help them.

One day he decided to become a human himself and live among them. 'And then,' thought God, 'they will understand how to live. They will be able to follow my example, and I will help them.'

Well, of course God couldn't stop being God and be a human instead – if he did that all the world would come to a sudden and nasty end.

So this is what God did. He spoke his great love for the world and his longing for the people, and the great love he spoke became a human baby, all ready to grow up in a human family, and show all the people what God was really like.

And do you know the name of that baby, born from the word of great love that God spoke?

The baby's name was Jesus, and we have just been celebrating his birthday! Jesus is God saying 'I love you'.

Praying

Jesus, you show us what God is like.
You show us that he loves us.
Thank you, Jesus!
Amen.

Activities

On the worksheet there are instructions for making a frame to put on a mirror. Whoever looks into the mirror will see someone God loves. There is also a dot-to-dot which helps us see something we couldn't see before and a picture which reinforces the teaching.

Print worksheet *Second Sunday of Christmas (C)* from CD-ROM.

Who is hidden here? Join the dots to see it.

Jesus is God saying

I ♡ you!

1 Colour the frame
2 Cut out the middle
3 Stick it on shiny mirror paper
4 Let your family and friends look in it

You will need

glue

crayons

scissors

paper

God is hidden, too. But we can see him in Jesus.

For parents
Look for things God has made which are good/faithful.
Read some stories of Jesus.
Pray with your child.

Jesus, you show us what God is like. You show us that he loves us. Thank you, Jesus. Amen.

The Epiphany

Thought for the day

Jesus, the hope of the nations, is shown to the world.

Readings

Isaiah 60:1-6
Psalm 72:(1-9) 10-15
Ephesians 3:1-12
Matthew 2:1-12

Aim

To become familiar with the story of the wise men finding Jesus.

Starter

Play pass the parcel. At the different layers have old bus and train tickets. The prize at the end is a star-shaped biscuit.

Teaching

Tell the children that today we are going to hear about a journey. It isn't a bus journey or a car journey or a train journey. This is a camel journey. (All pack your bags and get on your camels.) We are very wise people, but we don't know where we are going. We are looking for a baby king. And we are packing presents for him. (Pack gold, frankincense and myrrh.) Produce a star on a stick as you explain how a special star has started shining in the sky and we are sure it will lead us to the baby king. Lead off behind the star, riding your camels, and pretending to go over high mountains, through water, stopping for the night, and going to sleep and so on. At last you reach the town of Bethlehem (stick up a sign) where you find the baby king with his mum and dad. (Have a large picture, or one of the cribs made before Christmas.) We all get off our camels and give the baby our presents. The baby's name is Jesus and we have found him at last!

Praying

This is a prayer the wise men might have said. We have all been invited to find Jesus as well, so we can say it with them.

Thank you, Jesus,
for inviting me
to come and look for you.
I am glad I have found you!
Amen.

Activities

To emphasise that the journey of the wise men was probably a hard one, there is a maze to help the wise men find their way to Bethlehem. The star-making activity will need star templates, and ready-cut card for the younger children.

Print worksheet *The Epiphany (C)* from CD-ROM.

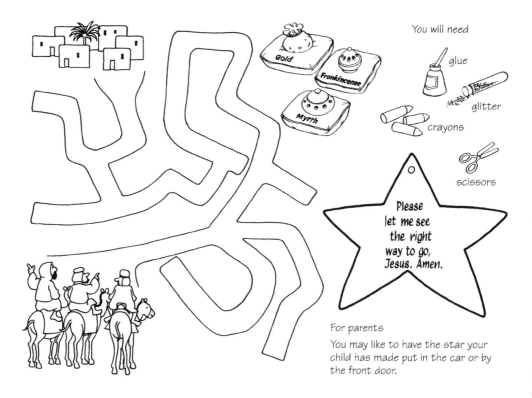

You will need

glue

glitter

crayons

scissors

Please let me see the right way to go, Jesus. Amen.

For parents
You may like to have the star your child has made put in the car or by the front door.

The Baptism of Christ
First Sunday of Epiphany

Thought for the day
Jesus is baptised, and God confirms his identity and his calling.

Readings
Isaiah 43:1-7
Psalm 29
Acts 8:14-17
Luke 3:15-17, 21-22

Aim
To know that God knows them by name.

Starter
Have a number of pictures or objects set out in the middle of the circle. The children guess the name you are thinking of by the way you describe the object or picture. Start with more general statements and get more specific, like this: 'I'm thinking of something which is round…and white…and you might put cornflakes in it.' They have to say the name, rather than pointing, unless they are very young.

Teaching
Have the children's names written out carefully on cards with a string attached so they can be worn. Hold up each one in turn and describe the person the name belongs to, by nature as well as looks, and with lots of positives. The children can join in by adding things they like about each one. When all the children are wearing their names, tell them how God knows each of us by name. He already knows all the things about us that we have talked about, and lots more as well.

Show a picture of a baby, a child, and an adult being baptised, and talk about God calling us by name to follow him. They may remember a Christening in the family, or one of the recent ones in church, and can tell the others what happened. Have a jug and a bowl of water so they can focus on that as they hear about Baptism.

Praying
Dear God,
you know my name
and you know me
and you love me.
I know your name.
I know you and I love you!

Activities

The name cards can be decorated with coloured sticky paper, finger-painting or with pens. On the sheet there are objects and people to name, and thank God for, and space to draw themselves doing something they like doing.

Print worksheet *First Sunday of Epiphany (C)* from CD-ROM.

Second Sunday of Epiphany

Thought for the day

As a marriage celebrates the beginning of a changed, new life for the bride and groom, so our loving, faithful God has chosen us and is ready to transform our lives for the good of the world.

Readings

Isaiah 62:1-5
Psalm 36:5-10
1 Corinthians 12:1-11
John 2:1-11

Aim

To be introduced to the story of the wedding at Cana.

Starter

Water play. Protect the floor and have a number of washing-up bowls with water, containers and sieves. Let the younger children enjoy filling and emptying. Older children can be encouraged to see how many small containers it takes to fill a larger one.

Teaching

Talk with the children about any weddings they may have been to and taken part in. Show a few wedding photos (preferably amateur ones which show people enjoying themselves rather than in set poses). Now tell them about the time Jesus and his mother were invited to a wedding. When you get to the part about the water jars, fill a large jug with water. Pour some into a wine glass as you tell them about the servants pouring it out. The fact that it is of course still water can lead on to what happened in Cana. I think this is far preferable to the red colouring stunts which only turn it all into a magic trick.

Praying

Thank you for the falling rain.
   wiggle fingers downwards
Thank you for the rising sap.
   draw fingers upwards over body, as if a tree
Thank you for the juicy fruit.
   hold arms out with fingers hanging down
Thank you for my favourite fruity drink!
Amen.
   pretend to drink it

Activities

On the worksheet they will be changing things and making them special, and this forms a basis for thinking about how God works in our lives. Instructions for making a clay or plasticine water pot are given on the sheet.

Print worksheet *Second Sunday of Epiphany (C)* from CD-ROM.

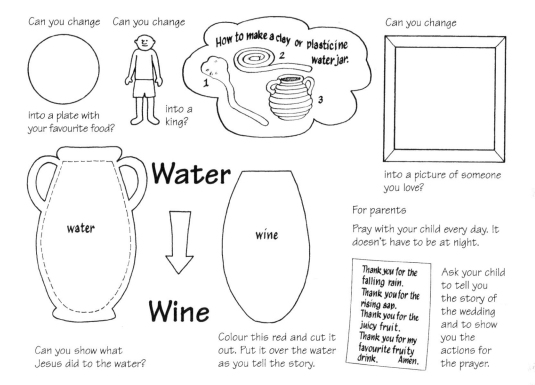

Can you change

into a plate with your favourite food?

Can you change

into a king?

How to make a clay or plasticine water jar.

Can you change

into a picture of someone you love?

For parents

Pray with your child every day. It doesn't have to be at night.

Water

water

wine

Wine

Can you show what Jesus did to the water?

Colour this red and cut it out. Put it over the water as you tell the story.

Thank you for the falling rain.
Thank you for the rising sap.
Thank you for the juicy fruit.
Thank you for my favourite fruity drink.   Amen.

Ask your child to tell you the story of the wedding and to show you the actions for the prayer.

Third Sunday of Epiphany

Thought for the day

The meaning of the scriptures is revealed to the people.

Readings

Nehemiah 8:1-3, 5-6, 8-10
Psalm 19
1 Corinthians 12:12-31a
Luke 4:14-21

Aim

For them to develop listening skills, both physically and spiritually.

Starter

Listen for your name. Sit in a circle. Have a plate of pieces of fruit and tell the children that one by one they can choose a piece to eat. You will call their name when it's their turn. For each one you can say something like, 'Max, you can jump to choose a piece of fruit now. Imogen, you can crawl to choose a piece of fruit now.' Speaking our name alerts us to listen, and God knows us by name.

Teaching

Give out percussion instruments (home-made shakers will be fine) to everyone and have a quiet bell yourself. Get everyone to play loudly, along with a track from a praise tape. Stop everyone and ask if anyone could hear the little bell. Play it on its own so they know what to listen for and then get everyone playing again, but listening out for the bell. Now collect all the instruments in and give the bell to a child to play while we all listen. Now it sounds quite clear, but before, when we were all making a noise, it was so quiet we could hardly hear it.

Stand at one end of the room facing the wall, and see if the children can creep up on you without you hearing them.

Sit in the circle again and try passing the bell (or a crackly, rustly bag) around the circle without it making any noise at all. All these things develop listening skills, both the attentiveness and concentration and also the body control. Praise the children for their success as some will find this quite a challenge. Tell the children how God helps us to know if something is right or wrong, and show this using puppets. Just as a puppet is thinking aloud about stealing something, or telling a lie or being unkind, ring the little bell. The puppet realises that something is wrong, and changes his/her action. Explain that God never forces us to make the right choice (that's for us to decide) but he does let us know what is right, to help us make the right choice.

Praying

Jesus, when you say
Stop! Think! Change!
   (ring the bell three times)
Help me to hear you
   (hands on ears)
and help me to do it.
Amen.
   (hands out, palms up)

Activities

The worksheet helps the children to explore how we hear best, both physically and spiritually. The instruments can then be used to make a storm, starting very quiet, building up and then dying away into silence.

Print worksheet *Third Sunday of Epiphany (C)* from CD-ROM.

Look at this picture. Edward is trying to tell his mum some news. Why can't she hear him?

Draw them in a quiet place so Edward can tell his news and his mum can hear it.

God lets us know what is right and what is wrong
(but we do need to listen!)

What is God saying?

For parents

Help your child to play a listening game this week. Here is a prayer to pray together.

Jesus, when you say,
STOP! THINK! CHANGE!
Help me to hear you
and help me to do it.
   Amen.

Fourth Sunday of Epiphany

Thought for the day

At eight days old, Jesus is presented in the temple, and at the Purification is revealed to Simeon and Anna as the promised Saviour who is able to reveal to us our true selves.

Readings

Ezekiel 43:27-44:4
Psalm 48
1 Corinthians 13:1-13
Luke 2:22-40

Aim

To know that Simeon had been waiting for the Saviour and knew it was Jesus.

Starter

A waiting game. Everyone gets into a space and sits down. The leader calls out, 'Ready . . . steady . . . hop/jump/walk!' and the children mustn't move until they have heard the full instruction. You can make it harder by sometimes giving the instruction quickly and sometimes slowly. Today we are going to meet someone who waited all his life for something, but at last he got it.

Teaching

Dress up one of the leaders as Simeon, or just tell the children we have a visitor today, and put on a head-dress and white beard as they watch. When you are ready, resume eye contact with them and say, 'Hallo, children, my name's Simeon. Can you say, "Hallo, Simeon"?' Say you want to tell them about something exciting that happened to you. Tell them how old you are, and explain that you love God and know you can trust him. You knew that one day God was going to send someone to save and rescue people, and God had told you that you would see this Saviour in person before you died. Go on to tell the children what happened on that day in the temple when Joseph and Mary brought Jesus in. Chat your story, involving the children, and try to get across your excitement at actually meeting the Saviour God had promised.

Praying

Leader	Simeon knew he could trust God.
All	We can trust God, too.
Leader	Simeon loved God.
All	We love God, too.
Leader	Simeon knew that Jesus had come to save us.
All	We know Jesus came to save us, too.

Activities

The worksheet goes over the story with a sequencing activity involving cutting and sticking. If you have nativity dressing-up clothes suitable for the children they can 'play' the story through in costume.

Print worksheet *Fourth Sunday of Epiphany (C)* from CD-ROM.

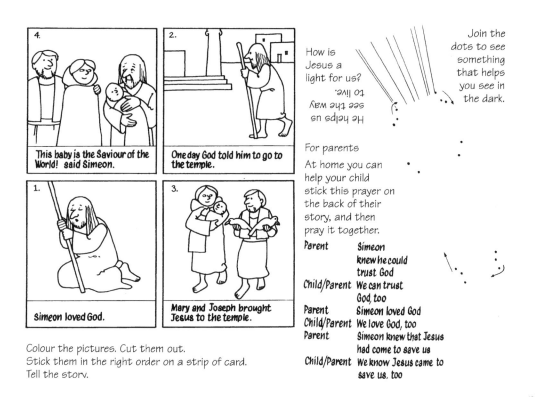

Colour the pictures. Cut them out.
Stick them in the right order on a strip of card.
Tell the story.

Sunday between 3 and 9 February

(if earlier than the Second Sunday before Lent)

Thought for the day

God calls his people and commissions them.

Readings

Isaiah 6:1-8 (9-13)
Psalm 138
1 Corinthians 15:1-11
Luke 5:1-11

Aim

To introduce them to the story of the catch of fishes.

Starter

Have a fish-catching game, either using magnets on strings and paperclips on the fish, or a bazaar-stall fishing game with floating fish which are caught with hooks. The fish for the magnet game can either be made beforehand or cut out ready and then coloured by the children.

Teaching

Tell the story with the children acting it out as you go along. They can find their way to their boat in the dark, push their boat out, throw out the nets, sit and wait, pull in the nets and shake their heads when they find no fish, throw the nets out again, wait and yawn, pull the nets in, and repeat this until morning comes and they rub their eyes. They can shade their eyes to see all the crowds coming, beckon Jesus and help him into the boat, and sit on the sand to listen. Then they push the boat out again, throw in the nets, wait, and pull them in full of fish! Tell the children how Peter was amazed at what had happened, and a bit frightened by it. Jesus told him he didn't need to be afraid, and invited Peter to follow him. Peter said yes, and spent the rest of his life following Jesus and telling other people about him.

Praying

Sing this prayer to the tune of *One, two, three, four, five, once I caught a fish alive*.

One, two, three, four, five,
thank you, God, that I'm alive!
Six, seven, eight, nine, ten,
here I am to help you, then.
What job can I do?
Love God as he wants me to,
show his love each day
living life the loving way.

Activities

On the sheet the children create a collage picture of the story. You will need some scraps of net curtain or the net bags that oranges come in and some fish cut from shiny paper.

Print worksheet *Sunday between 3 and 9 February (C)* from CD-ROM.

What a lot of fish!

To make the collage picture

1 Colour the picture
2 Stick on the fishing nets
3 Stick on lots and lots of fish

One, two, three, four, five,
Thank you, God, that I'm alive!
Six, seven, eight, nine, ten,
Here I am to help you, then.
What job can I do?
Love God as he wants me to,
show his love each day,
living life the loving way.

For parents

Please help your child learn this prayer by singing it together every day.

Cut out and colour this fish and put a paper clip at the mouth. Try catching it at home with a fridge magnet.

Sunday between
10 and 16 February

(if earlier than the Second Sunday before Lent)

Thought for the day

The challenges and rewards of living by faith.

Readings

Jeremiah 17:5-10
Psalm 1
1 Corinthians 15:12-20
Luke 6:17-26

Aim

To know that we can trust God.

Starter

Chickens. The children run and peck around until the mother hen clucks a danger warning. Whenever that happens, the chickens stop what they are doing and run to the safety of the mother hen (one of the leaders on a rug). When she tells them the danger is over, they can scatter again.

Teaching

Talk about how the chickens know they will be safe with the mother hen. They can trust her to look after them. Talk together about what happens if they fall over and hurt themselves, and draw their attention to the fact that because someone loves them, they look after them. Talk about the way they look after pets and the way they can look after their mums and dads and grandparents with hugs and helping them.

God looks after us all. He has given us a lovely world to live in, with food for us to eat, and all the things we need to make homes and clothes and toys and cars. That's because he loves us.

Praying

When I am afraid
I will trust in you, O God.
I will take shelter under your wings.

(From Psalms 56 and 57)

Activities

On the worksheet there are instructions for making a working model of chickens running to the safety of the mother hen's wings. You will need string and sticky tape, and may prefer to prepare the chicks and hen in card.

Print worksheet *Sunday between 10 and 16 February (C)* from CD-ROM.

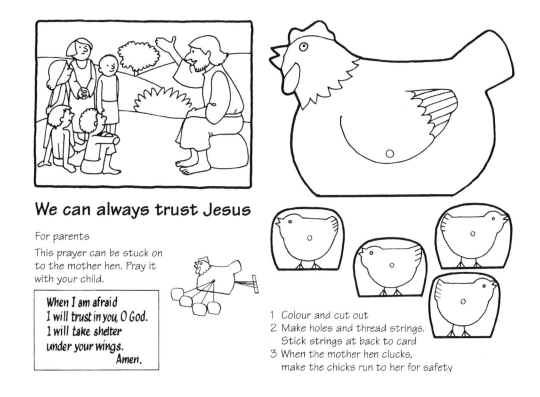

We can always trust Jesus

For parents

This prayer can be stuck on to the mother hen. Pray it with your child.

When I am afraid
I will trust in you, O God.
I will take shelter
under your wings.
Amen.

1 Colour and cut out
2 Make holes and thread strings. Stick strings at back to card
3 When the mother hen clucks, make the chicks run to her for safety

Sunday between 17 and 23 February

(if earlier than the Second Sunday before Lent)

Thought for the day

Jesus teaches us to love our enemies and forgive those who sin against us.

Readings

Genesis 45:3-11, 15
Psalm 37:1-11,39-40
1 Corinthians 15:35-38, 42-50
Luke 6:27-38

Aim

To learn to make up when things go wrong.

Starter

Let the children draw on chalkboards and rub it all out again. Or use the magic writer pads that enable you to erase what you have drawn.

Teaching

Talk about and demonstrate how we can rub out our mistakes on a chalkboard. Draw a nasty splodge as you talk about someone being unkind. But then they say, 'I'm sorry I was unkind.' If someone says that to us we can say, 'That's OK. I forgive you!' As you say it, rub out the splodge.

Jesus says, 'Forgive one another. Pray for those who are unkind to you.' When we do this we are rubbing out the unkindness and clearing the way to start again.

Praying

Thank you, God,
for forgiving me.
Help me to forgive as well.
Amen.

Activities

Help the children to make the two finger puppets from the worksheet and fix them on their fingers, so they can practise getting cross and making up again. They can also colour and fold the model on the sheet to see what a difference forgiveness makes.

Print worksheet *Sunday between 17 and 23 February (C)* from CD-ROM.

Colour the pictures. Cut out. Fold along the dotted lines. Now you can swing the middle flap over to make a 'before and after' story.

Colour the finger puppets. Cut out and stick round fingers with rubber bands or sticky tape.

For parents

Ask your child to show you how to put things right when we are unkind and pray this prayer together.

Thank you, God
for forgiving me.
Help me
to forgive
as well.
            Amen.

Second Sunday before Lent

Thought for the day

'He commands even the winds and the water and they obey him.'

Readings

Genesis 2:4b-9, 15-25
Psalm 65
Revelation 4
Luke 8:22-25

Aim

To introduce them to the love of God in his creation.

Starter

Have a hands-on exploration of creation. Provide trays of pebbles, sand, water (protect the surrounding areas or use the washbasins), different textures and different smells. Have books with pictures of animals, birds, fish and insects. The children can wander round touching and enjoying all the different objects.

Teaching

Talk about the different things they have explored and emphasise what a lovely, varied world God has made. Talk about how the world is like a garden God has made, with all these lovely things in it, and all the animals, and people to look after it. Talk over with them how we can look after it well.

Praying

Thank you, God,
for the sun and the rain,
for plants and animals and birds.
And, most of all,
thank you, God,
for making me ME!
Amen.

Activities

Give the children paper and paints to celebrate in art our creation and the way God provides for us. Mount the finished pictures and display them with photographs and today's prayer in an area of the church or hall.

Print worksheet *Second Sunday before Lent (C)* from CD-ROM.

Spot the difference

For parents
Pray this with your child and you can
both add in the particular things each
day for which you are thankful.

Thank you, God, for the sun
and the rain, for plants and
animals and birds. And most of
all, thank you God for making me ME!
Amen.

Sunday next before Lent

Thought for the day
God's glory makes Moses' face radiant, and it transfigures Jesus as he prays on the mountain. Our lives, too, can become increasingly radiant as the Spirit transforms us.

Readings
Exodus 34:29-35
Psalm 99
2 Corinthians 3:12-4:2
Luke 9:28-36 (37-43)

Aim
To look at how lives can shine with God's love.

Starter
Patches of sunshine. Have some cut-out circles of yellow paper scattered on the floor and explain that these are patches of sunshine in a dark wood. The children move and dance around to some music, and when the music stops they go and stand on a sunshine patch. Take away a patch each time so that in the end there is only one patch of sunshine left. Children not finding a patch to stand on are out.

Teaching
Talk about how much we need the sunshine. We need God's love to shine in the world too. God can help us to make our lives shine like patches of sunshine in the dark forest. Put out the sunshine patches again, and this time tell the children to stand in the darkness when you say something which is bad or sad, and go to a sunshine patch when you say something good and loving.

Bad and Sad
People hitting and hurting each other
Being grumpy and sulky
Being a pain
People not having anywhere to live
People telling lies
People not having enough to eat

Good and Loving
People saying sorry
Being friendly
Helping someone
People sharing their things with others
People telling the truth
People giving money to buy food for the starving

By physically moving into the sunshine when the 'shining lives' qualities are mentioned, the children will begin to understand the symbolism of radiant light in a spiritual sense. Jesus' life shone because of what he said and what he did. Our lives can shine with his love like patches of sunshine.

Praying

You will need the children to have made their sunshine mats for this. They start by standing on the mat and singing to the tune of *Twinkle, twinkle, little star*. At the darkness section the children move off the mat and walk around it, first one way and then the other, before moving back on to the mat for the last line.

We are sunshine in the darkness,
we are shining with your love.
Help us when we live in darkness,
help us when we live in darkness,
help all those who live in darkness
to shine like sunshine with your love!

Activities

Have some sheets of yellow paper with a wavy outline drawn on. Children old enough to use scissors can cut these out. Others will need help here. Or use white paper and let the children colour them with yellow crayons. The prayer from the sheet can be cut out and stuck on to the mat so that parents can sing the prayer with their children at home. The sheet also includes pictures of Jesus' shining life to colour, and a puzzle to see which behaviours belong to the 'light'.

Print worksheet *Sunday next before Lent (C)* from CD-ROM.

Cross out the unloving things and colour the sunshine things in bright colours.

Parents: Cut out, stick on the sunshine mat, and sing the prayer together.

We are sunshine in the darkness
We are shining with your love
Help us when we live in darkness
Help us when we live in darkness
Help all those who live in darkness
to shine like sunshine
with your love!

Draw in the child Jesus is making better. Then colour the picture.

Draw in Jesus giving the blind man his sight. Then colour the picture.

First Sunday of Lent

Thought for the day

Following his baptism, Jesus is severely tempted out in the desert, and shows us how to overcome temptation.

Readings

Deuteronomy 26:1-11
Psalm 91:1-2, 9-16
Romans 10:8b-13
Luke 4:1-13

Aim

To look at good ways of living.

Starter

Have a selection of balancing activities for the children to try. These could include walking between two chalk-drawn lines, climbing up to stand on a chair without using your hands, walking along a bench, standing on one leg, and walking along a piece of string laid along the floor.

Teaching

Talk about the balancing acts and how we had to try hard to stop ourselves falling and to keep our balance. In the way we live we have to try hard to do what is kind and loving and good. (Walk along the string line as you say this.) Sometimes we fall down on that (wobble off the string here), and end up being unkind and selfish. When that happens we have to put things right and get back to being kind and loving again. (Go back to walking along the string again.)

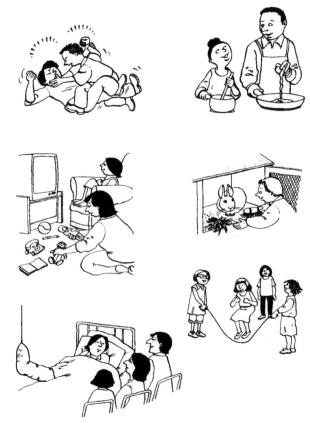

Have some pictures of people behaving well and badly. Show the pictures one by one, and decide together whether the people are walking God's way or not. If they are, put the picture on the string; if not, place it away from the string. Copy the pictures right or use your own ideas. They need to be pictures your particular group can relate to.

Praying

To the tune of *Here we go round the mulberry bush*. Act out the verses and add or alter them as appropriate for the group. The children's ideas can be incorporated too.

Help us, God, to share our toys,
share our toys, share our toys,
help us, God, to share our toys,
and live as Jesus told us.

Other verse ideas: to help our mums/help our dads; to look after our pets; to tell the truth

Activities

On the worksheet there is a chart to be filled in through the week to draw attention to their good, brave and honest behaviour, and a 'spot the loving living' activity. They can also be taught Jesus' summary of the law using their fingers. They simply touch each finger of one hand (as if counting) as they say the words 'Love God, love each other'.

Print worksheet *First Sunday of Lent (C)* from CD-ROM.

Second Sunday of Lent

Thought for the day
If only we will agree to put our faith in God, he will fill our lives with meaning and bring us safely to heaven.

Readings
Genesis 15:1-12, 17-18
Psalm 27
Philippians 3:17-4:1
Luke 13:31-35

Aim
To know that God makes promises and keeps them.

Starter
Pass the parcel. In the middle is a key with a promise that says, 'You will be able to give everyone here a sweet.' The key opens a box in which there are sweets for everyone (the right number exactly). The winner of the key gives the sweets out.

Teaching
Talk about how when *(John)* got the key it didn't look much like sweets for us all, but the message turned out to be true. By using the key John did end up with just enough sweets for all of us.

Share some promises the children know about, either ones they have made or those which have been made to them. Talk about what promises are, and how important it is not to break a promise and not to make a promise you can't keep.

God is very good at making promises and he always, always keeps them. The Bible is full of stories about God's promises and how they all came true. So we can trust God, because he means what he says.

And one of his big promises is to you and me. God has promised us that whenever we talk to him he will be listening, and whenever we need him he is there. God doesn't have to go to sleep, so we don't need to worry about waking him up, and he's never too busy to spend time with us.

Praying

Dear God,
I can't see you with my eyes
but I know you are here
because you promised you would be,
and you always keep your promise.
I'm glad you always have time to listen,
and you know what it's like to be me.
Amen.

Activities

The worksheet looks at promises and how they sometimes get broken by people. God's promise to Abram is explored, and the children can make a night sky full of stars with dark blue or black paper and stick-on gold and silver stars. The title from the worksheet can be stuck on to the sky picture.

Print worksheet *Second Sunday of Lent (C)* from CD-ROM.

Third Sunday of Lent

Thought for the day

We have God's invitation to come and drink freely of his Spirit, but if we keep refusing his offer it can eventually be withdrawn.

Readings

Isaiah 55:1-9
Psalm 63:1-8
1 Corinthians 10:1-13
Luke 13:1-9

Aim

To enjoy the gift of water and thank God for it.

Starter

Water play. Protect the children and the floor and have some bowls of water on low tables, plenty of sieves, and containers, and things that float and sink. Also water some plants and/or give a pet a drink.

Teaching

Talk about being thirsty and needing water. Whether we are plants or animals we all need water to live. Make up a picture of a blue river running through a green field, using coloured paper cut to shape. Put foil fish in the river, plants and trees near the water, foxes and badgers and birds all drinking the water. Stick each item on with a glue stick as you talk about it, and let the children help. You can all admire and talk about the finished picture. Water keeps us all alive. Jesus says, 'You need God like you need water'. This can be written as a title for the water picture, or for very young children the title can be 'Thank you, God, for water'.

Praying

We can drink it, swim in it,
cook and wash up in it,
fish can breathe in it.
What can it be?
It's water! God has given us water!
And we say thanks!
   (glug, glug)
Thanks!
   (swish, swish)
Thanks!
   (sizzle, sizzle)

Thanks!
   (splish, splosh)
Thanks!
   (bubble, bubble)

As the children make the sounds they mime the drinking, swimming, cooking and so on.

Activities

Using the worksheet the children can draw in the different animals, plants and birds on the pictures and discover someone who enjoys water by completing a dot-to-dot puzzle.

Print worksheet *Third Sunday of Lent (C)* from CD-ROM.

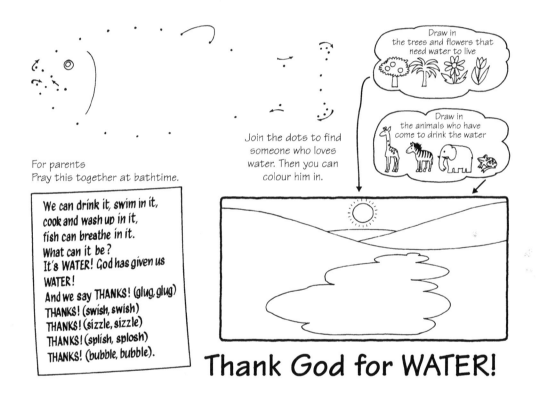

For parents
Pray this together at bathtime.

We can drink it, swim in it,
cook and wash up in it,
fish can breathe in it.
What can it be?
It's WATER! God has given us
WATER!
And we say THANKS! (glug, glug)
THANKS! (swish, swish)
THANKS! (sizzle, sizzle)
THANKS! (splish, splosh)
THANKS! (bubble, bubble).

Join the dots to find someone who loves water. Then you can colour him in.

Draw in the trees and flowers that need water to live

Draw in the animals who have come to drink the water

Thank God for WATER!

Fourth Sunday of Lent
Mothering Sunday

Thought for the day
While we are here in this life, given one another to care for, we can learn the lessons of mutual love and support and shared suffering.

Readings
Exodus 2:1-10 or 1 Samuel 1:20-28
Psalm 34:11-20 or Psalm 127:1-4
2 Corinthians 1:3-7 or Colossians 3:12-17
Luke 2:33-35 or John 19:25-27

Activities
Today is not one for learning separately but for celebrating together. Provide shakers and bells for the younger ones to play during one or two hymns, and streamers to wave. Gather the children round the altar for the eucharistic prayer and choose hymns where the meaning is accessible to everyone.

Have materials for making cards available for the very young.

Print worksheet *Fourth Sunday of Lent (C)* from CD-ROM.

Colour the picture, fold it into a card and have the message written for you inside.
Give it to your mum with a smile and a hug.

Thank you!

Colossians 3:12-17

PEBBLES

Fifth Sunday of Lent

Thought for the day
When we are privileged to share in Christ's suffering, we also share in his new life.

Readings
Isaiah 43:16-21
Psalm 126
Philippians 3:4b-14
John 12:1-8

Aim
To see that God is in the sad and hard times as well as the happy ones.

Starter
Have an assortment of junk, crayons, paint, wool and glue. Tell the children that all this is stuff that no one wants. It's stuff that people have thrown out as rubbish. But we can use it to make things. Set the children free to transform the junk, and then share and admire what we all managed to make.

Teaching
Talk about the fun we've had with some old boxes and thrown-out rubbish. God never thinks of anything or anybody as rubbish. He can make beautiful things out of everything. Show some seed. What does God make out of this dried up, dusty stuff? Flowers! (Show some pictures from a seed catalogue.) Show some vegetable peelings and old tea bags. What can God do with this smelly old stuff? Compost to help the tomatoes grow! (Show some ripe compost.)

It's the same with people. God doesn't think, 'Oh, they're too small for me. I can't work with them.' He thinks, 'Ah, good! Some small people to cheer someone up, or give their mum a hug, or teach the grown-ups. Just what I needed!' And he doesn't think, 'Oh, they're no good to me now they're old and can't get out much.' He thinks, 'Ah, good! Some old people who can't get out much, so they've lots of time to think and pray for the holiday club. Just what I needed!' For God nothing is rubbish and nobody is rubbish.

God can even use the times we are sad. He can even use the bad things like accidents and wars, and make something good come from them. Nothing and nobody is too bad for God to use, because he loves us all.

Praying

Loving God,
I am glad you love us so much.
I am glad I can help you now
as well as when I am grown-up.
You can use my sadness as well as my happy times
whenever you like.
Amen.

Activities

If the children need more time to finish their junk models they can do that now. The worksheet helps them think about the good that God can bring out of such things as moving house, a rainy holiday, and a time in hospital. Make sure they understand that God never makes bad things happen to us, but when they do happen he always works to use them for some good.

Print worksheet *Fifth Sunday of Lent (C)* from CD-ROM.

Palm Sunday

Thought for the day

As Jesus rides into Jerusalem on a donkey, and the crowds welcome him, we sense both the joy at the Messiah being acclaimed, and the heaviness of his suffering which follows. Jesus' mission is drawing to its fulfilment.

Readings

Liturgy of the Palms:
Luke 19:28-40
Psalm 118:1-2,19-29

Liturgy of the Passion:
Isaiah 50:4-9a
Psalm 31:9-16
Philippians 2:5-11
Luke 22:14-23:56 or Luke 23:1-49

Aim

To introduce them to the story of the entry into Jerusalem.

Starter

Stop, wave, shout hooray! When different signs are displayed the children 'Stop!' (a red circle), 'Wave!' (a cut-out or real palm branch), and 'Shout hooray!' (a crown). You can also sing a praise song, such as *Sing Hosanna*.

Teaching

Using upturned bowls and pots and a green cloth or large towel, let the children help make a model landscape. Boxes covered in white paper make the Jerusalem buildings, and the path down into the Kidron valley is a length of brown crepe paper or material. Cut out coat shapes of fabric which the children can lay down on the road in front of Jesus, and have a card cut-out of Jesus riding on the donkey which you can move along as you tell the story. Let the children all wave their paper palm branches, standing around the model. They will feel as if they are all part of the story.

Praying

Hooray for Jesus,
 riding on a donkey!
Hooray for Jesus,
 he is our King!
Hooray for Jesus,
 coming to Jerusalem!
Hooray for Jesus,
 he is our King!

Activities

Today the children may be joining in the parish procession, with streamer-waving, singing and dancing. They will also be preparing the model. Have large palm leaves drawn on green sugar paper. Older children can cut these out themselves, and those just mastering the scissors technique can make random cuts along the sides of the basic shape. Pictures to help with this and the houses are given on the worksheet. There is also a picture of the event which the children can complete by drawing in the people cheering Jesus on his way.

Print worksheet *Palm Sunday (C)* from CD-ROM.

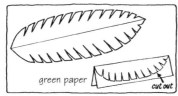

Palm branches

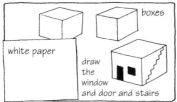

Houses

For parents
Pray this together when you can shake or jangle keys, or dried peas in a jar.

Hooray for Jesus riding on a donkey!
Hooray for Jesus he is our king!
Hooray for Jesus coming to Jerusalem!
Hooray for Jesus he is our king!

Can you help finish the picture?
Draw in the missing bits.
Draw in lots of people, cheering Jesus on.

HOSANNA!

Easter Day

If possible, it is recommended that the children and young people are in church with the other age groups today. Involve the children in some of the music and in the decorating of the church.

Thought for the day

It is true. Jesus is alive for all time. The Lord of life cannot be held by death. God's victory over sin and death means that new life for us is a reality.

Readings

Acts 10:34-43 or Isaiah 65:17-25
Psalm 118:1-2, 14-24
1 Corinthians 15:19-26 or Acts 10:34-43
John 20:1-18 or Luke 24:1-12

Aim

To enjoy celebrating that Jesus is alive.

Starter

Have an Easter egg hunt, preferably outside if this is safe and practical.

Teaching

You could tell the story gathered around an Easter garden that the children have helped to make.

Praying

Jesus died for us
  arms out, head down
Now he's alive for us
  jump up and clap hands over head
Hip, hip, HOORAY!
Jesus is alive today!
  raise arms

Activities

Use modelling clay or playdough for the children to make their own models of the garden, and the women coming to the empty tomb. On the worksheet there is a picture of the women visiting the tomb early on the first Easter morning.

Print worksheet *Easter Day (C)* from CD-ROM.

Where are the Easter eggs?

Can you find 10 eggs?

For parents
Pray with your child, using the actions.

Jesus died for us (arms out, head down)
Now he's alive for us (jump up and
clap hands over head)
Hip, hip, HOORAY!
Jesus is alive today (raise arms)

JESUS IS ALIVE!

Second Sunday of Easter

Thought for the day

Having seen Jesus in person, the disciples are convinced of the Resurrection. We too can meet him personally.

Readings

Acts 5:27-32
Psalm 118:14-29 or Psalm 150
Revelation 1:4-8
John 20:19-31

Aim

To experience that something can still be there even if we can't see it.

Starter

Playa peep-bo game with the younger children and a hunt-the-slipper game with the older ones. Point out that the slipper was there all the time, even before we found it.

Teaching

Spread out a towel, sheet or carpet tiles on the floor and copy the pictures (*right*) on to thin card. Gather the children around and tell the story of today's Gospel, using the pictures.

Praying

Dear Jesus,
I can't see you
but I know you are here.
I know you can hear me,
and I know you love me.
Thank you, Jesus!
Amen.

Activities

On the worksheet there is a dot-to-dot picture of Jesus to complete, and a picture to colour. Also there is an activity which helps the children appreciate their senses, and realise that sight is not the only way of knowing something is true. Possibilities for the seeing but not touching category would be the sun, moon and stars; hearing but not seeing might be someone's heartbeat, the wind, or thunder; touching but not hearing might be a table or a sandwich; and all three might be a person.

Print worksheet *Second Sunday of Easter (C)* from CD-ROM.

Join the dots to make Jesus appear.

For parents
To pray with your child

Dear Jesus,
I can't see you
but I know you are here.
I know you can hear me,
and I know you love me.
Thank you, Jesus! Amen.

Third Sunday of Easter

Thought for the day

Those who know Jesus and recognise that he is the anointed Saviour are commissioned to go out as his witnesses to proclaim the good news.

Readings

Acts 9:1-6 (7-20)
Psalm 30
Revelation 5:11-14
John 21:1-19

Aim

To get to know the story of today's Gospel.

Starter

Going fishing. Borrow or make the kind of magnet rod and lines which can catch paper fish with paperclips on their mouths. Have the paper fish cut ready so the children can decorate them and add the paperclips. Put the fish in a carton pond, and let fishing commence!

Teaching

Tell the story with the children all acting. They push the boat into the water, throw the net out into the water, wait, inspect the net, wait some more, and get fed up. Then catch sight of a man on the beach, cup your hand to your ear to hear what he says, pull in the net, throw it in the other side and haul in the massive catch. Realise that the man on the beach is Jesus, give a great shout, wade to shore and enjoy breakfast together.

Praying

Dear Jesus,
thank you for coming with us
to the shops/on the bus/to the dentist.
Wherever we go
you are always there for us.
Amen.

Activities

If you get enough small cartons, each child can colour one to make a complete fishing set to take home. The worksheet has the outline for a collage picture which can be completed by sticking on cotton wool clouds, shiny paper fish and a red shiny paper fire on the beach. There is also a fish jigsaw with the words 'It's Jesus!' on it.

Print worksheet *Third Sunday of Easter (C)* from CD-ROM.

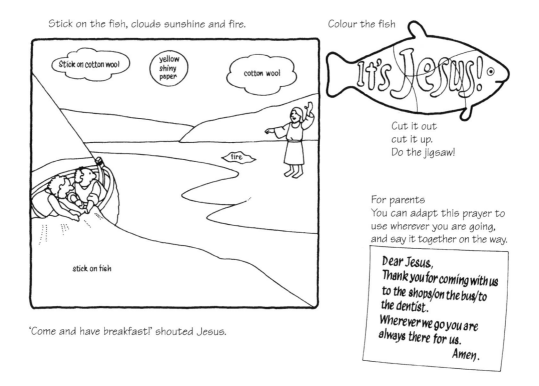

Stick on the fish, clouds sunshine and fire.

Stick on cotton wool

yellow shiny paper

cotton wool

fire

stick on fish

'Come and have breakfast!' shouted Jesus.

Colour the fish

It's Jesus!

Cut it out
cut it up.
Do the jigsaw!

For parents
You can adapt this prayer to
use wherever you are going,
and say it together on the way.

Dear Jesus,
Thank you for coming with us
to the shops/on the bus/to
the dentist.
Wherever we go you are
always there for us.
                    Amen.

Fourth Sunday of Easter

Thought for the day

Asked if he really is the Christ, Jesus directs his questioners to look at his life in action and see for themselves that he and the Father are one.

Readings

Acts 9:36-43
Psalm 23
Revelation 7:9-17
John 10:22-30

Aim

To get to know the story of Tabitha being brought to life again.

Starter

Have some simple lace stitching for the children to try. You can make your own sewing cards by punching holes in a greetings card picture, and providing lengths of coloured string with sticky tape wound round the end to make the threading easier.

Teaching

Tell the children that the person in today's story was also very good at sewing. Her name was Tabitha, and she enjoyed getting pieces of material and making them into all sorts of lovely things that people could use and wear. Show them the kind of things Tabitha might have made, such as clothes and sheets. Explain how, when Tabitha got very ill and died, her friends were very sad, and they asked one of Jesus' friends to come to the house. The friend's name was Peter and he came straight away. Tabitha's friends showed Peter the lovely things Tabitha had made, and they told him what a kind person she was, and how sad they were that she had died. Usually people who die go to live with Jesus in heaven, but this time God had another plan for Tabitha.

Now because Peter was such a close friend of Jesus, Jesus could work through him. Peter went upstairs and knelt down beside Tabitha's bed. He prayed and prayed, and then, in Jesus' name, he said to the woman, 'Tabitha, wake up'. And Tabitha opened her eyes and looked at Peter, and smiled! So Peter held out his hand and helped her up. Through Peter, Jesus had brought Tabitha back to life again. It was a sign that Jesus really was alive and working in his friends. And Tabitha's friends were all very happy. They thanked Peter, and I expect Peter said it was God they really needed to thank, so they all hugged Tabitha and thanked God for giving their friend back to them for a while longer. Perhaps Tabitha made Peter something to wear, as a thank-you present. What do you think she might have made for him?

Praying

Dear God,
you are so kind to us,
so good at knowing
what we need.
You are my God and my friend.
Amen.

Activities

On the worksheet there is a 'spot the difference' and a 'dot-to-dot' activity to encourage the children to talk about the story. They can also continue or develop the sewing, and have a sewing demonstration by a leader or a visitor from the church. It is important that the children understand that being brought to life is a very unusual event.

Print worksheet *Fourth Sunday of Easter (C)* from CD-ROM.

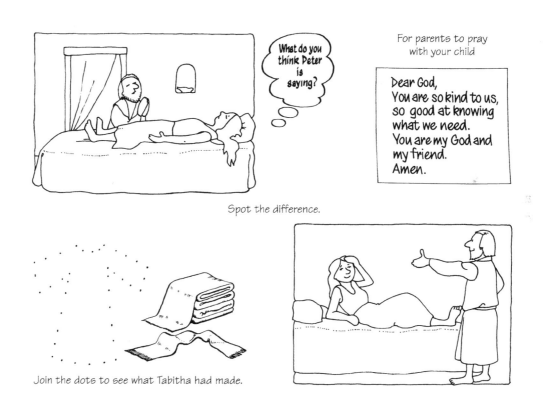

Spot the difference.

Join the dots to see what Tabitha had made.

Fifth Sunday of Easter

Thought for the day

Christ, breaking through the barrier of sin and death, allows us to break into an entirely new way of living which continues into eternity.

Readings

Acts 11:1-18
Psalm148
Revelation 21:1-6
John 13:31-35

Aim

To know that Jesus' friends love one another.

Starter

Sit in a circle and give everyone a chance to talk about their friends – what their names are and what they like playing together. Then play a circle game as friends together, such as 'The princess slept for 100 years', or 'in and out of the dusky bluebells'.

Teaching

Explain that today we are thinking about friends, and we're going to find out about Jesus and some of his friends. The children can do all the actions as you talk about the way Jesus and his friends went for walks together, listened to each other (cup hand to ear), talked together (open and close hands to make them 'chat'), laughed together and cried together. They sometimes went to parties and ate nice food together and drank refreshing drinks together. At the end of the day they got tired together (yawn).

Jesus loved his friends and he said to them, 'I want you to love one another like this. Even when you don't feel like it, I want you to be kind to one another and look after one another.' And that's what all Jesus' friends try and do.

Jesus has lots of friends. There are the friends who lived with him in Galilee, and there's all of us who follow Jesus today. We can be his friends as well – when we walk together, listen to each other, talk together, laugh together and cry together. And when we eat and drink, and when we get tired at the end of the day, Jesus is still with us, loving us.

Praying

I have a friend who is deeper than the ocean,
I have a friend who is wider than the sky,
I have a friend who always understands me,
whether I'm happy or ready to cry.
Jesus is my friend who is deeper than the ocean,
Jesus is my friend who is wider than the sky,
Jesus is my friend who always understands me,
whether I'm happy or ready to cry.

Activities

The worksheet has pictures to encourage the children to explore what it means to live in the loving way which marks us out as Jesus' friends, and they can fold, cut out and colour a string of Jesus' friends who are holding hands.

Print worksheet *Fifith Sunday of Easter (C)* from CD-ROM.

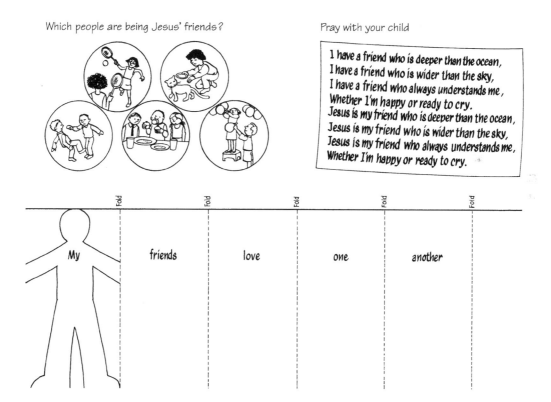

Sixth Sunday of Easter

Thought for the day

The continuing presence of God, as Holy Spirit, leads us, as Jesus promised, into a personally guided outreach to all nations.

Readings

Acts 16:9-15
Psalm 67
Revelation 21:10, 22–22:5
John 14:23-29 or John 5:1-9

Aim

To introduce them to the idea of going where God the Holy Spirit leads us.

Starter

Follow my leader. Choose several children to take turns at leading everyone around to music, walking, hopping or dancing in the way they choose.

Teaching

Talk together about when we say goodbye, and practise waving to one another and blowing kisses. Talk about feeling sad when the time comes for saying goodbye to friends or grandparents and we don't want them to go.

Explain how Jesus' friends didn't want him to go, and when the time came to say goodbye they were sad. They didn't look forward to being without him. Jesus wanted them to know that he would not be leaving them on their own. The Holy Spirit of God would be coming to be with them and lead them in the right direction.

Praying

As you lead the children through a drawn or marked pathway, lead them also line by line in this prayer:

Spirit of God,
lead me along the paths
of kindness
and love.
Amen.

Activities

The idea of leading is continued in the worksheet where they can take their finger for a walk through the country. There is also a matching activity to start you talking about keeping in touch with God so that we know where we are being led. Give the children the opportunity to ask for God's help and guidance in any areas of their life which they are a bit scared about, or which make them sad. Their recording of these places visually will be part of the prayer, and you can talk later about how God answered them. Children need to know right from the start that God can work with them and through them.

Print worksheet *Sixth Sunday of Easter (C)* from CD-ROM.

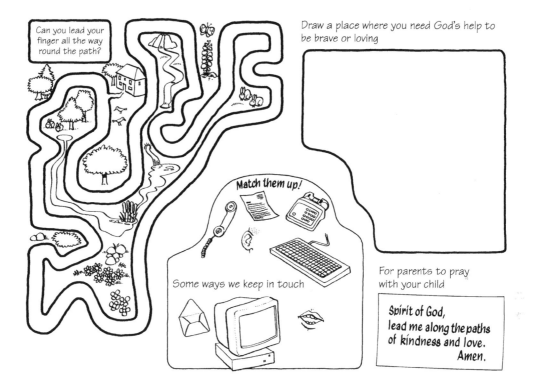

Ascension Day

Thought for the day

Having bought back our freedom with the giving of his life, Jesus enters into the full glory to which he is entitled.

Readings

Acts 1:1-11 or Daniel 7:9-14
Psalm 47 or Psalm 93
Ephesians 1:15-23 or Acts 1:1-11
Luke 24:44-53

Activities

It is likely that Ascension Day services for schools will not need a separate programme for children. However, I have included a drawing and colouring activity for today so that children in church can work at this during the sermon.

Here are some suggestions:

- Any artwork or writing that the children have done on what the Ascension is about can be displayed around the building, and time given in the service to looking at it.

- Have a beautiful helium balloon at the ready. Write on it an Ascension message that the children would like to send. After the service two representative children can let the balloon float away.

- Children can wave white and yellow streamers during some of the hymns.

Print worksheet *Ascension Day (C)* from CD-ROM.

PEBBLES

Seventh Sunday of Easter
Sunday after Ascension Day

Thought for the day

Jesus lives for all time in glory; we can live the fullness of Resurrection life straight away.

Readings

Acts 16:16-34
Psalm 97
Revelation 22:12-14, 16-17, 20-21
John 17:20-26

Aim

For them to know that Jesus is in heaven, and explore what heaven is like.

Starter

Sit in a circle and describe different children and objects by giving clues about them. The children have to guess who or what is being described. (I'm thinking of something that is warm ... and colourful ... and has a hole to put your head through. What could it be?)

Teaching

Young children may not have been involved in Ascension Day services so tell them today about the friends of Jesus getting used to seeing him alive after Easter. Now the time has come for Jesus to go into heaven, and his friends won't see him any more. Use pictures cut out of card and move them around on carpet tiles or towels on the floor, with the children gathered round the of the landscape. Pictures to copy are given (*right*). Cut out a large cloud to hide Jesus from their sight, and then take the friends back to Jerusalem rejoicing, before you add in the angels welcoming Jesus into heaven.

Praying

The angels said,
'Hello, Jesus. Well done!'
I want to say it too:
'Hello, Jesus.
Well done!'
Amen.

Activities

On the worksheet is a pattern for making angels. For the very young these will need to have been already copied and cut out. If you want to have lots of angels for each child use the template and cut the angels from that, perhaps using different colours of paper. Cotton or wool can be attached to the heads either by tying, or with sticky tape. Use shoe boxes for the surroundings of heaven, and white paper with cotton wool on it for the cloud. Use the picture of Jesus from the Ascension Day worksheet.

Print worksheet *Seventh Sunday of Easter (C)* from CD-ROM.

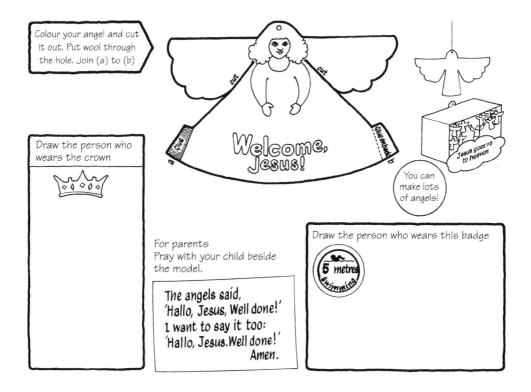

Day of Pentecost
Whit Sunday

Thought for the day
As Jesus promised, the Holy Spirit is poured out on the apostles and the Church is born.

Readings
Acts 2:1-21 or Genesis 11:1-9
Psalm 104:24-34, 35b
Romans 8:14-17 or Acts 2:1-21
John 14:8-17 (25-27)

Aim
To celebrate the birthday of the Church.

Starter
Jack in the box. Have everyone crouching down. The leader says, 'Ready, steady, Jack in the box!', and everyone springs up. Vary the length of time between the 'ready' and the 'steady' so the children are hanging on the leader's words, ready to spring into action, but not sure when to.

Teaching
Explain how Jesus' friends had been told to wait for the coming of the Holy Spirit after Jesus had gone into heaven. They were praying and waiting, and waiting and praying for over a week, and then suddenly the Spirit came to them all.

Bring in a birthday cake with two candles on it. If possible, have the cake in the shape of a church, or have a picture or model of a church on it. Explain to the children that today is like the birthday of the Church, not just of St Andrew's but all the churches everywhere in the world. Light the candles, each of which stands for about a thousand years. It is now about two thousand years since the Holy Spirit of God was poured out on Jesus' friends and the Christian Church was born.

As you talk about the handing-on of the Gospel, use a set of Russian dolls, and keep taking another one out. Those few people told lots of others about Jesus, and those others told lots more, and their children and their grandchildren, and then the grandchildren grew up and they told their friends and their children and their grandchildren. And soon more and more people all over the world knew about Jesus and the love God has for us. And they went on telling other people until eventually someone told us! So now we know about Jesus and God's love for us, and through our lives we'll tell our friends and our children and our grandchildren so they will know as well.

Sing 'Happy Birthday, dear Church', blow out the candles and share the cake.

Praying

Happy birthday, dear Church,
Happy birthday, dear Church.
Jesus' love is for ever,
Happy birthday, dear Church!

Activities

Have some fairy cakes already iced, and let the children decorate them ready to give out to everyone as birthday cake after the service. The worksheet has a picture to colour of the Church being born at Pentecost.

Print worksheet *Day of Pentecost (C)* from CD-ROM.

Trinity Sunday

Thought for the day

The unique nature of God is celebrated today, as we reflect on the truth that God is Creator, Redeemer and Life-giver.

Readings

Proverbs 8:1-4, 22-31
Psalm 8
Romans 5:1-5
John 16:12-15

Aim

To help them appreciate the wonder of God.

Starter

Let them make something, such as a picture, from all kinds of bits and pieces, such as wool, bottle tops, toffee wrappers and feathers. Or they can paint or print a picture. This activity needs to be fairly unstructured, so they express themselves in their pictures.

Teaching

Display all the pictures and admire them. Talk about how when we enjoy thinking of things and making them, we are doing what our God loves doing. He loves making things that are beautiful and huge and tiny. He loves making people, and watching over us as we grow and learn to do all sorts of things for ourselves, using the brain he has given us.

Pass round a few things God has made for the children to look at, touch and smell. Talk together about how lovely they are. (You might have a stone, a shell, a feather and a flower.)

Praying

Lord God,
I love the things you have made.
They show me your love.
Amen.

Activities

Give the children large letters to colour and stick these with their pictures on to a long roll of wallpaper which can be displayed in church. The finished message reads: 'Our God is wonderful!' The worksheet also has this message, together with a dot-to-dot which again puts them in the role of creator so they can appreciate God as Creator.

Print worksheet *Trinity Sunday (C)* from CD-ROM.

Our God is wonderful

Have you ever seen these?

Thank you God!

God made me, too!

To pray with your child

Lord God,
I love the things
you have made.
They show me
your love.
        Amen.

Sunday between 29 May and 4 June

(if after Trinity Sunday)

Thought for the day

The good news we have been given is not just for us, but to pass on to the rest of the world.

Readings

1 Kings 18:20-21 (22-29), 30-39 or 1 Kings 8:22-23, 41-43
Psalm 96 or Psalm 96:1-9
Galatians 1:1-12
Luke 7:1-10

Aim

To learn how to start spreading the good news.

Starter

Sit in a circle and pass the parcel. Put a Christian sticker in each layer, and a Bible story book in the middle.

Teaching

Talk about the way they have been passing the parcel on, so everyone gets a tum, and how good they were at that. Now we're going to pass our news on to each other, but we don't need to put it in a parcel. We can speak our news and everyone will be able to hear it at once. Have a sharing news session, making sure the children listen to each other by passing a 'talking shell/stone' around. Only the one holding this can speak.

Tell the children that you have a piece of very good news you want to pass on to them. Holding the talking stone/shell tell them that you have found out that God is real and that he loves us all. Following Jesus makes you very happy and helps you live a good life. Ask if any of them know that piece of good news as well.

Tell the children that there are quite a lot of people who don't know this good news yet, and they need people to tell them. What can we do about that?

Write their ideas down. It doesn't matter that they can't read them; they know adults write things down that are important, and will pick up on the truth that their ideas are being taken seriously.

Praying

Lord Jesus,
I am sad that some people don't know you yet.
Please bless them
and send someone
to tell them about you.
Amen.

Activities

This will lead on from the ideas the children have. You may be scribing messages to go with their drawings that can be copied and given to Baptism families, or people being married in your church. You may be making posters to be put up where the slimming and line-dancing classes are held. You may be taping their messages. Have an assortment of materials at the ready.

The worksheet has a 'message delivery' activity, an outline to use for messages, and a 'matching people with message' puzzle.

Print worksheet *Sunday between 29 May and 4 June (C)* from CD-ROM.

Sunday between 5 and 11 June

(if after Trinity Sunday)

Thought for the day

Our God is full of compassion; he hears our crying and it is his nature to rescue us.

Readings

1 Kings 17:8-16 (17-24) or 1 Kings 17:17-24
Psalm 146 or Psalm 30
Galatians 1:11-24
Luke 7:11-17

Aim

To get to know the story of the widow at Nain.

Starter

Sad and happy. Make a smiley face for one end of the room and a sad face for the other end. The children find a space in the middle. The leader calls out situations, and if it's something that makes them sad they run to the sad face; if happy, to the happy face. Situations may be eating chocolate, playing with friends, your pet being ill, going on holiday, having a tummy ache, and getting an invitation to a party.

Teaching

Bring the wall labels down and lay them on the floor together, back to back. Today we are going to hear about someone who started off being very sad (show this side) and Jesus helped to make her very happy (show the happy side.)

Tell the story, making sure the children understand what a widow is (otherwise they may assume you are talking about a window). When you tell them about her son dying, ask them how the mother was feeling, and show the sad face. How did Jesus know she was so sad? Let them add these details to the story. Take your time over telling them how Jesus raised the young man to life, pausing for a moment after he has said, 'Young man, get up'. When Jesus gives the young man back to his mother, look at the sad face again. Did the mother feel sad now? Change the face to match her joy.

Praying

Lord Jesus,
we pray for people who are sad.
Please help them to be happy again.
Amen.

Activities

Make masks using paper plates with the eyes already cut out. They draw a happy face on one side and a sad one on the other.

Print worksheet *Sunday between 5 and 11 June (C)* from CD-ROM.

Which is the odd one out?

Draw what the widow cooked for Elijah.

Which things would make Jesus 😊 happy?
Which things would make Jesus 😢 sad?

God loves us!

To pray with your child

Lord Jesus,
We pray for people who are sad.
Please help them to be happy again.
Amen.

Sunday between
12 and 18 June

(if after Trinity Sunday)

Thought for the day

God has the authority and the desire to forgive our sins completely and set us free from guilt.

Readings

1 Kings 21:1-10 (11-14), 15-21a or 2 Samuel 11:26–12:10, 13-15
Psalm 5:1-8 or Psalm 32
Galatians 2:15-21
Luke 7:36–8:3

Aim

To know that God loves us and forgives us.

Starter

Have a number of sorting-out games, such as getting different shapes into the right holes, sorting out a Happy Families set of cards into families, and tidying a muddle of a cupboard or dressing-up box.

Teaching

Talk about what a good job we did of sorting those things out and putting things right again. Whenever we do that we're being like God, because God loves putting things right and sorting out the messes we make in our lives. Let's look at the sort of things God puts right.

Using toys or puppets, have them acting out various situations where someone is behaving wrongly. For instance, one toy can be greedy and take all the cakes, so there aren't enough for the others; there may be two being nasty to a third, and leaving them out all the time; 'Mum' may leave the children playing, and one keeps kicking or saying nasty things to the other. Vary the situations to suit your group. At the end of each situation let the children say what the wrong behaviour was, and think how they should have behaved. (This may be fun to find out!)

Talk about how we all behave badly sometimes, and the good thing is that, as soon as we realise we have done wrong, we can say 'I'm sorry' to God and 'I'm sorry' to the people we have upset. And then it can be put right straight away so we can get on with enjoying life again.

Praying

Thank you, Jesus
for showing me
when I was being unkind.
I'm sorry I did it.
Thank you for forgiving me!

Activities

On the worksheet there are examples of unkind and selfish behaviour for the children to talk about, together with an activity to put right what is wrong. Even young children need to be taught about these things. It is important that the teaching is matched with friendly, trustworthy leaders and a secure, loving church environment. The children are invited to think of an area where they know they find it hard to behave well, and draw them doing it God's way. The process of drawing the right behaviour is positive reinforcement and will help develop good self-esteem.

Print worksheet *Sunday between 12 and 18 June (C)* from CD-ROM.

What's wrong here?
Let's put it right!

Me, doing it God's way

To pray with your child.

Thank you, Jesus,
for showing me when
I was being unkind.
I'm sorry I did it.
Thank you for
forgiving me!
Amen.

Sunday between 19 and 25 June

(if after Trinity Sunday)

Thought for the day

God is close through all our troubles, and can bring us safely through them.

Readings

1 Kings 19:1-4 (5-7), 8-15a or Isaiah 65:1-9
Psalms 42, 43 or Psalm 22:19-28
Galatians 3:23-29
Luke 8:26-39

Aim

To know the story of Jesus healing the man in the desert.

Starter

Make some paper chains, using either the ready-stuck kits or strips of different coloured paper and glue or staples.

Teaching

Wind all the finished paper chains around one of the children, and tell them that today's story is about a grown-up who had to be chained up to keep him from getting into danger.

Tell the story as if you are one (or two) of the villagers. When you mention the way this man had to be chained up, the child can break out of the chains, just as the man did. Get across in the telling that Jesus loved the man and felt sorry for the way he was chained up inside his illness. When the man is healed he can sit still and talk just like we can, and he asks Jesus if he can come with him. But Jesus has a job for him right here in his own town. He can tell everyone what God has done for him. That will make people listen, because they remember what he was like before Jesus healed him.

Praying

Lord Jesus,
thank you for being with us
when we are sad and upset.
Thank you for cheering us up.
Help us to cheer people up
when they are sad.
Amen.

Activities

On the worksheet there are bits of a person to be cut out and stuck together on the space provided. Younger children will need these cut out already, and if you prefer you can give the children card 'person chunks' to keep in a clear greetings card wrapper as a jigsaw to make up at any time. There is also an activity to spot the odd ones out, which will draw their attention to the way God asks us to welcome everybody in. With God, no one is left out.

Print worksheet *Sunday between 19 and 25 June (C)* from CD-ROM.

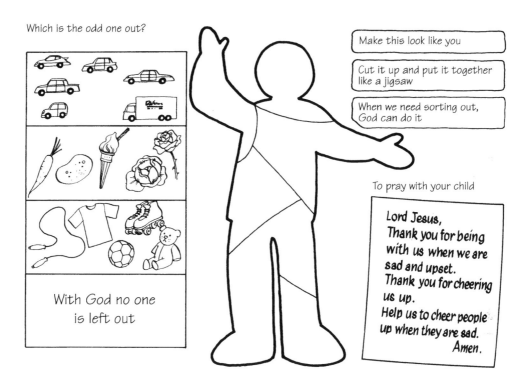

Sunday between
26 June and 2 July

Thought for the day

When we are called to follow Jesus, that means total commitment, with no half-measures.

Readings

2 Kings 2:1-2, 6-14 or 1 Kings 19:15-16, 19-21
Psalm 77:1-2,11-20 or Psalm 16
Galatians 5:1, 13-25
Luke 9:51-62

Aim

To understand that we are called to follow Jesus.

Starter

A *'you-do-as-I-do'* story. Here is one example. The actions are mostly obvious.
'I'll tell you a story. This story is new, so you listen carefully and do as I do.
This is Tom Thumb and this is his house.
These are his windows *(hands make glasses at eyes)*
and this is Squeaky, his mouse *(your little finger)*.
Early one morning the sun began to shine.
Squeaky mouse sat up in bed and counted up to nine.
One, two, three, four, five, six, seven, eight, nine! *(in a squeaky voice)*
Then he took a great big jump and landed on Tom's bed *(your left hand)*.
He quickly ran right up Tom's arm and landed on his head.
Squeaky pulled Tom's hair, Squeaky pulled Tom's nose,
till in the end Tom Thumb jumped up and put on all his clothes.
Then they sat down to breakfast and ate some crusty bread.
And when all that was over, Tom Thumb said . . .'
(back to the beginning)

Teaching

Have several chairs in a line, and prepare beforehand card church windows, door and tower clock as shown below.

By name, ask a particular child to sit on one of the chairs and hold a window. Continue to call by name for particular jobs until you have a complete church. Point out that you called them all to do particular jobs, and in doing them the children have become a church.

Jesus calls his followers to jobs that only we can do, and when we agree, and start doing them, we all become the Church of God. This Church isn't really a building, is it? It's a group of people. And that's what the Church is – a group of people called to do God's work in the world.

Praying

Jesus, you have called me to follow you,
and here I am!
Lead on, Jesus,
I'm right behind you.

Activities

Have a look at the pictures of some jobs people have been called to and talk about them, and people you know who do such jobs. Then they can draw a picture of themselves doing a job that God likes them to do. This may be any kind of caring, thoughtful behaviour.

Print worksheet *Sunday between 26 June and 2 July (C)* from CD-ROM.

333

Sunday between
3 and 9 July

Thought for the day

In Christ we become a new creation.

Readings

2 Kings 5:1-14 or Isaiah 66:10-14
Psalm 30 or Psalm 66:1-9
Galatians 6:(1-6) 7-16
Luke 10:1-11, 16-20

Aim

To get to know the story of Naaman.

Starter

Do some magic painting, where the water has the effect of bringing the invisible colours to life. Split a book of pictures among the group and provide water and brushes.

Teaching

You could tell the story with a suitably dressed Action Man as Naaman, washing him seven times in a bowl of water!

Praying

Lord Jesus,
I pray for all the people
who are sad and lonely.
I know you love them
as much as you love me.
Amen.

Activities

The worksheet gives instructions for making a model of Naaman with and without his spots, so they can 'play the story' at home. Provide a container for the pieces.

Print worksheet *Sunday between 3 and 9 July (C)* from CD-ROM.

To pray with your child

Lord Jesus,
I pray for all the people
who are sad and lonely.
I know you love them as
much as you love me. Amen.

Colour this Naaman. Cut him out and stick
him on card. Dip him into the water 7
times. Only bring him out 6 times.

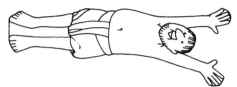

On the 7th dip bring this Naaman
up out of the water!

Can you put in the dots?

Have this line cut for you

Colour this blue
and stick on to card

Sunday between 10 and 16 July

Thought for the day
Straighten your lives out and live by God's standards of love.

Readings
Amos 7:7-17 or Deuteronomy 30:9-14
Psalm 82 or Psalm 25:1-10
Colossians 1:1-14
Luke 10:25-37

Aim
To know the parable of the good neighbour.

Starter
Have a free play session with games such as dressing-up, which encourage the children to play together as well as alongside each other.

Teaching
Tell the story of the good neighbour, involving the children as the characters and helping them act it out. Teach them the summary of the Law to the tune of *London's burning*:

You shall love the
(hands on heart)
Lord your God with
(point upwards)
all your heart and
(hands on heart)
all your mind and
(hold head with hands)
all your strength! All your strength!
(show biceps)
And love your neighbour, and love your neighbour.
(arms round one another's shoulders)

Praying
Lord Jesus,
with my lips
I can tell you I love you.
With my life
I will show you I love you!
Amen.

Activities

The worksheet encourages the children to look at the way people look after others, and there is a picture to finish and colour of the mugged man in the story being looked after by the good Samaritan. Help the children to talk about ways they can be good neighbours.

Print worksheet *Sunday between 10 and 16 July (C)* from CD-ROM.

What has happened here?

Draw the child being looked after

To pray with your child

Lord Jesus,
Help me to be kind
and helpful, and use my
strength to make a
better world.
Amen.

What goes in here?

MILK

Colour this picture of the man being looked after by a kind person.

Add a

a

and a

Sunday between
17 and 23 July

Thought for the day

Against impossible odds God has reconciled us to himself, in Christ.

Readings

Amos 8:1-12 or Genesis 18:1-10a
Psalm 52 or Psalm 15
Colossians 1:15-28
Luke 10:38-42

Aim

To look at the value of listening.

Starter

Play this game in which they have to listen carefully to the instructions. You give them an instruction of where to move to, followed by the way to do it, such as: 'Go to the front wall as aeroplanes; go to the back wall as window cleaners.'

Teaching

Get everyone to find their ears, and talk about what they are for. Try covering and uncovering ears to hear the effect, notice how loud it sounds if you rub your own ear, but if someone else does it to theirs you can hardly hear it at all. Enjoy the gift of hearing and listening that God has given us, and share your favourite sounds. Think about what sounds you hear when you first wake up.

Then do some exercises to train your listening. Sit very still and listen to all the sounds around for a minute, then share what you heard. Whisper something very quietly and see if you can hear it (it might be something funny, or an instruction to touch their toes with their hair). Have a 'news time', with everyone listening carefully to whoever is speaking.

Tell the children about the way all the grown-ups and children used to come out and listen to Jesus, because they found what he said so helpful.

Praying

Thank you, God,
for my ears to listen with.
Help me to get really good at listening
to you and to other people.
Amen.

Activities

Have a recording of different sounds and see if the children can guess what they are. On the worksheet there are objects drawn for which they can make the sounds, and the picture of a park encourages them to imagine what sounds they would hear if they were in that place.

Print worksheet *Sunday between 17 and 23 July (C)* from CD-ROM.

Sunday between
24 and 30 July

Thought for the day
Keep asking for God's Spirit and he will keep pouring out his blessing on you.

Readings
Hosea 1:2-10 or Genesis 18:20-32
Psalm 85 or Psalm 138
Colossians 2:6-15 (16-19)
Luke 11:1-13

Aim
To know that we can ask God for things, and seek him.

Starter
Play hide and seek, either with people, or hunting for a shoe.

Teaching
Talk about asking for things from our parents. If you asked for some bread, would they give you a stone? If you asked for fish and chips, would they give you snake and chips? If you asked for an egg, would they give you a scorpion? You can laugh together over these, and they will see that although they might look a bit alike, their parents would give them what was good for them, not something that was bad for them. Why? Because their parents love them.

Explain that one day Jesus was teaching the people to pray, and he looked at how good parents are at giving good gifts to the children they love. Well, he said, it's just the same only more so with God. He is a very loving parent to all his children, and we can trust him never to give us anything that would be bad for us.

Jesus wants us to ask him about things, and to ask for his help, and to ask for the things we need. If we ask for something that might not be best for us at the moment, he will probably say, 'No' or 'Not yet'. As we learn to ask for things that he wants for us as well, we shall find that he often says, 'Yes, I'd like that too.' He might even ask our help in getting things done.

Praying
Our Father in heaven,
please give us
all we need today.
Amen.

Activities

On the worksheet there are activities to reinforce the asking, seeking and knocking. They can also make a model of an opening and closing door.

Print worksheet *Sunday between 24 and 30 July (C)* from CD-ROM.

Can you find 6 ⌷ hidden in this picture?

For parents to pray with your child

Our Father in heaven, please give us all we need today.
                    Amen.

Cut along the dotted line. Then you can knock and open the door

Sunday between 31 July and 6 August

Thought for the day

True richness is not material wealth; true security is not a financial matter.

Readings

Hosea 11:1-11 or Ecclesiastes 1:2, 12-14; 2:18-23
Psalm 107:1-9, 43 or Psalm 49:1-12
Colossians 3:1-11
Luke 12:13-21

Aim

To know that God looks after us like a loving parent looks after a young child.

Starter

If you have a parent who would be willing to bath a baby with the children there, that would be lovely. Or play a matching parents and babies game. Give each child the picture of an animal, and they have to go round the room looking for the baby picture that matches their adult animal.

Teaching

Talk about the different ways in which the people who love us look after us. On the worksheet there are some pictures to start you off. Tell them how God said to his people, 'I love you like that!' Teach them this song, sung to the tune of 'Three blind mice' and putting in all the children's names.

God loves Oliver.
God loves Louise.
God loves Jordan.
God loves Daisy.
He knows when they're friendly
and when they get mad,
he knows when they're happy
and when they are sad,
if they help each other it makes him feel glad,
'cos God loves us!

Praying

Dear Jesus,
your love makes me rich.
Thank you for giving me
so much love to love with!

Activities

The worksheet gets the children thinking of three people they love, and drawing what they would like to give them if they could give them anything at all. This will help them to pray for their three people, and help develop their ability to think in out-giving mode. If you have a garden or outside area they can gather some small flowers (daisies, buttercups, dandelions and bindweed are fine) and make a posy of them in wet cotton wool and foil to take into church and lay as thank-offerings in front of the altar. They can take their flowers home with them afterwards.

Print worksheet *Sunday between 31 July and 6 August (C)* from CD-ROM.

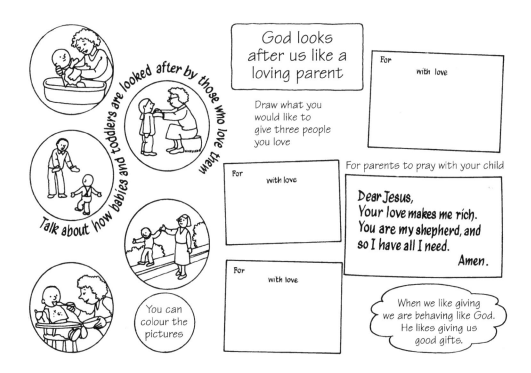

Sunday between
7 and 13 August

Thought for the day

Have faith in God, and get yourself ready to meet him.

Readings

Isaiah 1:1, 10-20
Psalm 22-23
Hebrews 11:1-3, 8-16
Luke 12:32-40

Aim

To know that God can be trusted.

Starter

Play 'Simon says'. Point out that we had to make sure we only listened to Simon's instructions. We knew if we did that we wouldn't get it wrong.

Teaching

Bring a clock along, with the time an hour fast. Bring one of those pop-up toys which you press down and they suddenly surprise you by popping up before you expected.

As you start, pretend to have just noticed the time on the clock and the time gives you a shock – it's already time we were in church! Then you check with your watch and are very relieved that the clock must be wrong. You know you can trust your watch because you checked that against the television just before you came out.

Talk about there being some things you get to know you can trust, and other things let you down. Share stories about car breakdowns, toys that break, and so on.

We can trust God because he doesn't have 'off' days or go into a sulk. He doesn't move away just when you're getting to know him, and he doesn't go away on holiday. He doesn't have times when you can't get in touch with him. He's always there for us and always fair and loving. So we can trust God with all our fears and our hopes and dreams, all the things that upset us and all the things we're looking forward to. We can trust him with our secrets. He will stay our friend right through to when we're grown up, right to when we get old and even when we've died – he'll still be our friend. By the time we die we will have got to know and love him very well, and he will welcome us into heaven to enjoy being with him for ever.

Praying

Dear Jesus,
it's good to know
I can trust you.
You are always there for me.
Thank you!

Activities

If you can borrow a parachute, you can play some games which build trust and co-operation – working together to make a ball bounce high, and creating a 'mushroom' shape and running underneath it one by one. Or help one another to complete a floor jigsaw. The worksheet gives them space to create a composite picture of themselves and their life, putting in such things as their favourite colours and animals, pastimes and people.

Print worksheet *Sunday between 7 and 13 August (C)* from CD-ROM.

Sunday between 14 and 20 August

Thought for the day

When we fix our eyes on Jesus our lives will reflect his nature.

Readings

Isaiah 5:1-7 or Jeremiah 23:23-29
Psalm 80:1-2, 8-19 or Psalm 82
Hebrews 11:29–12:2
Luke 12:49-56

Aim

To learn that God likes us and wants the best for us.

Starter

Pass the parcel. Make sure everyone has a turn (if necessary, have several parcels with several small groups). Each layer contains a freezer label with 'I'm special' written on it. Eventually every child is wearing one.

Teaching

Pass round a flower each for the children to hold, and talk together about what it is like – what its petals and leaves look like, what it smells and feels like, and so on. Marvel over all the care that God has taken in bringing a flower like this into being.

Now pass round something else to enjoy and notice, such as feathers, stones or vegetables. Again draw their attention to all the care God has taken over these things.

Collect everything in and say we've got another collection of beautiful, amazing things God has made. Get everyone to stand up in the circle and hold hands. At the moment they are making a sort of chain, but they aren't daisies. At the moment they are quiet, but they can speak. What – or who – can they be? It's us!

Sit everyone down and go round the group picking out one nice thing about everyone, and then enthuse together over the loving care God has taken over each one of us. No wonder God likes us and thinks us all very special.

Praying

Thank you, God,
for making me
and knowing me
and liking me.
It's special being special!

Activities

Make finger-print pictures, using shallow trays of paint and hand-washing bowls between colours. Some suggestions for making their prints into people and objects are given on the worksheet.

Print worksheet *Sunday between 14 and 20 August (C)* from CD-ROM.

Why is this day special

For Anne and Mike?

Why is this day special for Oliver?

Some ideas

Thank you God for making me and knowing me and liking me. It's special – being special!

For parents to pray with your child

This is me on my special day

My finger-print picture

Sunday between 21 and 27 August

Thought for the day

God sets his leaders apart to challenge prejudices and assumptions, and alert people to the truth.

Readings

Jeremiah 1:4-10 or Isaiah 58:9b-14
Psalm 71:1-6 or Psalm 103:1-8
Hebrews 12:18-29
Luke 13:10-17

Aim

To know that God loves us right from before we were born and all through our lives, and he has a plan for us.

Starter

Moving in style. The children move around the room in the ways that the leader calls out. They can roll like little babies, crawl like older babies, be learning to walk like toddlers, jump and skip like children, ride bikes like older children, ride skateboards like teenagers, drive cars and lorries like grown-ups, and walk with a stick like elderly people.

Teaching

Talk about the way we went right through a person's life in the game. Go over the stages with them, getting the children to remember what they were and helping them get the order right. Out of all those ages in our life, when is it that God loves us? Is it when we're babies? Or when we've grown up? Or when we're old?

God loves us in all the ages, because he loves us all the time! Right from before we've even been born, God knows us and loves us. Tell the children that God loves them now, and he'll still be friends with them and loving them when they get old and perhaps have grandchildren of their own. Ask them to think of the oldest person they know. God loved all these people right back when they were tiny babies, and even before that!

Praying

You can sing and dance this prayer*

Oh, oh, oh how good is the Lord, (3)
I never will forget what he has done for me.
He loves all the babies, how good is the Lord (3)...
He loves all the toddlers, how good is the Lord (3)...
He loves all the children, how good is the Lord (3)...
He loves all the teenagers, how good is the Lord (3)...
He loves all the grown-ups, how good is the Lord (3)...
He loves the old people, how good is the Lord (3)...

*Children's Hymn Book, No. 164. Published by Kevin Mayhew Ltd.

Activities

Draw round the children on sheets of lining paper or wallpaper. The children can then colour themselves in. Write across the paper person, 'God has got a plan for me!'

Print worksheet *Sunday between 21 and 27 August (C)* from CD-ROM.

Sunday between
28 August and 3 September

Thought for the day

When we live God's way, both individually and as a community, we will be greatly blessed.

Readings

Jeremiah 2:4-13 or Ecclesiasticus 10:12-18
Psalm 81:1, 10-16 or Psalm 112
Hebrews 13:1-8, 15-16
Luke 14:1, 7-14

Aim

To know the story of the guests choosing the most important seats.

Starter

While the music plays, pass round a grand hat or a crown. Whenever the music stops, whoever is wearing the hat or crown stands up, and all the others bow and curtsey to them, saying, 'Yes, your majesty; no, your majesty!'

Teaching

You can either use puppets to tell the story today, or an assortment of character toys, some of which are very new and posh, while others are well loved, old and tatty. Lay a low table with a cloth and plates of drawn food, and arrange all the chairs around it. One by one the characters come in, talking to themselves about the party, and admiring the food.

One of the new, posh ones looks to see which the most important seat is, and decides to sit there because they are so important.

One of the old and tatty well-loved ones comes and looks for the lowest, least important seat, because they are conscious of being old and worn, and not very grand.

When the host comes in they go to the old, worn one and give him a big hug, really pleased that he has been able to come to the party. They ask him to come up and sit with them at the top of the table, as he's so important, having been such a good friend for years. When they get to the top of the table the hosts find the posh guest sitting there and ask them to move down so their special guest can sit there instead. The posh guest voices her embarrassment as she moves down and the old worn one takes his place at the top of the table.

This story teaches us not to think we're far more important than anyone else and deserve better than anyone else. Instead of rushing for the best place, or the biggest cake, or the first go, sometimes we need to enjoy giving the best to other people.

Praying

Big and small,
short and tall,
you made us all,
you love us all!
Amen.

Activities

On the worksheet the children are putting the guests in the right places, and the food on the plates. Also, they can paint or model some food on a paper plate to remind them of the story. Today's prayer can be written out on the back of the plate.

Print worksheet *Sunday between 28 August and 3 September (C)* from CD-ROM.

Sunday between 4 and 10 September

Thought for the day
Following Jesus is expensive – it costs everything, but it's worth it.

Readings
Jeremiah 18:1-11 or Deuteronomy 30:15-20
Psalm 139:1-6,13-18 or Psalm 1
Philemon 1-21
Luke 14:25-33

Aim
To know that it is worth the cost to follow Jesus.

Starter
Play shops, with play money, boxes and cartons, cut-out fruit and some paper bags.

Teaching
Talk about going shopping, and what they like buying and what they don't like buying. Talk about how we sometimes see things we would like, but we can't have them because they cost too much.

Tell the story, with the aid of a few appropriate props, of a child who sees a toy she really loves and would like for her birthday. Her mum tells her that she won't be able to have it as it costs too much money. The child keeps thinking about the toy, and decides she wants it so much that she doesn't mind not having any other presents, and no birthday treat, if that means she can have it. Her mum and dad talk it over with her. They don't want her to choose to do without those things and then be upset when she has only got one toy. The child is certain that this toy is worth it, so her mum and dad arrange for her to have the toy she wants so much. And the child is so happy with this one thing that she doesn't mind having no other presents and no birthday treat.

Following Jesus is really wonderful. It's wonderful having Jesus as our friend and knowing he loves us all the way through our life and wherever we travel to. But when we follow Jesus, we choose to do without some things.

We choose to do without being selfish, even when we want to be. We choose to do without being unkind, even when we feel grumpy. We choose to do without wanting things all the time, even if we like them.

But it's worth doing without these nasty things, because being with Jesus makes us so happy.

Praying

Jesus, I love you
and I will live like you,
even when it is easier not to.
Amen.

Activities

On the worksheet there is a picture to colour of Jesus with the children, and the children can draw themselves in the picture.

Print worksheet *Sunday between 4 and 10 September (C)* from CD-ROM.

Sunday between 11 and 17 September

Thought for the day
Jesus does not avoid the company of sinners but befriends them.

Readings
Jeremiah 4:11-12, 22-28 or Exodus 32:7-14
Psalm 14 or Psalm 51:1-10
1 Timothy 1:12-17
Luke 15:1-10

Aim
To know the story of the good shepherd and the lost sheep.

Starter
Hide and seek, using a model sheep.

Teaching
Let the children help make a landscape from upturned bowls draped with a green sheet or towel. Use model sheep, either plastic ones or home-made from thin card and cotton wool. Bushes and shrubs can be small house plants in pots, such as spider plants and money trees.

When the landscape is set up, tell the story, moving the sheep around as you talk about the normal daily routine for the shepherd caring for his flock, and the lost sheep being found and brought safely home.

Praying
Good shepherd,
thank you for looking after us.
Help us to look after each other.
Amen.

Activities
The children can make sheep masks using the instructions on the worksheet, and search for lost sheep in a picture which can then be coloured in.

Print worksheet *Sunday between 11 and 17 September (C)* from CD-ROM.

How to make a sheep mask

cotton
wool
cut out

punch
hole

cut

paper
plate

cut along here

Cut shape from a
paper plate; draw on the face, cut eye
holes and stick on cotton wool. Secure
round the head with wool.

To pray with your child

Good shepherd,
thank you for looking
after us.
Help us to look after
each other.
Amen.

Can you find the lost sheep? How will the shepherd
get to it? Colour the picture

Sunday between 18 and 24 September

Thought for the day

If you cannot be trusted with worldly riches, or even small amounts of money, then you will not be trusted with spiritual riches either.

Readings

Jeremiah 8:18–9:1 or Amos 8:4-7
Psalm 79:1-9 or Psalm 113
1 Timothy 2:1-7
Luke 16:1-13

Aim

To learn that we are to be good 'caretakers' and look after things as well as people.

Starter

A potato and spoon game. For each small group of children (2-4 in a group), place a bowl at each end of the room. In one of the bowls there is a potato and a spoon. The first person carries the potato in the spoon from one bowl to the other. The next carries it back to the first bowl, and so on. They can all have two turns. This can either be competitive or simply an activity which several groups happen to be playing at the same time, depending on the age of the children.

Teaching

Talk about how careful they all had to be to walk along holding the potato in the spoon without it falling off. Think how careful we have to be carrying a bowl of cereal, or a drink of juice. We have to really think about what we are doing. If we start thinking about something else, we can end up spilling it all over the floor!

Jesus told his friends that God takes great care making us and looking after us, and he wants us to take great care of things as well. Show a picture of different age groups working or playing together. He wants us to look after one another. (How?) Show a globe. He wants us to look after our world. (How?) Show a toy and a jacket. And he wants us to look after any things we are given to use or play with. (How?)

Praying

Dear God,
thank you for all the things I have been given
to use and to play with.
Help me to look after them well
and be ready to share them with others.
Amen.

Activities

There is space on the sheet for the children to draw the things to use and to play with that they like most, and some pictures of things being looked after well and badly, so they can develop their understanding of what good stewardship means.

Print worksheet *Sunday between 18 and 24 September (C)* from CD-ROM.

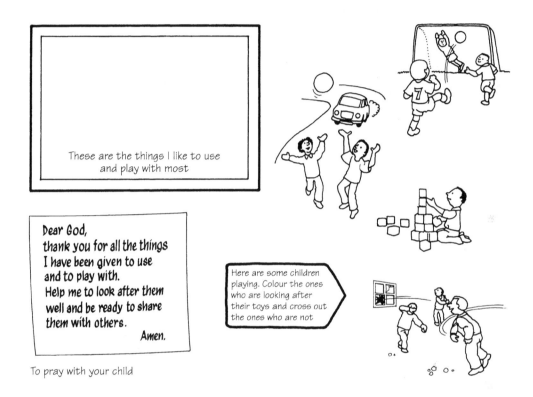

These are the things I like to use
and play with most

Dear God,
thank you for all the things
I have been given to use
and to play with.
Help me to look after them
well and be ready to share
them with others.
                              Amen.

To pray with your child

Here are some children
playing. Colour the ones
who are looking after
their toys and cross out
the ones who are not

Sunday between
25 September and 1 October

Thought for the day
Wealth can make us complacent so that we fail to notice the needs of those around us.

Readings
Jeremiah 32:1-3a, 6-15 or Amos 6:1a, 4-7
Psalm 91:1-6, 14-16 or Psalm 146
1 Timothy 6:6-19
Luke 16:19-31

Aim
To know that we are to notice one another's needs.

Starter
Spot the difference. The children hide their eyes while you change something (you might take a shoe off, or swap your watch to the other wrist) and then they have to guess what is different.

Teaching
Tell a story about a child noticing someone's need. Here is one possibility:

Emily and her dad were doing the shopping. It was the big weekly shop in the supermarket to get things like toothpaste, cereal, toilet paper and bread. Emily had got the list, and Dad was pushing the trolley.

The shop was full of people, some of them filling plastic bags with apples and potatoes, and others trying to work out the cheapest way to buy cheese. They were so busy with what they were choosing to buy that no one noticed a sticky white line on the floor by the cat food.

At least, nearly no one noticed. Emily saw it and wondered what it was. As she went to find the rabbit and chicken flavour (her cat's favourite) she followed the sticky white trail, and smelt the smell of concentrated washing liquid. So that's what it was! Emily could see the trail disappearing round the corner into the lemonade and coke part of the shop.

'Dad!' said Emily. 'Look!'

Dad looked.

'Mmm, well spotted, Emily,' he said. 'We had better follow that trail and find out why it's there.'

'It's concentrated washing liquid I think,' said Emily.

'I think you could well be right,' said Dad.

They pushed their trolley round the corner. There, just between the large bottles of lime and lemon and the small bottles of blackcurrant and apple was a woman pushing a trolley. And on the front of the trolley was a refill of concentrated washing liquid, leaking white sticky stuff along the floor as the trolley went along. Anyone could slip over on it and hurt themselves.

Emily and her dad showed the woman the white sticky trail.

'Oh good heavens, fancy that!' said the woman. 'Fancy me not noticing! What a good thing you noticed it before anyone hurt themselves.'

Dad and Emily smiled at each other.

The woman and Emily and her dad told the shop assistants and helped them mop up the mess with paper towels. The manager put down some orange cones saying 'Wet floor' on them, so people would know it wasn't safe to walk there yet.

Talk about how good it was that Emily noticed, and share any stories the children want to tell about times they have noticed when people need help.

God wants us to notice things and be ready to come to the rescue.

Praying

Dear God,
use our eyes
to see the needs around us
and use our hands to help.
Amen.

Activities

On the sheet there is a picture on which to spot various needs, and a pair of glasses to make.

Print worksheet *Sunday between 25 September and 1 October (C)* from CD-ROM.

Sunday between 2 and 8 October

Thought for the day
God hears our distress and our crying, and feels it with us.

Readings
Lamentations 1:1-6 or Habakkuk 1:1-4; 2:1-4
Lamentations 3:19-26 or Psalm 137, or Psalm 37:1-9
2 Timothy 1:1-14
Luke 17:5-10

Aim
To learn about perseverance.

Starter
Have some buckets and beanbags, so the children can try throwing the beanbags into the buckets.

Teaching
Make up an obstacle course which a soft toy, such as a bear, could negotiate with a bit of help from his friends. This might include something high to balance along, a dark tunnel he must hurry through on his own, and something to climb up.

Make a bear walk the obstacle course, talking to himself in a growly voice as he goes along. He is sometimes scared and anxious by the height, sometimes frightened and sad about being alone in the dark, and sometimes finding it all an uphill struggle. There are also parts of his journey with fun and excitement and good views. Through all the difficult parts the bear bravely perseveres. The children can applaud him when he eventually reaches the end of the course.

Talk about how the bear kept on going, even when he was scared or tired. That's what God wants us to do in life.

Praying
Make a ring of string which everyone holds and passes through their hands as they pray:

Lord, help me to keep trying
again and again and again!
Lord, help me to keep loving
on and on and on.
Amen.

Activities

On the worksheet there is an obstacle course for the children to make their fingers walk along, and a 'keeping on and on' game to make, for which they will need string.

Print worksheet *Sunday between 2 and 8 October (C)* from CD-ROM.

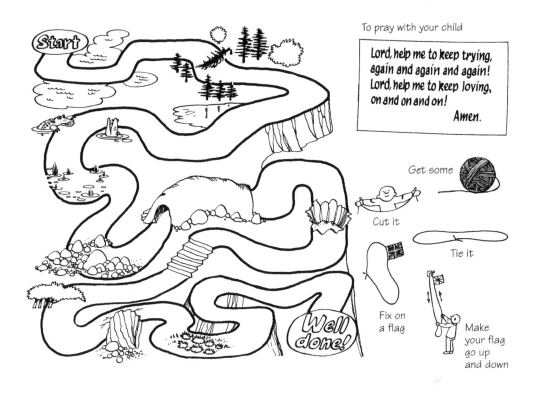

Start

To pray with your child

Lord, help me to keep trying, again and again and again! Lord, help me to keep loving, on and on and on!
Amen.

Get some

Cut it

Tie it

Fix on a flag

Make your flag go up and down

Well done!

Sunday between 9 and 15 October

Thought for the day

God can always use even seemingly hopeless situations for good.

Readings

Jeremiah 29:1, 4-7 or 2 Kings 5:1-3, 7-15
Psalm 66:1-12 or Psalm 111
2 Timothy 2:8-15
Luke 17:11-19

Aim

To know that Jesus healed the ten lepers and one said 'thank you'.

Starter

Provide a selection of sorting-out games and toys, such as building something from a jumble of bricks or boxes, putting shapes in the right holes, and jigsaw puzzles. Today we are going to look at the way Jesus sorted out ten problems all at once!

Teaching

Using the carpet tiles surface, tell the story of today's Gospel. You will need cut-outs of the lepers, a distant village, some trees, Jesus, the priest, and the leper who said 'thank you'. You can base them on the pictures below. The road to the village can either be a cloth, or strip of paper.

Praying

When we are sad
   (chin in hands):
you cheer us up
   (trace big smile with finger).
When we cry
   (fists in eyes):
you brush our tears away
   (brush face with hands).
When we feel weak
   (go droopy):
you make us strong
   (show muscles)
and we say THANK YOU!
   (shout)

Activities

There is a picture of the lepers throwing off their bandages happily when they are healed which the children can colour, after they have counted the lepers and various other things

Print worksheet *Sunday between 9 and 15 October (C)* from CD-ROM.

To pray with your child

When we are sad (chin in hands)
you cheer us up (trace big smile with finger)
When we cry (fists in eyes)
you brush our tears away (brush face with hands)
When we feel weak (go droopy)
you make us strong (show muscles)
and we say:
          THANK YOU!

How many?

Here I am saying 'THANK YOU'

People who said 'thank you'

Sunday between
16 and 22 October

Thought for the day

Don't get side-tracked; always pray and don't give up.

Readings

Jeremiah 31:27-34 or Genesis 32:22-31
Psalm 119:97-104 or Psalm 121
2 Timothy 3:14–4:5
Luke 18:1-8

Aim

To look at the value of regular prayer.

Starter

Here we go round the mulberry bush. With one of the regular morning jobs being: 'This is the way we pray to God on a cold and frosty morning'.

Teaching

Bring a large circle of card split into the four seasons, and a circular band of paper showing the regular events of a day, based on the pictures right.

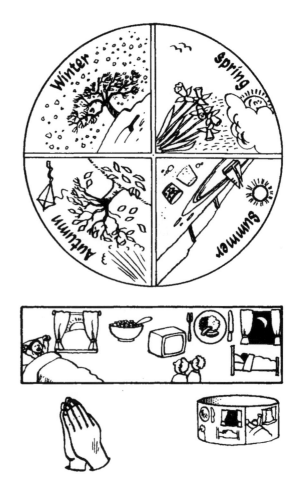

Turn the chart round like a wheel, and talk about the seasons and the way the same thing happens every year. Then point out that the days all have a pattern as well. Move the band round so that they can see the same pictures coming up day after day. There are some things we do every day.

Jesus tells us that we should make praying part of our daily pattern too. Have the praying picture, and stick it on the band in the morning, before eating, and before sleeping. Then turn the whole thing round a few times so they get the idea of the ongoing pattern.

Praying

When I wake up I say:
Good morning, Jesus!
Help me live your way today.
When I sit down to eat I say:
Thank you for this food.
Before I go to sleep I say:
Goodnight, Jesus.
Thank you for looking after me.

Activities

The worksheet helps them make their own day's band to use, and there is some pictorial teaching on how to pray.

Print worksheet *Sunday between 16 and 22 October (C)* from CD-ROM.

Sunday between 23 and 29 October

Thought for the day

When we recognise our dependence on God we will approach him with true humility and accept his gifts with joy.

Readings

Joel 2:23-32 or Ecclesiasticus 35:12-17 or Jeremiah 14:7-10, 19-22
Psalm 65 or Psalm 84:1-7
2 Timothy 4:6-8, 16-18
Luke 18:9-14

Aim

To know that we are to let God into our life as the earth lets in water.

Starter

Play with water and have lots of sponges, so they can try transferring water from one container to another using the sponges' soaking and water-holding quality.

Teaching

Have a tray of dry earth, and point out how nothing will grow in it if it stays as dry as this all the time, because things need water to grow. We can't grow any goodness in our lives if we don't get showered with God's love.

But that's all right, because God is always there showering us with his love. As you talk, shower the earth with a watering can. He gives us a beautiful world to live in, fruits and vegetables and animals and families to enjoy and look after. He gives us life, and minds to think with, and bodies to move around with.

All the time we keep ourselves open to God like this earth is open to the water, he can fill our lives with his love and we will grow more and more loving and truthful and good.

Praying

Thank you, God,
for the rain that falls.
   make fingers into falling rain
Thank you for trees that grow so tall.
   stretch up
Thank you for this life you have given us all!
   move and dance about

Activities

Use the wet earth to plant some bulbs to be ready in the spring. The worksheet has a picture to colour and add the raindrops. Provide raindrops cut from shiny blue and silver wrapping paper for this.

Print worksheet *Sunday between 23 and 29 October (C)* from CD-ROM.

Stick on the raindrops

Can you see

6 trees

10 apples

1 river

2 clouds

1 tractor

Thank you, God,
for the rain that falls. (make fingers into falling rain)
Thank you for trees that grow so tall. (stretch up)
Thank you for this life you have given us all! (move and dance about)

To pray with your child

All Saints' Day
Sunday between 30 October and 5 November

Thought for the day
In Christ we are chosen to be God's holy people.

Readings
Daniel 7:1-3, 15-18
Psalm 149
Ephesians 1:11-23
Luke 6:20-31

Aim
To find out what saints are and why we are celebrating today.

Starter
Give out balloons to throw and catch.

Teaching
Talk about the balloons and how much better they are with air inside them. Although we can't see the air we know it is there because the balloons get bigger when you blow air into them. We can't see God's love, either, but when it fills us we grow into loving people. We need God's love in us.

There is a name for people who have spent their lives being filled with God's love. We call them Saints. Saints are close friends of God who want to live God's way so much that they don't mind what happens to them so long as they can carry on being friends with him. Some saints have bravely stood up for what is right. Some have spent their lives looking after the very poor, or those with dangerous illnesses. Some saints have helped lots of people to know and love God better.

Today is like a party to celebrate all the saints, and thank God for what he can do in our lives.

Praying
Sing *Oh, oh, oh, how good is the Lord* (see page 349 for words) dancing to it in a circle.

Thank you, God,
for your friends, the saints.
Help us to get to know you more
and enjoy being your friends.

Activities

They can make the worksheet into a pop-up picture of the saints cheering us on our way to heaven.

Print worksheet *All Saints' Day (C)* from CD-ROM.

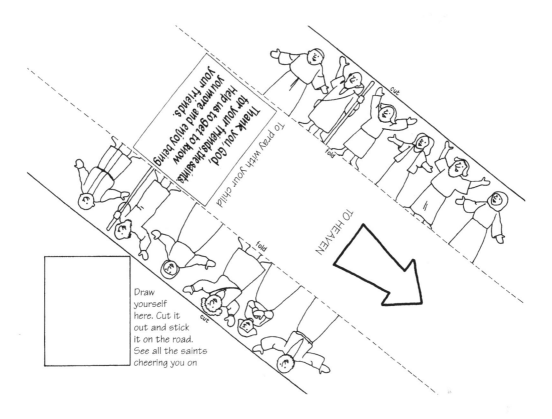

Fourth Sunday before Advent
Sunday between 30 October and 5 November
For use if the Feast of All Saints was celebrated on
1 November and alternative propers are needed.

Thought for the day
Jesus came to search out the lost and save them. Through him we come to our senses and make our lives clean.

Readings
Isaiah 1:10-18
Psalm 32:1-7
2 Thessalonians 1:1-12
Luke 19:1-10

Aim
To be introduced to the story of Zacchaeus.

Starter
Spot the birds. Fix a number of bird pictures high up around the room. Show the children an example of what they are looking for, and set them off hunting for the pictures, but don't tell them they will have to look up to see them. Let them discover that for themselves.

Teaching
Prepare the tree by fixing a card or thick paper tree outline to a chair, so that when Zacchaeus stands on the chair you can just see his face over the top of the tree. Give Jesus and Zacchaeus head-dresses to wear, and have all the other children standing at the side of the road as Jesus comes walking through their village. Let Zacchaeus lead Jesus and his friends across the room to his house (some chairs can make the walls) where they sit down to eat. Then they can come outside for Zacchaeus to announce to all the people waiting outside that he is changing his life. He's going to stop cheating people out of their money, and pay back all his debts four times over. All the people can give him three cheers and a round of applause.

Point out that although Zacchaeus was short, he wasn't too short to work with God. They may be short, but they are not too short or too young to work with God either.

Praying
Look, Lord,
I may be short
but I am not too short
to be your friend.
I want to be in your team
and work with you today.

Activities

They can all make a tall tree with Zacchaeus in it to remind them of the story. You will need a length of wallpaper for each child, cut into a trunk, and the tree's crown.

Print worksheet *Fourth Sunday before Advent (C)* from CD-ROM.

Third Sunday before Advent
Sunday between 6 and 12 November

Thought for the day
Life after death is not wishful thinking but a definite reality.

Readings
Job 19:23-27a
Psalm 17:1-9
2 Thessalonians 2:1-5, 13-17
Luke 20:27-38

Aim
To know that Jesus told us life goes on after death.

Starter
Place some tiny cakes decorated with chocolate drops in a box or tin, and have an extra packet of chocolate drops with you. Tell the children that there is something nice in the tin. Can they see it, without taking off the lid? No. Do they trust you to tell them the truth? (I wonder!) Do they believe that there really is something nice in the tin?

Assure them that there really is something nice in it, and you are going to give them a little idea of what it is like. Now give each child a chocolate drop to enjoy. What do they think is in the tin? Well, it's certainly something to do with chocolate drops. Open the tin so they can all see. It's like chocolate drops but even better, because there's a whole cake, decorated with a chocolate drop for everyone. Now you can give them out one by one, so that everyone has one.

Teaching
When Jesus was walking about on our earth he told his friends that life goes on after our bodies wear out and die. He told them heaven was a nice place to be, and they would be very happy there. (As you say this, hold the closed tin.)

Can we trust Jesus to tell us the truth? Yes, we can.

So if Jesus said there is life after we die, and people are happy there, can we believe him? Yes, we can.

What will it be like? (Pick up the empty packet of chocolate drops.) Jesus gives his friends some clues, and he lets us feel the joy and happiness and peace and love of heaven sometimes. Heaven will be like that only much, much better!

Praying
Be near me, Lord Jesus, I ask thee to stay
close by me for ever and love me I pray.
Bless all the dear children in thy tender care
and fit us for heaven to live with thee there.

Activities

There is a dot-to-dot angel to complete, and then they can draw and paint heaven in their favourite colours. If you want to make this a collage picture, bring along an assortment of different colours and textures for them to use.

Print worksheet *Third Sunday before Advent (C)* from CD-ROM.

Heaven goes

∴n and

∴n and ∴n

To pray with your child

Be near me, Lord Jesus, I ask thee to stay close by me for ever and love me I pray. Bless all the dear children in thy tender care and fit us for heaven to live with thee there.

I think heaven might look like this

Second Sunday before Advent
Sunday between 13 and 19 November

Thought for the day

There will be dark and dangerous times as the end approaches, but by standing firm through it all we will gain life.

Readings

Malachi 4:1-2a
Psalm 98
2 Thessalonians 3:6-13
Luke 21:5-19

Aim

To know that God is a fair judge.

Starter

Weighing and sorting games, using lots of different items, such as stones, vegetables, pasta, bricks, saucepans and feathers. Sort according to shape, use or colour. Use balance scales, or hang two baskets at either end of a broom handle and hold it in the middle. The children can try to balance the baskets.

Teaching

Using toys or puppets, act out several situations which are not fair. Tell the children to shout out 'That's not fair!' as soon as they spot something which isn't. Then talk about why it isn't fair, and act out the same situation, this time making it fair. Here are some ideas for situations:

- Three sweets are shared out between three toys with one toy having two sweets and one having none.
- It's clearing-up time and one toy is allowed to carry on reading while the others have to do all the tidying up on their own.
- The toys are playing 'catch' and one says he hasn't been caught when really he has.

Our God always judges justly, or fairly. He always knows both sides of the story, and he is always fair. So we can trust him.

God has made us able to tell what is fair, so that we can play fairly and grow wise, choosing to do what is right and just. God wants us to stand up for what is fair. He doesn't want people to treat each other badly and unfairly.

Praying

Dear God,
you are a good judge.
You are always fair.
Help me to be fair as well.

Activities

They can make their own set of balances to use at home. They will each need two yoghurt pots, wool, and half a pea stick. The worksheet gives instructions.

Print worksheet *Second Sunday before Advent (C)* from CD-ROM.

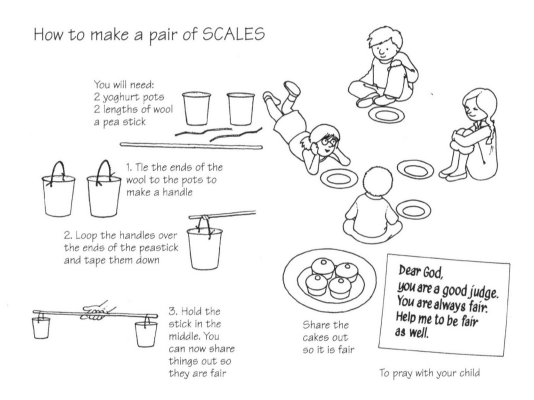

How to make a pair of SCALES

You will need:
2 yoghurt pots
2 lengths of wool
a pea stick

1. Tie the ends of the wool to the pots to make a handle

2. Loop the handles over the ends of the peastick and tape them down

3. Hold the stick in the middle. You can now share things out so they are fair

Share the cakes out so it is fair

Dear God,
you are a good judge.
You are always fair.
Help me to be fair as well.

To pray with your child

Christ the King
Sunday between 20 and 26 November

Thought for the day

This Jesus, dying by crucifixion between criminals, is the anointed King of all creation in whom all things are reconciled.

Readings

Jeremiah 23:1-6
Psalm 46
Colossians 1:11-20
Luke 23:33-43

Aim

To know and celebrate that Jesus is our King.

Starter

Scatter different coloured and named circles all over the floor, one for each person. Everyone starts by standing on their own circle. When the music starts, everyone moves and dances around. When the music stops, they go and stand on their spot. A matching set of named circles (small ones) are in a basket, and one is drawn and that person is given a crown to wear. When the music starts this time, everyone follows what the King or Queen does. The crown is changed each time the music stops, and you can easily give everyone a go by removing their name from the basket once it has been chosen.

Teaching

Hold the crown and talk about what kings are often like in fairy stories, establishing that they are usually the most important person in the kingdom, with lots of power and lots of money.

As Christians, we belong to a kingdom. It's a kingdom of love and joy and peace and goodness and forgiveness. Anyone in any country can be part of this kingdom, if they ask to be. It's a kingdom which grows bigger and bigger as more people get to meet with God. And our King is someone who was born in a stable, and died on a cross, and came back to life again. Do you know his name? Yes, it's Jesus. And if we are part of the family of God, which we are, that means we are princes and princesses in the kingdom of God!

Praying

Dear Jesus,
you are my friend
and yet you are a King!
I am glad I live in your kingdom.

Activities

The worksheet can be decorated and turned into a crown, which the children can wear as they sing some songs to celebrate, such as:

- *Who's the king of the jungle?*
- *I rejoice in making Jesus happy*
- *I'm H-A-P-P-Y*
- *If you're happy and you know it*

Print worksheet *Christ the King (C)* from CD-ROM.

Dear Jesus, you are my friend and yet you are a King!
I am glad I live in your kingdom.

Jesus is my friend and my king
signed

You Can Drink It

Music for Sunday between 10 and 16 July (Year A)

God has pro-vi-ded us wa-ter! Wa-ter of life!

2. It's as hard as rock,
   yet it flows down a mountain,
   and clouds drop drips of it —
   what can it be?

3. It's as light as snowflakes
   and heavy as hailstones,
   as small as dewdrops
   and big as the sea.

Text: Susan Sayers
Music: Susan Sayers, arr. Noel Rawsthorne
© Copyright 1986 Kevin Mayhew Ltd.

All That We Can Hear

Prayer for Second Sunday before Lent (Year B)

All that we can hear and ev-'ry-thing we can see, in-clud-ing
me, we all of us spring from God, who cares for each of us un-
end-ing-ly. Let the whole earth sing of his love!

Words: Susan Sayers
Music: Susan Sayers, arr. Noel Rawsthorne
© Copyright 1986 Kevin Mayhew Ltd.